Breaking Through
Bureaucracy

Breaking Through Bureaucracy

A New Vision for Managing
in Government

Michael Barzelay

with the collaboration of Babak J. Armajani

UNIVERSITY OF CALIFORNIA PRESS

BERKELEY LOS ANGELES OXFORD

University of California Press
Berkeley and Los Angeles, California

University of California Press, Ltd.
Oxford, England

© 1992 by
The Regents of the University of California

Library of Congress Cataloging-in-Publication Data

Barzelay, Michael.
  Breaking through bureaucracy : a new vision for managing in
government / Michael Barzelay with the collaboration of Babak J.
Armajani.
       p. cm.
  Includes bibliographical references (p.   ) and index.
  ISBN 0-520-07800-4 (cloth : alk. paper).—ISBN 0-520-07801-2
(paper : alk. paper)
  1. Bureaucracy—Minnesota. 2. Administrative agencies—Minnesota—
Management. 3. Executive departments—Minnesota—Management.
4. Minnesota—Politics and government—1951-   5. Organizational
change—Minnesota. 6. Bureaucracy—United States. 7. Public administration. I. Armajani, Babak J. II. Title.
JK6141.B37 1992
353.9776'01—dc20   91-39396
                                                                  CIP

Printed in the United States of America

The paper used in this publication meets the minimum requirements
of ANSI/NISO Z39.48-1992 (R 1997) (*Permanence of Paper*). ∞

Contents

Foreword

Ideas matter—and scarcely less in "practical" than in academic affairs (though less explicitly, to be sure). This is Michael Barzelay's central motif in *Breaking Through Bureaucracy*, with specific reference to American public management.

In the spirit of Keynes's famous comment that "practical men, who believe themselves to be quite exempt from any intellectual influences, are generally the slaves of some defunct economist,"[1] Barzelay argues that elected officials, senior appointed executives, and media commentators, whose views tend to shape organizational arrangements and oversight practices in the American public sector, are themselves typically slaves of obsolete ideas—in this case, not economic but managerial.

The ideas that still dominate our public management practice, Barzelay maintains, are squarely rooted in the politics-administration dichotomy, a legacy of Progressive reform in the early twentieth century. Nothing new here, you might say; the politics-administration dichotomy was long ago assigned to the dustbin of history. But not so. Barzelay demonstrates that, whatever its status among theorists, the politics-administration dichotomy remains alive and well in the world of practice. He goes on to illustrate the ways in which it contributes to those characteristics of American public administration that we, as citizens, find most exasperating.

This is just the beginning, however. Barzelay understands that it is impossible to dethrone an old mental set (or paradigm, as he calls it, following Thomas Kuhn) except by replacing it. He also realizes that a mental set that has manifested the tenacity of the politics-administration dichotomy has probably satisfied some important stakeholder needs. A viable replacement must satisfy these needs at least as effectively as the original paradigm, and preferably more so. Barzelay goes beyond criticism to inquire deeply into what these needs are and then to construct a public management paradigm for our time.

For the benefit of readers unfamiliar with the intellectual history of American public administration, a few words of semantic clarification may be in order. The politics-administration dichotomy is the idea that policy making and policy execution are distinct activities, which, in a well-ordered polity, are assigned to separate groups of public officials. Prescriptive arguments rooted in this idea typically specify that elected legislators should confine themselves to policy making, whereas appointed administrators should confine themselves to policy execution.

It has long been commonplace among scholars to speak of the politics-administration dichotomy in the past tense, as an artifact of Progressive reform, doubtless useful in its day as an ideological weapon against political machines but hopelessly flawed as a description of what was or ever could be. What has been less frequently observed, however, is the persistence of a mental set, or paradigm, organized around the politics-administration dichotomy that still dominates American popular thought on the topic of public management.

The core problem addressed by this "bureaucratic" paradigm (Barzelay's label) is democratic accountability. The solution, devised as an alternative to partisan patronage and ad hoc meddling, is that execution of the laws should be organized as a ministerial activity. The laws should be crystal clear; their execution should be thoroughly routine. The aims of managerial reform, quite simply, should be honesty, efficiency, and a day's work for a day's pay. The demons to be slain are corruption, arbitrariness, and sloth. There is no room in this paradigm for bureaucratic intelligence or creativity, because these imply discretion, an invitation to the above-mentioned demons. The appropriate instruments of reform, it follows, are top-down controls: precise rules to cover as many circumstances as possible, investigators to weed out corruption, and close oversight by staff units in the immediate entourage of the chief executive.

Public management ideas are generally imports from the world of business. The bureaucratic paradigm is no exception. If it is rooted politically in Progressive reform, its business roots are in the movement for scientific management. The central problem addressed by scientific management was how to maximize assembly-line productivity. Its solution was to carry out time-and-motion studies of worker movements to identify the most efficient repetitive motions and then to ensure that workers consistently adhered to these procedures.

Business concepts vary widely in the ease with which they can be transplanted to the public sector. The bureaucratic paradigm found fertile soil. Elected officials concerned about losing control as government grew rested easier in the knowledge that new instruments of control were at hand. Voters angry at the thought of bureaucratic corruption and waste (a media staple from early on) readily accepted the idea that tight, "business-like" controls might yield some improvement.

Nearly a century has passed since the origins of this paradigm, and the business world has moved on. Its managerial focus today is far more sharply on how to stay ahead of fast-moving competitors than on how to maximize simple static efficiency. What most distinguishes great corporations, it is generally agreed, is their capacity for continuous, customer-sensitive adaptation and innovation. This is not to suggest that efficiency is passé. But efficiency in the production of obsolete products is today recognized as a shortcut to corporate bankruptcy.

In striving to achieve this new, far more complex vision of effective management, today's cutting-edge business leaders have come to recognize that top-down management has severe limitations. The approach can work when customer needs and production processes are highly stable. However, when the challenge is to keep abreast of changing customer needs, to develop new products more rapidly than competitors, and to achieve constant productivity gains, top-down management cannot do the trick. No small group of managers can possibly know enough, or generate enough creative ideas, to achieve organizational competitiveness. Neither, through strategies of tight control, can managers elicit the type of worker commitment required to achieve ever-increasing standards of product quality.

So the focus of management reform in the business sector has shifted from tight control to motivating employee commitment, tapping employee knowledge, and unleashing employee ingenuity. In pursuing this vision, business leaders increasingly seek to involve lower levels in their organizations in decision-making responsibilities, especially in the area of direct customer interface, while at the same time relying on recruitment, training, socialization, and incentives to ensure adherence to company objectives.

Until now, remarkably little attention has been paid, by either scholars or practitioners, to the implications for the public sector of this new business managerial vision. The reason, perhaps, is that it is difficult to image how a paradigm so "loose" in its control mechanisms could possibly satisfy demands for accountability in the public sector.

Barzelay has taken up this challenge. Moreover, he has done so empirically. He has observed a real-world effort to adapt key elements of this vision for public application. In the course of doing so, he has paid particularly close attention to argumentation—to the criticisms directed at his subject innovators, to the justifications that have worked for them, and to the whole dynamic by which ideas contend in the world of public management.

He has found that tensions between accountability and performance are considerably more soluble than one might expect. After all, business leaders are scarcely prone to relinquishing those elements of control they consider vital. The relevant focus in comparing paradigms is not the degree but rather the type of control—as well as what top managers consider their most critical tasks. Barzelay's greatest contribution, in my view, is to demonstrate that the aim of reconciling accountability, delegation, and stimuli for employee creativity in the public sector is thoroughly realistic, and to provide empirical illustrations of practical means by which it may be pursued. I shall not attempt to summarize his argument here, as I could not do it justice in this brief space. Let me note simply that I think anyone with a serious interest in this theme will find *Breaking Through Bureaucracy* a fount of fresh, persuasive insights.

To note that *Breaking Through Bureaucracy* is a work of empirical scholarship is not to say, of course, that it is about average practice. Barzelay's approach is to learn from pathbreaking practice, all the while considering how it might fare in other settings. He is the first to acknowledge that in focusing as he does on a single case—and Minnesota at that, where "good government" has thrived for generations and scandal is the exception rather than the rule—he is directing our attention to an outlier. Barzelay's main concern, however, is with what could and should be. In this view, contemporary average practice and its roots in history are background features rather than the central topic of inquiry.

It bears mention in this context that Barzelay's research has been funded by the Program on Innovations in State and Local Government, a joint venture of the Ford Foundation and Harvard University's John F. Kennedy School of Government. The Innovations program includes both a nationwide competition each year for innovative programs in state and local government (with prizes of $100,000 for each of the ten winners) and a program of research. Barzelay first became aware of the Minnesota initiatives described in this volume after a subset of them received a 1986 Innovations award. He was motivated initially just to write a case study for instructional purposes, but as he probed, his theoretical antennae began to quiver—and continued to do so through five years of subsequent study. The clear, indeed elegant, line of argument that drives *Breaking Through Bureaucracy* may strike, in retrospect, some readers as obvious. In prospect, however, it was anything but, even to those who had partially sensed and begun acting on it in practice.[2]

Barzelay's concern from relatively early on was to articulate, and thereby help diffuse, good practice as well as to build theory and curriculum. This blend of academic and practical concerns typifies the scholarship funded by the Innovations program and reflects a judgment by those who administer the program (of whom, admittedly, I am one) that, in general, the most fruitful path to public management theory is to observe practice closely and, more specifically, that the best way scholars can help improve public management is to search out, observe, and think hard about "best" practices.

While constantly shuttling between his academic and practitioner reference groups during the years that *Breaking Through Bureaucracy* was in gestation, Barzelay was taken by the unconventional idea that he might write a single book for both areas. At the same time, he became sharply aware of the divergent interests and stylistic preferences. Public managers, he concluded, read primarily in search of ideas and techniques they might apply. Stylistically they prefer to learn from case examples written in plain language, with a minimum of abstract analysis and formal documentation. Scholars, however, read in search of generalizations about reality, interesting new data, rigor in argumentation, conceptual precision, and explicit linkages to prior theory and research.

Barzelay was eager to communicate with both of these target audiences simultaneously. In considering how to do so, he arrived at the following hypotheses: first, that many practitioners are eager for serious analysis, particularly if it is directed to their central concerns, presented in everyday language, and liberally peppered with real-world examples; and second, that the objectives of scholars can be met by adhering to defensible norms of professional social inquiry. His particular solution in the pages that follow is to relegate those aspects of the analysis most likely to interest academics, and nearly all of his documentation, to an extensive set of footnotes. Somewhat to my surprise (O.K., I was a skeptic), this combination works extremely well. Both scholars and practitioners should find the main text a thoroughly good read, while scholars will find their distinctive concerns addressed fully in the endnotes—which virtually add up to a parallel book!

Alan A. Altshuler

Preface

Making the operating institutions of government work better is a challenge that Americans have taken up throughout the twentieth century. The movements for civil service reform, the short ballot, state government reorganization, professional city management, and budget reform kicked off the tradition of reform. Then came the integrative idea of administrative management articulated at the end of the 1930s and since restated innumerable times. In the 1960s and 1970s, a new generation of Americans engaged in public affairs developed and applied a range of tools, including systems analysis, policy analysis, program budgeting, and program evaluation, to improve the results of government programs.

Once again, Americans are taking up the challenge of improving the performance of public sector organizations.[1] Some are pursuing their aims with the aid of concepts the tenor of which is different from bureaucratic ideas of authority, responsibility, efficiency, and control. These concepts include customers, service, quality, value, flexibility, innovation, empowerment, and continuous improvement. Informed by these and other concepts, some public officials at all levels of government are experimenting with innovative solutions to long-standing operational problems. Meanwhile, however, other public managers dismiss the excitement about these concepts as just another fad.

To those who dismiss the new ideas, *Breaking Through Bureaucracy* offers several arguments illustrated by real-world experience to raise in their minds the possibility that a new paradigm about managing government operations is coming together and that it might have the staying power of the system of ideas bequeathed by the reformers. To the increasing number of public officials and citizens who already embrace these ideas, this book offers not only examples of specific workable strategies for important organizations within the governmental structure but also an analysis of how these ideas—linked together—challenge the bureaucratic paradigm that has guided practice since early in the century. To those who are reticent to move firmly into either camp, this study provides empirical evidence for the argument that at least some important recurring problems in government are likely to be solved by putting the new concepts into practice.

THE FOCUS

The kinds of problems examined in this book are wholly familiar to anyone working in government. They arise in the course of routine interactions between line employees, who directly produce the outputs of government agencies, and staff employees, who control the inputs. Many of the latter group of employees work in, or are influenced by, centralized staff agencies. In a well-known book written by and for public managers, Gordon Chase and Elizabeth Reveal summed up the staff/line relationship this way:

> In practice the overhead [staff] agencies are often obstacles to efficient management in government. . . . The combination of complexity, obscurity, and tedium means that overhead agencies can maintain an enviable isolation from accountability. . . . Overhead agencies use a variety of tactics to frustrate the public manager and maintain control over money and people. . . . The more rigid the overhead system, the more hurdles there are. . . . In such systems the merits all too often become irrelevant as the process becomes an end in itself. . . . For the seasoned public manager it is the part of the job that either finally wears you down to acquiescence or constantly recharges your batteries through sheer provocation.[2]

Unlike the book just cited, *Breaking Through Bureaucracy* is not a primer on the facts of life in government; rather, it pays close attention to concerted efforts in one state government to break through the bureaucratic and political constraints that make it unnecessarily hard for line agencies to produce outcomes that citizens value. These efforts began in the early 1980s in the staff agencies of Minnesota. Staff agency executives, eventually supported by overseers and operating-level managers and employees, identified their customers, clarified accountability relationships, redesigned operating strategies, introduced choice and competition in internal service relationships, and devised management processes that focused attention on results rather than inputs. By the end of the decade, this experience had attracted the attention of many public managers and educators throughout the nation.[3]

This book argues that the reigning bureaucratic paradigm, though it promises good government, actually tends to produce weak, misplaced, and misguided accountability. It examines how specific organizational strategies that go against the grain of the bureaucratic paradigm offer workable solutions. To help readers apply this approach in their settings, this book highlights arguments made in favor of the unconventional solutions, important details of implementation, and measured results. *Breaking Through Bureaucracy* concludes by identifying principles for managing staff/line/overseer relations and by placing concepts often maligned as faddish in the context of the historical evolution of managerial ideas.

LINKING RESEARCH TO PRACTICE

The origins of this book can be pinpointed with unusual accuracy. In the fall of 1986, during my second year on the faculty at the John F. Kennedy School of Government, I became involved with the Innovations in State and Local Government program, a joint venture between the Ford Foundation and the School. My first assignment was to develop a teaching case about the State of Minnesota's Striving Toward Excellence in Performance (STEP) program, which had received an Innovations program award several months earlier. I repeatedly interviewed Department of Administration Commissioner Sandra J. Hale, Deputy Commissioner Babak Armajani, and other individuals involved in the STEP program. From these interviews in 1986, I learned much about the vision, practical difficulties, and demonstrated possibilities of promoting innovation from within government.

I soon turned my attention to conducting research on innovation in public management, and I began to take more seriously than ever the notion that in this field, academics can and should learn from practitioners. This notion was deeply embedded in the Kennedy School's culture as I experienced it and represented a major premise of the Innovations program. As a scholar, I thought that it would be a good idea for me to form some kind of intellectual partnership with an innovative practitioner. From my work on the STEP case, I had an informed hunch that Babak Armajani would be a suitable intellectual partner from the world of practice. When I asked him to play this imprecise role, Armajani graciously entertained the idea.

By that time, Armajani, as assistant and then deputy commissioner, had been working for nearly five years to improve the management of Admin's centralized purchasing, data processing, general services, and other operations. The need to make improvements had been painfully evident, as recounted in the stories leading off chapter 2. The direction of change, as explained in chapter 3, had been guided by many of the principles advocated by the STEP program as well as by additional ideas, such as holding service providers accountable to customers and introducing marketlike forces within government. My first exposure to what had been taking place at the frontiers between Admin, overseers, and line agencies came when Armajani sent me a document that explained the department's emerging strategy (reproduced as appendix 1). I was intrigued by the ideas of identifying customers, separating service from control activities, and governing service activities as either utilities or marketplace enterprises. Drawing on my studies of politico-economic systems and management, I asked him scores of conceptual and practical questions about the ideas put forward in that document. The answers persuaded me that examining innovative solutions to recurring problems along the staff/line frontier would be productive of valuable research on public management.

Just a few months later, Armajani became deputy commissioner of Revenue. At Revenue, Armajani and a network of collaborators inside and outside the agency applied some of the same concepts and reasoning to the enterprise of bringing citizens' behavior into compliance with norms. Out of these and other concurrent deliberations in which he played a leadership role came such ideas as "serving collective customers" and "winning adherence to norms" as well as operational strategies to put them into practice in staff and line contexts. In January 1991, Armajani left state government due to a change in administration.

From Armajani's perspective, the collaboration provided an occasion and stimulus to refine and integrate some of the general concepts, arguments, and strategies—such as those linked to the idea of marketplace dynamics—that he had been developing while solving problems in the Department of Administration. Developments in Admin operations along with similar shifts in organizational strategies in the central personnel and finance agencies have served as the principal factual context for our joint effort to understand how ideas and actions can bring about desirable organizational change in government—whether in the staff agencies or in agencies delivering services to the public directly. We were fortunate that other individuals—especially Jeff Zlonis, Larry Grant, Elaine Johnson, and Judy Pinke—spent untold hours relating their experiences to us and criticizing the conceptual schemes we developed in order to discern what was innovative about the family of organizational change efforts taking place in the staff agencies.

Although my relationship to these change agents and to Armajani was hardly arm's length, I saw my role as an academic researcher based at a professional school of government; I was never engaged as a consultant to Minnesota state government, and all the costs associated with my research and writing were borne by the Innovations program and the John F. Kennedy School of Government. What made this kind of collaboration possible was Governor Rudy Perpich's support for fresh thinking in state government, Admin Commissioner Sandra J. Hale's encouragement of the interactive research process, the organizational culture of the Kennedy School, and the institutional support of the Ford Foundation.

During hundreds of conversations during the 1987–91 period,

Armajani and I convinced each other of many things. For example, Armajani persuaded me that the customer was a powerful and important concept in government. I convinced him that some difficulties in using the customer concept in government could be overcome by drawing on emerging findings about concept formation made by cognitive scientists. As another example, he persuaded me that acceptance of the kind of reasoning and practices he championed in government was rooted in a different paradigm from the one that influenced the thinking and behavior of government officials and politicians. After inquiring into the origins of staff agencies, I persuaded him that the paradigm he struggled to replace was a by-product of a specific historical process and that advocates for change should provide good reasons for believing that the new paradigm was better than the sophisticated one developed initially by early twentieth-century reformers. Many of the conversations about these matters took place while we were collaborating on a paper, "Managing State Government Operations: Changing Visions of Staff Agencies," which was published as a coauthored article in the *Journal of Policy Analysis and Management* in 1990.

Our method of working on that paper was to discuss thoroughly all points made in the multiple outlines and drafts I wrote. When we decided to move ahead on a book, we proceeded more or less as before. By the time a draft was complete, it was apparent to others and to me that the term *coauthor* did not properly characterize our nonstandard working relationship, and Armajani consented to the suggestion that he be identified as my collaborator. Armajani also deferred to my determination to craft arguments that would survive the scrutiny of academicians in the fields of public policy, management, and government. I therefore refined the argument and both expanded and reorganized the work in major ways before publication. In this key phase of the book's development, my collaborator was involved in some respects but not all. Although Armajani agrees with all major points made in this book, if he were to express his and our ideas in writing, the approach and style would be vastly different. The author should therefore be held solely accountable for any gaps between the aims and actual accomplishments of this book.

Acknowledgments

Our collaborators in the interactive research process were Larry Grant, John Haggerty, Peter Hutchinson, Elaine Johnson, Jim Kinzie, Joe Kurcinka, Connie Nelson, Judy Pinke, Julie Vikmanis, and Jeff Zlonis. In addition to writing background papers cited in the endnotes and discussing many arguments advanced here, this group held my feet to the fire as I tried through successive drafts to write a book that meets the needs of practitioners. They should be pleased to learn that the term *epiphenomenal problem solving* was finally expunged from the text.

My feet were repeatedly held to a different kind of fire by Charles E. Lindblom, Eugene Bardach, Aaron Wildavsky, Mark Moore, Marc Zegans, Mary Jo Bane, Alan Altshuler, Robert Behn, Rogers M. Smith, Steven Kelman, Richard Elmore, and Robert Reich. Their comments on the penultimate draft were especially valuable. Gene Bardach's willingness to provide detailed written criticisms on that draft, as well as speedy comments on new and rewritten chapters, went well beyond even the espoused norms of the community of scholars.

Helpful comments on earlier drafts were also provided by Hale Champion, Dan Fenn, David Bishop, Marshall Bailey, Miguel Angel Lasheras, Fred Thompson, Lee Friedman, Alasdair Roberts, Andrew Stone, J. Austin Burke, and James Clark. Quality research assistance was provided by David Snelbecker and Miriam Jorgensen.

We would like to thank all those who attended a June 1989 conference on managing state government operations held at the John F. Kennedy School of Government—especially Peter Zimmerman, associate dean for Executive Programs, and Julia

Elliott, who jointly organized the two-day event. Participants included the collaborators listed above, Rudy Perpich, Sandra J. Hale, John James, Tom Triplett, John Brandl, David Bishop, Kevin Kajer, Steven Ordahl, Mary Faulk, Lias Steen, Otto Brodtrick, Brain Marson, the late Stephen B. Hitchner, Jr., James Verdier, Rogers M. Smith, Jerry L. Mashaw, Robert Leone, and several Kennedy School colleagues.

Along the way, I had the opportunity to teach multiple cases about the Minnesota experience to over one hundred federal managers participating in the Kennedy School's Senior Executive Fellows programs in 1989 and 1990. I would like to thank them for their good humor and for highlighting those aspects of the cases that were most relevant to them. During the past year, Robert Kowalik, veteran street-level bureaucrat, trained linguist, and friend, sharpened my thinking about paradigms and helped me appreciate how the ideas in this book could be made relevant in a setting as different from Minnesota as Massachusetts. Throughout the writing process, no one has provided more quality feedback on matters of substance, organization, and style than Catherine S. Moukheibir. She also helped me to interpret critical comments provided by academics and practitioners on earlier drafts and to translate them into strategies for producing a book satisfactory to both groups of readers.

Armajani extends his personal gratitude to John James, who as commissioner of Revenue fully supported his deputy's continued involvement in both staff agency change efforts and the collaboration leading to this book.

Just after this book was accepted for publication, C. E. Lindblom repeated to me advice given to him by J. K. Galbraith forty years before: take a "finished" manuscript and rewrite it completely. The opportunity to do so came during the fall semester of 1991, thanks to Kennedy School Deans Robert D. Putnam and Albert Carnesale's support for faculty development. The people of Bruner/Cott & Associates generously permitted me to use office space at an undisclosed Cambridge, Mass., location while I produced the final version.

I dedicate this book to the professional educators who have done the most to develop my intellectual capacities and discipline my writing. Of these I woud like to mention here, with warm thanks and a pledge to continue doing the same for my own students, Peter S. Bennett, George B. Dantzig, Scott R. Pearson, Robert O. Keohane, Robert Packenham, Albert Fishlow, Juan J. Linz, Martin Shubik, Raymond Vernon, Mark H. Moore, and, not least, Charles E. Lindblom.

PART ONE

. . . .

Setting the Agenda

CHAPTER ONE

Beyond the Bureaucratic Paradigm

Imagine how government would work if almost every operating decision—including the hiring and firing of individuals—were made on partisan political grounds; if many agencies spent their entire annual appropriations in the first three months of the fiscal year; if appropriations were made to agencies without anyone having formulated a spending and revenue budget for the jurisdiction as a whole; and if no agency or person in the executive branch had authority to oversee the activities of government agencies.

This state of affairs was, in fact, the norm in the United States in the nineteenth century. That it sounds so chaotic and backward to us is due to the success of early twentieth-century reformers in influencing politics and administration at the city, state, and federal levels. As a result of their influence, most Americans take for granted that administrative decisions should be made in a businesslike manner, that the executive branch should be organized hierarchically, that most agency heads should be appointed by the chief executive, that the appropriations process should begin when the chief executive submits an overall budget to the legislature, that most positions should be staffed by qualified people, that materials should be purchased from responsible vendors based on objective criteria, and that systems of fiscal control and accountability should be reliable.[1]

The political movements favoring this form of bureaucratic

3

government emerged partly in response to the social problems created by the transformation of the United States from an agrarian and highly decentralized society to an urban, industrial, and national society.[2] For government to address social problems in an efficient manner, reformers said repeatedly, government agencies needed to be administered much like the business organizations that, at the time, were bringing about the industrial transformation.[3] For Americans supporting the reform and reorganization movements, bureaucracy meant efficiency and efficiency meant good government.[4]

Bureaucratically minded reformers also placed a high value on the impersonal exercise of public authority. To this end, they argued that actions intended to control others should be based on the application of rules and that no action should be taken without authorization. When officials' actions could not be fully determined by applying rules, professional or technical expertise was to be relied on to make official action impersonal.[5] This outlook extended to hiring and purchasing. The consistent application of universal rules embodying the merit principle was expected to assure that government officials would act competently on behalf of the public interest, while simultaneously undermining the power of the party machines that dominated politics *and* administration.[6] The consistent application of universal rules in purchasing was expected to reduce government's operating costs and to have similar political consequences.[7]

The values of efficiency and impersonal administration along with prescriptions for putting them into practice in government constituted a compelling system of beliefs in the early twentieth century. This system may be termed the *bureaucratic reform vision*.

PERSISTENCE OF THE BUREAUCRATIC PARADIGM

The bureaucratic reform vision lost its hold on the political imagination of the reform constituency once civil service and executive budgeting had been put into place and the Great Depression posed new and pressing collective problems. As a belief system about public administration, by contrast, the bureaucratic reform vision survived—although not wholly intact—such political changes as the Great Society and Reaganism and a series of efforts to improve management in government including systems analysis, management by objectives, and zero-based budgeting. Among the legacies of the bureaucratic reform movements are deeply ingrained habits of thought.[8] These habits of thought and the belief system that supports them are referred to in this book as the *bureaucratic paradigm*.[9]

In order to probe whether the bureaucratic paradigm is a good guide to public management a century after the reform movements began, it is important to be aware of the key beliefs it contains. The following beliefs are among those embedded in the bureaucratic paradigm that deserve close scrutiny.

- Specific delegations of authority define each role in the executive branch. Officials carrying out any given role should act only when expressly permitted to do so either by rule or by instructions given by superior authorities in the chain of command. Employees within the executive branch are responsible to their supervisors.

- In exercising authority, officials should apply rules and procedures in a uniform manner. The failure to obey rules should be met with an appropriate penalty.

- Experts in substantive matters—such as engineers, law-enforcement personnel, and social service providers—should be assigned to line agencies, while experts in budgeting, accounting, purchasing, personnel, and work methods should be assigned to centralized staff functions.

- The key responsibilities of the financial function are to prepare the executive budget and to prevent actual spending from exceeding appropriations. The key responsibilities of the purchasing function are to minimize the price paid to acquire goods and services from the private sector and to enforce purchasing rules. The key responsibilities of the personnel function include classifying jobs, examining applicants, and making appointments to positions.[10]

- The executive branch as a whole will operate honestly and efficiently as long as the centralized staff functions exercise unilateral control over line agencies' administrative actions.

UNRAVELING THE BUREAUCRATIC PARADIGM

The bureaucratic paradigm has been criticized by intellectuals since the 1930s. Some criticized the idea that the formal organization is the principal determinant of efficiency and effectiveness.[11] Some urged that control be viewed as a process in which all employees strive to coordinate their work with others.[12] Some voices criticized the idea that the exercise of unilateral authority within hierarchies was a recipe for good government.[13] More argued that the meaning of economy and efficiency within the bureaucratic paradigm was conceptually muddled.[14] Many came to recommend that budgeters analyze social benefits and costs of government programs instead of focusing attention only on expenditures.[15] Some raised concerns about the tendency of line agency employees to adjust to staff agency's administrative systems by becoming constraint-oriented rather than mission-oriented.[16] A few intellectuals also found evidence for the proposition that the workings of some administrative systems contradicted common sense.[17] Many of these insights and arguments have been incorporated into mainstream practitioner and academic thinking about public management. Nonetheless, many of the beliefs of the bureaucratic paradigm have escaped serious challenge.[18]

The most important recent conceptual challenge to the bureaucratic paradigm arising in the world of practice is the notion that government organizations should be customer-driven and service-oriented. A recurring aspiration of public managers and overseers using these concepts is to solve operational problems by transforming their organizations into responsive, user-friendly, dynamic, and competitive providers of valuable services to customers. Thinking in terms of customers and service helps public managers and overseers articulate their concerns about the performance of the government operations for which they are accountable. When supplemented by analysis of how these concepts have been put into practice in other settings, reasoning about customers and service helps managers generate alternative solutions to the particular problems they have defined as meriting attention. In many instances, the range of alternatives generated in this fashion is substantially different from that yielded by reasoning within the bureaucratic paradigm.[19]

Many public officials, alert to the power of these conceptual resources in the contemporary United States, are identifying those whom they believe to be their customers and are using methods of strategic service management to improve their operations.[20] For example, the U.S. Army Recruiting Command has developed an extremely sophisticated strategy to attract its external customers—qualified young Americans—to join the military.[21] This strategy is designed to satisfy these customers' needs for guaranteed future employment, occupational training, immediate income, self-esteem, individuality, and fair treatment so as to meet the internal customers' needs for a high-quality workforce. The Army recruiting operation's key service concept—reinforced by television advertising—is to provide external customers a "guaranteed reservation" for "seats" in training programs for specific military occupations. To support this service concept, Army contractors engineered a sophisticated information system known as REQUEST. Operated by specialized recruiters referred to as guidance counselors, the REQUEST system customizes the Army's offer of multiyear membership, employment, training, immediate cash, and other benefits. The more attractive the recruit—as judged from a battery of standardized tests—the better the offer. This example plainly illustrates how one government organization, in attempting to implement public policies—in this case, maintaining a large standing army capable of fighting wars and staffing it with volunteers—puts the customer-service approach into practice.[22]

Strategic service management is also practiced in situations where the government/citizen transaction is involuntary and when obligations are being imposed. An example of this kind of situation is the operation of taxation systems. Some revenue agencies now identify taxpaying individuals and businesses as their customers; others identify the collective interests of the people who pay taxes and receive government services as the customer, while conceiving of service provision as a way of cost-effectively facilitating voluntary compliance.[23] Such revenue agencies are making operational changes—for example, simplifying tax forms, writing instructions in plain English, providing taxpayer assistance, and building the capacity to produce timely refunds—with the aim of making it easier and more rewarding for people to comply with their obligations. This approach to managing revenue agencies puts into practice in a compliance context two key principles of service operations management: first, that customers participate in the production and delivery of services, and, second, that the service-delivery process tends to operate more smoothly when customers understand what is expected of them and feel that the organization and its service providers are making a reasonable effort to accommodate their needs.

FORMULATING AN ALTERNATIVE

The concept of a customer-driven service organization is thus a tool used increasingly by public officials to define and solve problems.[24] At a higher level of generality, this concept also provides many of the resources needed to formulate a coherent alternative to the bureaucratic paradigm.[25] The outlines of this alternative and its mode of identifying and attacking the vulnerabilities of the bureaucratic paradigm are already coming into focus. The following paired statements highlight the main rhetorical battle lines:[26]

- A bureaucratic agency is focused on its own needs and perspectives. A customer-driven agency is focused on customer needs and perspectives.

- A bureaucratic agency is focused on the roles and responsibilities of its parts. A customer-driven agency is focused on enabling the whole organization to function as a team.

- A bureaucratic agency defines itself both by the amount of resources it controls and by the tasks it performs. A customer-driven agency defines itself by the results it achieves for its customers.

- A bureaucratic agency controls costs. A customer-driven agency creates value net of cost.

- A bureaucratic agency sticks to routine. A customer-driven agency modifies its operations in response to changing demands for its services.

- A bureaucratic agency fights for turf. A customer-driven agency competes for business.

- A bureaucratic agency insists on following standard procedures. A customer-driven agency builds choice into its operating systems when doing so serves a purpose.

- A bureaucratic agency announces policies and plans. A customer-driven agency engages in two-way communication with its customers in order to assess and revise its operating strategy.

- A bureaucratic agency separates the work of thinking from that of doing. A customer-driven agency empowers front-line employees to make judgments about how to improve customer service and value.[27]

The fact that this kind of rhetoric is coming into common use suggests that a new alternative to the bureaucratic paradigm— one that builds on much prior practical and intellectual work— is now available. As this alternative becomes well-formulated and well-accepted, it may become the frame of reference for most efforts to diagnose operational problems in the public sector and to find solutions to them. The time is ripe, therefore, to define as carefully as possible what this alternative is. *Breaking Through Bureaucracy* takes on this task.[28]

In characterizing the post-bureaucratic paradigm, this book draws a series of contrasts with its bureaucratic predecessor at two different levels of generality. At the general level, the two paradigms are compared on their respective claims about how government production processes should be managed, how control should be exercised, and what ideas public employees should care deeply about. At the specific level, the two paradigms are compared on their claims about how relations among centralized staff agencies, line agencies, and overseers should be managed.[29]

TARGETING THE STAFF AGENCIES

Staff/line/overseer relations are an ideal focus for our attention because their historic pattern constitutes a major obstacle to continued experimentation with the customer-service approach. Staff agencies exercise enormous influence over the management of government operations because overseers give them authority to control all the inputs to line agency production processes: money, labor, information systems, data, office space, materials, equipment, training, travel, and the like. Staff agencies tend to exercise their authority in accord with laws and regulations whose consequences are rarely subjected to systematic analysis. Furthermore, staff agencies are generally known for their lack of responsiveness to what line agencies ask of them.[30] Absent a change in their operational routines, staff agencies are the likely bottlenecks in the process of putting the post-bureaucratic paradigm into practice. This bottleneck is illustrated and analyzed in chapter 2.

Breaking Through Bureaucracy then explores an exemplary effort to eliminate this potential bottleneck, which, as mentioned in the preface, took place during the 1983–90 period in Minnesota state government. This effort initially foundered on resistance to change. Many staff agency employees were horrified by the idea that they should be responsive to line agencies. The head of purchasing insisted that if his unit were responsive, line agencies would buy Cadillacs instead of Chevrolets. Personnel experts envisioned the demise of "the system" of rules protecting merit employment, equal access, and affirmative action. Information managers worried that agencies did not have the expertise to manage information resources efficiently and effectively.

These fears reflected the cultures of the organizations for which such individuals had worked for most of their careers. They had internalized the values of impersonal administration and economy and efficiency, as well as the reformers' belief that line agencies were staffed by people who would subvert the public interest if not strictly controlled by central authorities. To them, being responsive to agencies implied abandoning their missions.

In instigating organizational change, executives in the Department of Administration made use of the conceptual resources discussed above.[31] At first, most managers looked puzzled when asked to identify their customers. "It was an interesting question to them, but it wasn't one that had been thought through at all," recalls the assistant commissioner of administration for agency services at the time.[32] The term *customer* was simply not part of the working vocabulary of the department.[33]

When pressed, a common response of staff employees was that the public as a whole is the customer. The executives were not satisfied with this answer. They knew that line agencies were angered by poor service quality, rising costs, and counterproductive rules, and that certain legislators were alarmed that control over line agencies was not being effectively exercised. Department of Administration executives therefore insisted that each staff agency decide whether line agencies or overseers were their customers.

Managers and employees working for internal services, such as the central motor pool and the central office-supply store, had always thought of themselves as providing services to users. They were willing to conceptualize users as clients but resisted the idea that users were customers to whom they would be accountable. The customer concept was even more problematic for staff units who were control-oriented. Their purpose was not to satisfy agency needs; indeed, some employees working in these areas said their purpose was control. Department of Administration executives argued instead that the purpose of control activities is to meet the governor's and legislature's needs for analysis of administrative policies, generalized compliance with statewide norms, and information that helps overseers hold line agencies accountable directly for their performance. They argued that overseers are the customers of control activities, just as line agencies are the customers of service activities.

Executives became increasingly confident in using the customer concept. They insisted that staff personnel identify their customers. They claimed that the principal responsibility of each staff agency's employees is to serve their customers. They made sure that employees knew what their customers believed constituted service quality. All the while, they had to explain why it is appropriate for staff agency employees to be accountable to either overseers or line agencies as customers.

The arguments crafted by executives made more sense to staff agency employees as they became more familiar with them. One manager recalls that for two years he thought the deputy commissioner was "totally off his rocker," but that one day he "woke up and decided he was absolutely right."[34] Many others also came to similar conclusions. Filling some key middle-management slots with individuals who understood and agreed with this new way of thinking and working was instrumental to deepening its acceptance.[35] Many other factors also came into play. Not least among them was building the organizational and technological supports that enabled staff employees to succeed in the eyes of their customers.

CHAPTER TWO

The Need for Innovative Strategies

In championing the bureaucratic reform vision, early twentieth-century politicians like Minnesota Governors A. O. Eberhart, Theodore Christianson, and Harold Stassen argued that reorganization, an executive budget, and civil service reform were needed for state government to serve the public interest. The rhetoric they crafted to justify the solutions of reorganization and reform aimed to stir moral outrage on the part of the public as a whole. There were plenty of villains in the tales they told.[1] In comparison with the high politics of reorganization and reform, the improvement of staff/line/overseer relations in Minnesota during the 1980s is a story of quiet problem solving. Ritual dismay, interspersed with outrage, did nonetheless put in an appearance, creating an impetus for breaking through bureaucracy.[2]

ROUTINE TROUBLE ALONG THE STAFF/LINE FRONTIER

Situation Normal, All Fouled Up

Supplying Computers for the Classroom. In the mid-1980s personal computers were transforming the business world. To satisfy the demand for skilled computer users and to attract students, Normandale Community College developed an aggressive strategy of offering hands-on computer training. A new computer course was planned and promoted in the fall catalogue. In January, nine months before the semester's start, Normandale asked central purchasing to supply the fifty personal computers needed in the lab. Two weeks before the class was due to begin, the computers had yet to arrive.

To get action, instructors at the college urged the chancellor of the state's community college system to intervene on their behalf. The chancellor called the deputy commissioner of administration—who oversaw purchasing—and demanded to know why the computers had not been delivered. The deputy commissioner asked his procurement director why action had not been taken on the Normandale request. The procurement director responded: "The state expects to purchase several hundred personal computers this year. We can get a better price if we bid them all at one time. Therefore, we have been holding the community college requisition, along with several others, until we can take best advantage of the potential economies of scale. This is the purpose of central procurement."[3] Nothing could be done at that stage to fill the request within the constraints of the purchasing system, and Normandale was forced to cancel the computer course because of the lack of equipment.

Typewriters.   An office supervisor in the Commerce Department decided that it was time to replace the stock of manual typewriters with electric ones. A committee of typists in the department recommended that IBM Selectrics be purchased. They liked the fact that Selectrics had an excellent maintenance record and featured an easy correction device that would substantially improve their productivity. This line of typewriters was requisitioned through central purchasing. The buyer, following regulations, proceeded to write broad specifications for this request. The contract was awarded to the lowest bidder. As a result, a different kind and brand of typewriter, Adler, was purchased. Within six months, Commerce Department executives complained about tremendous problems with the chosen typewriters. The Adlers needed frequent repair. Replacement ribbons were difficult to find. More seriously, many typists refused to accept the machines, even if it meant continuing to use their manual typewriters. The office supervisors recommended that the Adlers be shelved and that Selectrics be leased.[4] The commerce commissioner said he would support this recommendation unless central purchasing approved the purchase of Selectrics.[5]

Specifying Scientific Instruments. A similar problem occurred when the Health Department requisitioned for a highly technical application a particular brand of microscope that happened to be manufactured in Germany. An American-made microscope incapable of performing the required functions arrived. "Buy American" statutes did not apply in this case, although buyers felt it prudent to act as though they did. The microscope remained in a Health Department storage closet.

Red Herring. Two Beluga whales were the featured attraction at the Minnesota Zoo. They were fed a particular variety of red herring. Acting in the presumed interests of the taxpayers and the zoo, a buyer in central purchasing found an alternative type of herring at a lower price. Zookeepers were shocked when the shipment arrived: the herring were toxic to the whales. A new shipment of the proper herring had to be rushed to the zoo at great expense.

Black Pens. One day, the Department of Administration's executive responsible for office supplies was heard cursing in his office. A colleague asked why he was angry. The executive responded that he had to use half a dozen black pens to compose a memo of two paragraphs. The subject of the memo: complaints about the quality of state pens.

Getting Programs Up and Running. During the 1984 legislative session state funds were appropriated to the Department of Trade and Economic Development and positions were authorized for a major new program. Although expectations of legislators were high and the program was a priority of Commissioner Mark Dayton, it had not begun by the subsequent legislative session. The reason: the Department of Employee Relations (DOER)—the central staff agency that operated the civil service system and managed labor relations for the state—had not yet classified the newly authorized positions. The recruitment and examination of candidates awaited conclusion of the classification process. On hearing of the delay in starting the new program, legislators demanded an explanation from the line agency's commissioner. Commissioner Dayton decried the slowness of the staffing processes. Attention turned to DOER. But DOER's managers demonstrated that normal procedures had been followed. Angry legislators did not know whom to blame.

Giving the System Time to Work.   In the early 1980s, it took an average of ninety days to classify a new position, sixty days to administer examinations, forty-five days to produce a financial report on the previous month's activity, ninety days to fill a requisition for a product stocked by a vendor, sixty days to complete a simple in-house printing job, up to one year to be assigned a motor-pool vehicle, sixty days or more to pay a vendor, four months to have an electrical outlet installed, six months to a year to obtain a copying machine, and thirty days to get routine vacuuming done.

Spending Money as Planned.   It was common practice for agencies in Minnesota, as elsewhere, to spend their entire appropriations during what is known as the budget execution process, even if ways could be found to operate more cost-effectively during the year. The incentives of the budgetary system all pushed in the direction of spending rather than economizing. First, state employees regarded an increase in appropriations to be a principal measure of an agency's success. Second, unspent appropriations were cancelled, hence unavailable to the agency in subsequent years. Third, overseers were likely to "reward" an agency for economizing on costs by reducing future appropriations. This state of affairs—in which managerial attention was rationally focused on spending rather than on creating value net of cost—was lamented by a number of staff agency executives, whose backgrounds included experience in business and education in public policy analysis. However, because the executives were taught by political and bureaucratic veterans to attribute the situation to the inescapable political economy of government spending and accounting, they learned to view this system of perverse incentives as part of the landscape.

The Infectious General Fund Mentality. Department of Administration executives were alarmed to discover that managers of their agency's general service activities also focused attention on spending rather than on creating value, even though they did not face the same perverse incentives as did managers of programs financed by appropriations. The method of financing most general services was known as revolving funds, which meant that they generated revenues by selling services to other agencies and kept their books using the accrual method of business rather than the cash method of government.[6] If these internal service activities generated an excess of revenues over expenses by economizing, the "savings" would be carried on the books as retained earnings and would be available for use in subsequent years. But the general fund mentality, ardently advanced by the Department of Finance, suggested that revolving fund managers were successful only when they broke even. If internal service activities happened to be making a profit, a committee met to determine how to increase spending fast enough to break even during the same year. No consideration was given to decreasing the rates line agencies were charged for the services they consumed, nor were expenditures justified on the basis of their rate of return. From the perspective of executives in the 1980s, internal service activities were businesses within government, and this was not a way to run a business.

Freeze: That's an Order! Shortly after taking office in 1983, Governor Rudy Perpich signed an executive order imposing a general freeze on hiring, on purchases of equipment, on travel by state employees and professionals, and on signing technical contracts. This move was the governor's response to a short-term fiscal shortfall and also played to the gallery of people who believed that government is wasteful. The freeze called for the central staff agencies—Finance, Administration, and Employee Relations—to give prior approval to any exception to the executive order. It required commissioners of the various departments to review all such requests personally and to submit a memorandum justifying exceptions as emergencies.

Within hours of the freeze announcement, the state's staff and line agencies were preparing to do battle with one another. Staff agencies began to develop rules, procedures, and guidelines to enforce the freeze order. Line agency commissioners began to develop criteria and guidelines for declaring a freeze-breaking administrative decision an emergency. Meanwhile, a much larger group of state managers planned how their purposes could be advanced despite the freeze. Many of these managers, mindful of the need for immediate savings but resentful of the lack of opportunity to use their judgment in solving this problem, scrutinized the first round of memoranda from freeze enforcers looking for loopholes. They wasted no time preparing elaborate justifications for exceptions to the freeze orders, first for their agency's commissioner and subsequently for the staff agencies.

In response to the first batch of requests for exceptions to the freeze, enforcers in the staff agencies issued additional rules. Subsequent rounds of increasingly lengthy memoranda were disseminated to armies of program managers, who sought new ways to circumvent or challenge the freeze. Despite strongly stated admonitions to the contrary, thousands of requests for exemptions poured in within a few weeks of the executive order. Considerable management resources were devoted to the administration and circumvention of the freeze in the months that followed. Rather than focusing on producing results for citizens, and in direct contravention of the reason behind the freeze, the state's executives and managers were engaged in a widespread bureaucratic skirmish.

Knocking Heads.   During a legislative hearing on allegations of excessive use of office space by the Department of National Resources, an angry state senator demanded answers from the commissioner of administration: "We're only in session for about six months. You're here full time. We expect you to watch over the other agencies to assure us that they are conducting their affairs according to norms that we have established. Next time you come back here, commissioner, I want to know how many heads you have knocked."[7]

Each year, the staff agencies were called on to solve numerous problems in line agencies. Often overseers failed to communicate their concerns and expectations directly to the line agencies concerned. Line agencies frequently eschewed responsibility for correcting problems and resisted staff agency efforts to bring about change. Sometimes, staff agency executives felt they were pushing on a string.

The conventional practice of using staff agencies to hold line agencies accountable for their administrative decisions by knocking heads left an indelible mark on the culture of virtually every unit within the staff agencies, including routine service operations. Recalls the Department of Administration's then–assistant commissioner with responsibility for the motor pool:

> I remember hearing a lot of complaints about service in the central motor pool and discussing this issue with the manager. I explained that service is really important and that our customers have to be satisfied. The motor pool manager said he totally agreed, and he then recounted the story of someone returning a car filled with wrappers after having been to McDonald's and what he did about it. He said, "I cleaned the car and took all this stuff, put it in a box, mailed it to the guy who messed up the car, and told him, this is no way to treat a state vehicle." [8]

In the mind of the assistant commissioner, there was something fundamentally wrong with a system that would lead a normal human being to put a higher priority on seeking justice for a state vehicle than on treating fellow state employees with ordinary respect.

The Major Point of the Stories

Those who have worked in government can readily draw on their own experience to supply further evidence for the argument that routine staff/line/overseer relations all too often produce unsatisfactory outcomes.[9] In talking about these outcomes, Americans generally use the term *inefficient*—a favorite epithet of the bureaucratic reformers—or the more vivid language of disgust, anger, and moral outrage. For purposes of defining and diagnosing the kind of situations illustrated above, the abstract concept of inefficiency is too blunt an instrument, while the vivid con-

cepts expressing sentiments are unwieldy. The recurring unsatisfactory outcomes of staff/line/overseer relations are more usefully categorized and labeled as summarized here.

*The needs of line agencies' customers—usually citizens—are un-
met, and their legitimate expectations are dashed.* This outcome is
illustrated by the cancellation of the Normandale Community
College computer course—which upset students' plans to take
the course—as well as by the delays in getting the new Department of Trade and Economic Development program off the
ground—which annoyed the legislators who spoke on behalf of
the program's customers.

The cost of providing government services is unreasonably high.
This outcome resulted when materials and equipment selected
by central purchasing went to waste because they did not fit
adequately into line agency production processes: the Adler
typewriters that Commerce Department secretaries would not
use, the American-made microscope that could not perform the
highly technical task for which it was ordered by the Health
Department, and the herring that the Beluga whales could not
eat. In these cases, central purchasing succeeded in minimizing
the cost per unit of input to line agency production but raised
the cost per unit of output delivered by the Commerce Department, the Health Department, and the zoo to their customers.
This same kind of outcome also resulted from the unnecessarily
high costs of the inputs—like centralized data processing—that
line agencies received from those service activities whose managers had internalized the general fund mentality. During the
governor's freeze, furthermore, line agency managers were frequently denied the opportunity to take actions they believed
would reduce both the unit costs of their services and annual
expenditures.

*Dissatisfaction with both the governing process and public ser-
vice becomes widespread.* Overseers worry that even their seemingly most powerful means of providing direction to agencies
and holding them accountable—such as imposing a general freeze
or changing the level of appropriations—are not up to the task.
Out of frustration, they demand that the staff agencies knock the
heads of line agency managers and employees, who naturally

retaliate by taking advantage of inevitable loopholes in rules enforced by staff agencies and communicate their feelings toward centralized service providers by such physical metaphors as rubbish left in motor-pool vehicles. Common sense suggests that in this system of intergroup relations neither chief executives nor legislators nor line agency executives nor front-line employees serving the public can do their jobs to their own satisfaction (let alone to one another's). Morale of politicians, no less than of public employees, is a proximate casualty. Erosion of service quality and cost-effectiveness, as well as pride in governmental institutions, cannot be far behind.

ARE RECURRING TROUBLES CONDITIONS OR PROBLEMS?

An ordinary citizen or elected official might react to many of the stories sketched above by shaking his or her head, remarking that the people working for state government must be bunglers, lamenting the nature of government and bureaucracy, calling the whole situation unfortunate, and then expressing concern about the *real* problems of crime, unemployment, and declining SAT scores. When this is the response, the unhappy situations portrayed above are not viewed as problems to be solved but as conditions to be endured, much like aging, frictional unemployment, and continental drift.

For a situation to be defined as either a problem or condition, people have to decide whether it can and should be improved.[10] Whenever there is any uncertainty about what can and should be done about a situation (and in complex situations such uncertainty abounds), deciding whether it is a condition or problem is a judgment call.[11] With the possible exception of iconoclasts, every individual's judgments are influenced to some degree by arguments that others make about the same situations or about situations resembling the one of concern.[12] Some arguments are simple; others are more complex. Some are laden with facts; others are grounded in strongly held values.[13] Some open up new lines of thinking; others have the effect of diverting thinking.[14] Some arguments are crafted to persuade people to regard situations as problems (think back to the civil rights movement or the origins of the environmental movement).[15] Unsatisfactory situations are often perpetually perceived as conditions because the argument that efforts to solve the so-called problem are likely to be futile or counterproductive is widely accepted.[16] Thus, if a situation is judged a condition, problem-solving efforts are likely to be feeble or nonexistent. If it is judged a problem, enough attention can be focused to make a difference.

A major empirical argument of *Breaking Through Bureaucracy* is that situations resembling those described above frequently recur in American government.[17] A major evaluative argument of this book is that these recurring situations are problems in the social-scientific as well as in the ordinary sense of the term. Some of these problems are harder to solve than others, though none is trivial.[18] Some of them are so formidable that even the best efforts to solve them may come to naught, making it reasonable to recategorize such recurring situations as conditions or predicaments.[19] Anyone who cares about government operations and their consequences should value intelligent efforts to solve these problems.

CONDITIONS, NOT PROBLEMS

The Bureaucratic Paradigm as a Source of Argument

The fact that routine troubles along the staff/line frontier in government have persisted for decades suggests that some people do not buy the argument that such recurring situations are problems. The reason may be that arguments defining these routinely troubling situations as conditions are based on the widely accepted premises of the bureaucratic paradigm. To see how arguments drawn from the bureaucratic paradigm can serve to rationalize undesirable outcomes, let us revisit the case of the canceled computer lab at Normandale Community College.[20] Suppose that a hypothetical cool-headed critic interviewed a defender of central purchasing in this case. The conversation might proceed as follows:

CRITIC: Central purchasing did not act on Normandale's purchase order for more than nine months. That's incompetence and inefficiency, pure and simple.

DEFENDER: The fact of the matter is that the price paid by a buyer of a commodity is generally lower when an order is large than when it is small. Government should take advantage of all types of economies of scale, including those deriving from market power, since the public has an interest in economical and efficient government.

CRITIC: But users of line agency services have an interest in their being provided on time. Doesn't this figure into the public interest?

DEFENDER: In the United States, government officials must espouse and live by the principles of economy and efficiency. The public never objects to making government more efficient. Getting a better deal on a purchase is what most people think of when they think of being thrifty. Besides, everyone pays taxes and only a few benefit from the delivery of any particular government service. Therefore, the general interest in buying any given commodity at the lowest possible price dominates the special interest in timely delivery of services.

CRITIC: How could the public interest have been served if Normandale's students lost the opportunity to learn to use computers? They were hurt; the state economy has lost the benefit of their improved training; the instructors were penalized; Normandale's reputation was tarnished.

DEFENDER: The answer lies in law and policy. In 1939, the state legislature gave the commissioner of administration the authority to make all purchases exceeding $50. This authority is delegated to central purchasing. The statutes give us explicit authority to combine purchases. The modern history of legislative action and executive orders shows that the goal of central purchasing is to reduce the cost of operating government by minimizing expenditures on goods and services purchased from the private sector. Our authority has never been successfully challenged: we still make all purchases exceeding $50.[21]

CRITIC: Which part of the statute says that central purchasing should not buy computers more frequently than once a year?

DEFENDER: How often to purchase any commodity is a determination made either by the director of central purchasing or by a lower-level official to whom he redelegates the authority delegated to him by the commissioner of administration. As earlier argued, a key criterion is reducing the price the state pays for what it buys. Another consideration is the cost of administering central purchasing. Because expenditures are appropriately kept to a minimum, only a handful of senior buyer positions are available and staffed. These experts do not have the time to make such a determination very often. They cannot provide special consideration to cases like Normandale's. Remember that the state purchases billions of dollars of goods and services every year.[22]

CRITIC: Why not assign the responsibility for deciding when to purchase computers to the more numerous front-line employees in the purchasing area?

DEFENDER: To delegate the authority to make such determinations to lower-level staff would be inappropriate.[23]

CRITIC: The fact of the matter is that central purchasing used poor judgment in holding up the purchases of computers for so long. No line agency should have to plan specific computer purchases more than nine months in advance. Central purchasing should be held accountable for Normandale's having to cancel the computer lab.

DEFENDER: Not at all. Central purchasing and the community college have different roles and responsibilities. The role of central purchasing is to make purchases for the state; its responsibility is to keep costs down. The community college should give central purchasing whatever amount of time it needs to carry out its responsibilities.[24]

As sympathetic as one might be to Critic's questions and accusations, Defender's argument cannot be dismissed as unreasonable. Indeed, within the context of the bureaucratic paradigm, Defender's argument is cogent. Here is how the argument works: As a matter of law, the state is to execute purchase orders exceeding $50 only when doing so is deemed appropriate by officials to whom statutory authority is delegated. As a matter of fact, this authority is delegated to central purchasing. As a matter of democratic administrative theory, central purchasing is accountable to the commissioner of administration and the governor for adhering to law and implementing policy.[25] As a matter of policy, state government is to operate economically and efficiently. As a matter of economic fact, suppliers charge less when buyers purchase in quantity. Given policy and fact, central purchasing should execute purchase orders for any single commodity in large batches.[26]

The argument continues: As a matter of ordinary prudence, lower-level buyers are not to be entrusted with authority to make sizeable purchase decisions. As a matter of fact, central purchasing has limited resources to do a lot of work. Therefore, central purchasing should attend only once in a while to the question of when best to buy batches of computers. Again as a matter of ordinary prudence, everyone concerned about this question should defer to purchasing officials, who are experts in applying law and policy to this factual context and others like it. Again as a matter of fact, central purchasing's officials determined that it was inappropriate to purchase computers during the nine months between Normandale's request and the start of the fall semester. Hence, central purchasing's conduct was justified. Q.E.D.

Any savvy bureaucrat can formulate—within the framework of the bureaucratic paradigm—similar internally consistent arguments justifying the conduct of staff agency officials in each of the troubling situations depicted above.[27] Whatever the motives for making these arguments, their consequence is to categorize such situations—and by extension the outcomes they generate—as conditions rather than as problems. The question is whether these arguments should be judged persuasive.

Social Science as a Source of Argument

The case for categorizing the Normandale incident as a problem rests on two kinds of claims. The first claim is that, all things considered, buying the computers on time would have been desirable; the second is that changing the way central purchasing operates is feasible. The argument supporting the first claim could proceed along the following lines:

> Central purchasing should enable state government to deliver results citizens value. Minnesotans value a competitive workforce as well as getting a good deal on the things bought either by government or themselves. Defender is right that the unit price of computers falls when purchased in quantity. But the question is whether central purchasing does everything it can to create both kinds of desired results and whether it makes the right choices when trade-offs have to be faced. And the answer to both questions appears to be "no." Taking advantage of technological innovation in the purchasing field would make it possible to get a good deal on computers and hold the Normandale class; even if technological change were impossible, it would be easy to show that the timing of central purchasing's execution of requisitions for computers is far from optimal.[28] On this reading of the situation, central purchasing should purchase computers for Normandale on time.

The tougher argument to make persuasive is that improving the situation is feasible. If this second argument fails, the claim that recurring troubles along the staff/line frontier are problems fails as well. One reason why this second argument is harder to make is that social scientists have produced a gold mine of evidence for the claim that good ideas are hard to implement in government.[29] Here is how Social Scientist might therefore respond to the argument that central purchasing can and should do better:

> I am skeptical about Defender's argument and am willing to accept, at least provisionally, the claim that central purchasing should do better.[30]
>
> Unfortunately, attempts by policymakers to make central purchasing do the right thing will be futile.[31] The first reason is politics. Central purchasing needs more resources in order to do its work; since it has no constituency, the legislature will never ap-

propriate the necessary funds or allocate the necessary positions.[32] The second reason has to do with the nature of organizations.[33] What happened in this case can be traced to purchasing's standard operating procedures. These routines, in turn, are supported by the organizational culture. In this culture, saving money is celebrated and responding to line agency pressures is shunned because of organizational capacity problems, the inescapable development of bureaucratic personalities in complex organizations, the psychic income that low-status officials derive from saying "no" to requests, and the organization's fear of having to be equally responsive to all requests for special consideration.[34]

Furthermore, organizational cultures are stable.[35] This case is no exception: buyers still seem to believe in the bureaucratic reform notion that minimizing the cost of filling a purchase order is necessarily economical and efficient. No one will do the hard work needed to change this organizational culture. The director of purchasing is a dyed-in-the-wool defender of the status quo. Executives come and go. Policymakers like to make policy and serve the public; they are not rewarded for improving a back-office operation like purchasing.[36] What we know about politics and organizations is thus discouraging. Recurring situations like this one—however lamentable from a rational point of view—are therefore conditions, not problems.[37]

Despite their rival views about how central purchasing should have managed this situation, Defender and Social Scientist thus reach the same ultimate conclusion: this manifestation of trouble along the staff/line frontier is a condition, not a problem. They reach this conclusion, interestingly, by traveling along different paths: the one presupposing the validity of the bureaucratic paradigm, the other selectively mining empirical social science. Anyone who believes that carefully investigated empirical generalizations should be considered when making judgments about unsatisfactory situations in and around government must take Social Scientist's argument seriously, just as anyone who values tradition must take seriously the force of Defender's argument.

PROBLEMS, NOT CONDITIONS

Similarly, anyone who is concerned, incensed, or morally outraged by recurring situations like the canceled computer class and its corresponding outcomes should listen not only to Defender's and Social Scientist's arguments but also to those making the opposite case. Progressive Thinker, for example, would argue that Social Scientist is unduly pessimistic. Central purchasing will eventually change its ways; history is definitely on the side of such a change.[38] Progressive Thinker, unlike Social Scientist, believes politics are conducive to transforming the organizational culture of operations and central purchasing:

> Scholars have long argued that politics in the West are no longer shaped by ideology but by interests and postmaterialist values.[39] Citizens are concerned—often dissatisfied—with the availability and quality of their public services.[40] Customer service to citizens can even become a key political issue during an era in which politicians campaigning for high office promise no less and no more than competence. Just look at British Prime Minister John Major's declaration of a service-oriented "citizen's charter" in the run-up to the first parliamentary elections held after the Thatcher era.[41] If central purchasing continues to generate horror stories, politicians will make the connection between its routines and citizen dissatisfaction, and they will ask for some kind of remedy.
>
> Furthermore, deep historical processes are also transforming bureaucratic politics in a favorable direction.[42] Managerial ideology and practice in the private sector have shifted from emphasizing high-volume, standardized production to emphasizing high-quality, customer-oriented production.[43] Espoused theories and practices of American public administration are never too far behind.[44] In fact, some federal and state agencies are fiercely competing to win the President's Award for Quality.[45] Many more are at least espousing the principles of "total quality management."[46] An orientation to quality and service thus makes good bureaucratic politics.[47] Some day this political ethos will infect the back-office operations of government—like central purchasing—as well as its citizen-contact operations. And when it does, even Defender will think twice before making the kind of argument we heard earlier.

Progressive Thinker, unlike Social Scientist, takes account of the ongoing revolution in information technology and takes an upbeat view of the trends:

> New and rapidly emerging mathematical and computational aids to rational decision making have vastly expanded the capac-

ity of formal organizations to solve problems.[48] It must be only a matter of time before central purchasing's hand calculators are replaced by computers and its paper inflow is transformed into electronic data. Once this happens, its bureaucratic reform organizational culture is vulnerable. The application of information-processing technology typically engenders a new approach to organizational behavior, one in which relationships are intricate, collaborative, and bound by the mutual responsibilities of colleagues. Some enthusiasts even say that "as the new technology integrates information across time and space . . . , managers and workers each tend to overcome their narrow functional perspectives and create new roles that are better suited to enhancing value-adding activities in a data-rich environment."[49] The old routines and culture cannot survive the arrival of computers and data networks.

Progressive Thinker also forecasts trends in workforce values that will further undermine the culture of control and bureaucentrism, which pervades the existing organization:

> The current head of purchasing began his career in 1960. For all practical purposes, his world-view was formed in the 1940s and 1950s. A level or two down in the organization are people who came of age in the late 1960s. We all know that these generations have different values and outlooks.[50] The younger ones dislike control-oriented organizational cultures. They believe in empowerment of employees and responsiveness to customers.[51] If the information-technology revolution fails to conquer the bureaucratic reform culture, generational replacement surely will.[52]

From this perspective, unstoppable forces of politics, technology, and demography assure that troubles along the staff/line frontier not only are problems (rather than conditions) but are problems that will be remedied in due course. After listening to Progressive Thinker wax lyrical about the forces that will eventually transform central purchasing's culture, one might react in any number of ways. For instance, one might question the realism of his view of historical change: Progressive Thinker's evolutionary vision has a lot in common with Karl Marx's revolutionary vision. Most of the time, historical reality is far less neat than either supposes: in reality, sociopolitical change is often partial, grudging, and with a lot of unfinished business left behind.[53] This reaction suggests that solving particular and general problems in the purchasing operation will not be as easy as armchair theorizing. But it leaves intact the argument that these recurring troubles along the staff/line frontier are problems.

Even if they agree with his outlook, some listeners may become impatient with Progressive Thinker. Because of their personal experience or intellectual commitments, they might be so enervated by the consequences of central purchasing's adherence to the bureaucratic paradigm that they urge politicians and public managers to accelerate history, ushering in the new era as soon as possible.

The Possibilist Contribution

On hearing these critiques of Progressive Thinker, another listener tries to formulate a more realistic scenario. In sketching it, Possibilist's immediate purpose is to persuade the skeptical that the historical forces identified by Progressive Thinker can be brought to bear on operations like central purchasing sooner rather than later through effective leadership and management. Because Possibilist's aim is to convince his audience that recurring troubles along the staff/line frontier are problems, all he needs to argue is that such a scenario could conceivably be played out; he does not need to argue that it will probably happen.[54]

Suppose the governor convenes a cabinet meeting about efficiency issues in state government and begins to hear about routine troubles along the staff/line frontier. He might think that he needs to appoint a commission to look into the situation, something like an economy and efficiency commission, but with a more appealing name. Suppose he then recruits several public-spirited business executives to serve on the Governor's Task Force on the Quality and Value of Public Services. Reflecting the changing makeup of the state economy, some of these executives run major service enterprises. Suppose that in the spirit of collaboration the governor asks several cabinet members (from both staff and line agencies) to join the Task Force and that to promote executive/legislative cooperation he invites a former colleague in the state senate to be a member. Wishing to include other levels of government, the governor also recruits to the Task Force the commander of a major military installation in the state. At the kick-off meeting, the governor makes it clear that he is willing to support the

Task Force's recommendations as long as they resemble good business practice in the best-managed service enterprises, industrial concerns, or government agencies. A press conference announcing this major new initiative is then held.

Some members of the audience are skeptical about whether such a task force could be appointed anywhere in the United States; none is willing to name a state in which a governor would likely commit political suicide by convening one. Possibilist continues:

> Now suppose that the chancellor of the community college system testifies about the case of the canceled computer class—and a dozen incidents like it—on the third day of Task Force hearings. During the subsequent executive session, these complaints are discussed with purchasing officials. Members soon come to the conclusion that nothing has been done to solve the recurring problem. And suppose that Task Force members then begin to take responsibility for finding a solution. Exercising leadership, the president of a far-flung service enterprise asserts that purchasing decisions should be decentralized to the agencies. The state senator quickly objects, first noting that taxpayers want the state to buy materials and equipment cheaply and, second, asserting that the only way to economize is to centralize purchasing. After a moment of silence, the commissioner of human services suggests that the group think about how the state might derive the benefits of both centralization and decentralization.
>
> The commissioner of transportation then recalls a recent visit to a neighboring state during which she learned that her counterpart agency issued bids every year for huge but indefinite quantities of resurfacing materials, and counties were able to order these materials directly from the low-bid contractor whenever they wanted to. She suggests that their own state look into this way of acquiring materials. The Army base commander immediately supports this idea, noting that it exemplifies a valuable principle of management: standardize what needs to be uniform (like the basic terms of a contract) and allow field operations to customize the rest (like the timing of purchases and deliveries). He goes on to illustrate this principle by talking about how the Army handles its nationwide recruiting.[55] And he concludes by suggesting that this principle be applied to all the problems the Task Force is examining. A month later, the Task Force gives the governor a draft recommendation calling on central purchasing to make use

of indefinite-quantity contracts for computers and other kinds of materials, equipment, and services.

After listening attentively to Possibilist's line of reasoning, Social Scientist raises a substantial objection:

> For all your hypothetical storytelling, you haven't argued anything more than I did earlier. Rational and informed people, like the members of the elite Task Force, shouldn't have a hard time coming up with good recommendations for the governor. But we all know that generating policy ideas is one thing; getting them implemented by organizations like purchasing is another.[56] You still haven't convinced me that my futility argument is off-base.

Surprised by Social Scientist's reasonable objection, Possibilist engages in on-the-spot reflection about the ultimate force of his own argument:[57]

> You seem to have in mind a general scenario in which people resist implementing good ideas that were "not invented here." Given that career purchasing officials did not participate in the Task Force's brainstorming meeting, I understand why you doubt central purchasing will build indefinite-quantity contracting into its organizational routines.[58] In the spirit of open-minded inquiry, I am even willing to concede that the Task Force's highly conventional strategy for improving management in government will fail to bring about meaningful and lasting change.[59] Yet I cannot bring myself to conclude, as you have, that troubles along the staff/line frontier are conditions, not problems.

Stimulated by the challenge, Possibilist experiments with another scenario:

> I can also envision how the proponents of indefinite-quantity contracting might be able to recover from this inauspicious start of the change process. Suppose that staff agency executives who oversee purchasing are as skilled at managing change as dozens of public sector executives who have successfully improved the performance of such line activities as law enforcement, regulation, defense, taxation, economic development, and human services.[60] And what if we suppose that Progressive Thinker's thumbnail sketch of trends in politics, technology, and workforce values is essentially accurate. Now, can't you imagine a case in which entrepreneurial staff agency executives—with history on

their side—work earnestly over several years, using all the tools of management in the public sector, to influence the thinking and behavior of the entire purchasing operation? Can't you imagine not only acceptance of indefinite-quantity contracting but a wave of internally generated efforts to identify and prevent troubles along this segment of the staff/line frontier? Are you really willing to argue that this scenario is implausible?

Social Scientist begins to wonder whether her futility argument can withstand this possibilist incursion. She is willing to agree that the scenario is plausible, hence willing to admit that situations like the missing computers are problems. But she is not convinced that more complex troubles along the staff/line frontier are also problems rather than conditions.

Possibilist's Empirical Inquiry

Drawing on his knowledge and imagination, Possibilist could engage in many more rounds of argument with Social Scientist and others who believe that the other recurring troubles along the staff/line frontier should be categorized as conditions, not problems. But Possibilist's audience may grow weary of his method of sketching hypothetical scenarios in order to argue that these recurring situations are problems. He therefore wants evidence of real-world efforts to define recurring troubles along the staff/line frontier as problems. Thinking ahead to a time when Defender is unwilling to use the bureaucratic paradigm to justify unsatisfactory situations and when Social Scientist is reticent to make futility arguments, Possibilist wants to know what difference changing staff agency institutional frameworks, cultures, and routines might make. The most ample information and evidence he finds for advancing these purposes is culled from the state of Minnesota during the 1983–90 period.

PART TWO

Breakthroughs
Are Possible

CHAPTER THREE

Inventing Strategies

Starting in the 1910s, Minnesota governors took it for granted that one of their responsibilities as chief executive was to increase the economy and efficiency of state government.[1] Although routine efforts to improve management in government were the responsibility of the commissioner of administration, many governors also convened special commissions—comprised mostly of businessmen—to find ways to cut costs and make government run in a more businesslike fashion.[2] Working within this tradition, Governor Wendell Anderson, for instance, created a Loaned Executives Action Program (LEAP) in the early 1970s, and Rudy Perpich, after succeeding Anderson as governor in 1976, appointed a private citizen to head his Task Force on Waste and Mismanagement.[3]

The Task Force made numerous recommendations, among them reducing travel allowances, curtailing training, and downsizing the central motor pool.[4] As a measure to reduce government paperwork, the Task Force recommended that the state stop buying file cabinets. To lower the state's electricity bill as well as the cost of cleaning coffee-stained carpets, the Task Force prohibited the use of electric coffee pots in state buildings.

SETTING THE TONE: THE STEP PROGRAM

Much to the surprise of wary state employees who remembered the Task Force on Waste and Mismanagement, the ritual of creating economy and efficiency commissions was abandoned during Perpich's first full term as an elected governor (1983–87). In the spring of 1985, following substantial planning work by Department of Administration (Admin) executives, state employees were invited to submit proposals for projects that would improve their work units' performance. Project proposals were to be submitted first to each agency's commissioner for approval, then reviewed by the steering committee of a program named STEP (Striving Toward Excellence in Performance), which the governor himself cochaired. The initial response of state employees was positive: eighty-four project nominations were submitted to the STEP program, and thirty-six proposals were selected by the STEP steering committee as the first year's projects. Approval by this committee showcased STEP projects, most of which dealt with otherwise hidden aspects of state government operations.[5]

Politics: The Governor's Conversion

What caused Perpich to support STEP instead of another task force on waste and mismanagement? First, some of the recommendations of the Task Force had tarnished his image in the media and alienated state employees, many of whom lived in districts that failed to support him in the 1978 election. After studying the votes, Perpich attributed his defeat in that election partly to his support for such measures as banning electric coffee pots from state office buildings.[6] Second, after the election Perpich himself experienced what it was like to be an employee of a large organization, subject to directives coming from the top. For more than two years, Perpich represented Minneapolis-based Control Data Corporation in Eastern Europe. During this period, Perpich's office in Vienna received an order from headquarters that alcoholic beverages neither be stored on company premises nor be consumed at lunch. His European colleagues were outraged at the directive and staged an ultimately successful job action to rescind it.[7]

Perpich campaigned for governor again in 1982 and this time was successful. The governor wanted to shy away from the employee-beating tone of the Task Force on Waste and Mismanagement and wondered how those elements of Control Data's management style that he admired might be usefully applied in state government. Instead of directing his appointees to reduce the cost of government, Perpich encouraged them to improve the management of state government. The mandate he gave to Commissioner of Administration Sandra J. Hale was "to help make Minnesota the best managed state in the nation."[8]

Elaborating the Mandate

Forgoing another economy and efficiency commission made it possible for Perpich's appointees to develop innovative ways to help the governor perform his duties as head of administration.[9] In developing a management initiative for the governor, Commissioner Hale met frequently with many of the state's prominent business executives. Her strategy was to trade ideas about how to improve the management of an organization as complex as state government. Some business executives considered government and business so fundamentally different that the potential gains from exchanging ideas on management struck them as insignificant. But the chairman of Minneapolis-based Dayton Hudson Corporation, William Andres, reasoned that his organization was a good deal like government in that it employed large numbers of people, most of whom served the public face-to-face. Hale eventually persuaded Andres, who also served as chairman of the state's big-business association, to represent the business community on the steering committee formed in 1984 to oversee the STEP program and evaluate STEP project proposals.

The STEP steering committee differed from a conventional economy and efficiency commission in several respects. First, it focused on improving the quality and cost-effectiveness of government rather than on producing cuts in expenditures. Second, the initiative for making change was placed in the hands of state employees rather than outsiders. Third, its membership—union officials, commissioners, and businesspeople—was broad, and it was cochaired by Governor Perpich and Andres, rather than being headed solely by a private citizen. Finally, the steering committee's endorsement was designed in part to raise the likelihood that the appropriations committees of the legislature would allow work units and agencies to reinvest cost savings in the same programs and services rather than reallocate them, thereby encouraging state employees to participate in the STEP program.[10]

From Theory to Practice

In planning the STEP program, some officials and their private sector contacts worked hard to translate many concepts that belonged to contemporary paradigms of management in the private and nonprofit sectors to state government.[11] The concepts included mission, strategy, customer service, creating value, managerial discretion, employee involvement, team building, experimentation, marketing, choice, competition, productivity investments, work measurement, and employee recognition. In inviting submissions to the STEP program, the Department of Administration urged state managers to use their STEP projects as an opportunity to test a series of hypotheses about management in government. These hypotheses were:

- Closer contact with the customer provides a better understanding of the customer's needs.

- Increased employee participation taps the knowledge, skills, and commitment of all state workers.

- Increased discretionary authority gives managers and employees greater accountability for a bottom line.

- Voluntary partnerships allow the sharing of knowledge, expertise, and other resources.

- Using state-of-the-art productivity improvement techniques yields results.

- Improved work measurement provides a base for planning and implementing service improvements and gives workers information about their performance.

Department of Administration officials invited all state employees to propose projects that would generate a measurable improvement in the delivery of state services. Each proposal, they believed, should be designed to improve operating results—for example, improving service levels or decreasing the

cost per unit of service—without entailing increased appropriations and should focus on building the capacity to achieve these
results through team building, training, and voluntary partnerships with the public and private sectors. Each proposal had to
identify members of a project team as well as a project manager
and outline the team's plans to test the new STEP hypotheses.
Admin's staff worked with the people who proposed the projects
to ensure that these hypotheses would be tested and that the
proposals specified how the change process would be managed.
(In 1986, Minnesota received an Innovations in State and Local
Government Award from the Ford Foundation for the STEP program.)

INTRODUCING MARKETPLACE DYNAMICS

Marketing as Two-Way Communication

Perpich's first full administration quickened the pace of changes
begun under the previous administration.[12] Soon after taking
office, Admin executives arranged to visit each major agency,
billing the event as an agency relations meeting. During these
meetings, complaints were heard about virtually every area of
Admin's work, including plant management, procurement, information management, the motor pool, and printing.[13] Jeff
Zlonis, then manager of agency relations, summarized the state
of Admin's relationship with line agencies in his report on agency
relations meetings:

> The agency relations visit reports were quite controversial. The
> reports, printed on colored paper to attract attention, included
> the comments of line agency managers, and were distributed
> throughout the department. Negative comments were not edited,
> except to remove overly abusive language. Some of the depart-
> ment managers complained bitterly about line managers' criti-
> cism of their services being published for others in the depart-
> ment to see. This was precisely the idea, however. We wanted to
> create a climate in which the line managers' opinions had a good
> deal of value and impact.[14]

The concept of agency relations meetings began to take root.
By the second year, department managers from the career ser-

vice and others asked whether they could attend the annual sessions. Department executives welcomed their participation. Despite the fact that criticisms at agency relations meetings was sometimes severe, attendance by Admin managers increased over the years.

Funding Bases

Before 1983, internal service activities—such as information management, printing, and the motor pool—were managed much like activities funded through legislative appropriations, even though most were financed by revolving funds and operated on a fee-for-service basis. Admin executives saw no reason why these units should operate much like generally funded activities. On the contrary, they believed that these units should seek to market their services to line agencies and that they should be accountable for creating value net of cost.

The early steps taken by Admin executives to rid revolving fund activities of what they called the general fund mentality included asking managers to find out what line agency customers wanted and how much it would cost to meet their needs, and then to determine what rates were appropriate. They also directed managers to focus cost control efforts on reducing overhead expenses. In the case of the Information Management Bureau's data-processing activity, Admin executives announced that they would recommend against Department of Finance approval of proposed rate increases for the subsequent fiscal year and that, nonetheless, they would hold managers accountable for generating sufficient revenues to cover expenses. This stark mandate signified the executives' complete rejection of the earlier methods of rate setting and spending, and it set in motion a variety of efforts to reduce overhead while maintaining service levels. As it turned out, the data-processing activity broke even without the aid of rate increases during that fiscal year.

Competition

The assistant commissioner of administration for agency services also pressured the managers reporting to him to recognize that users almost always could find substitutes for the services provided by the department. For example, agencies could increase their use of photocopiers if they were dissatisfied with the services of central printing. Or state employees could use their personal automobiles and be reimbursed, instead of using a motor-pool car. In some cases, the assistant commissioner pushed his managers to find ways to operate as though they were competing with alternative providers of the same service.

In a number of cases, including typewriter repair, management consulting, micrographics, and data entry, the department decided to allow agencies to purchase from outside vendors the same services as those provided centrally. In each case, the executives knew of no a priori reason why agencies should not be able to choose between private providers and Admin. None was viewed as a control function, and the argument that central provision enabled the state to capture potential economies of scale seemed weak. In each case, the department's executives committed themselves to closing down the operation if it could not successfully compete with private providers. In one such example—typewriter repair—despite efforts to improve the fifty-year-old operation, expenses continued to exceed revenues, and the department stopped providing this service to agencies within two years.[15] In contrast, the department's management consulting operation grew, despite the fact that agencies could buy services from private providers.

The general pattern during this period was to manage internal services as value-creating businesses, whether or not they actually competed with private vendors supplying the same service. Through experimentation with marketplace dynamics the agency's executives gained experience holding operating managers accountable for meeting line agencies' expectations for service and cost. It was believed that by striving to meet these expectations, Admin would make a significant contribution to improving management in state government.

Overcoming Legislative Distrust

The legislators most interested in Admin's operations were members of the State Departments Division of the House Appropriations Committee, which had jurisdiction over the Department of Administration. This subcommittee had a reputation for careful scrutiny of funding proposals submitted to them as part of the biennial budget process.[16]

When subcommittee members accused the department of providing low-quality services, executives accepted the criticism and even sent along copies of reports from agency relations meetings that documented the problems. In an effort to provide additional information about revolving funds, the department began to distribute reports of rate increases and changes in retained earnings to committee members on a regular basis. The department's credibility seemed to be strengthened when line agency complaints to legislators about poor service quality became less frequent. Some subcommittee members also seemed to be impressed when executives decided that the department could not compete effectively with private vendors for typewriter repair services and closed down this internal service activity. Finally, to build confidence in the management of revolving funds, executives requested that a transfer of retained earnings to the statewide general fund be made from the revolving fund operated by the department's public documents center. This accounting transaction gave control over monies earned by this center back to overseers, who could then appropriate it as they saw fit.

REVITALIZING PERSONNEL ADMINISTRATION

In the traditional civil service system, almost all positions in Minnesota state government were filled through the same rigid process, which required many months to complete. As a consequence, personnel was regularly under pressure to speed up the hiring process.[17] During the 1970s and 1980s, personnel executives responded with a variety of statutory and regulatory initiatives that made it possible, under certain conditions, to bypass some or all steps in the hiring process.[18] Although these officials never abandoned their commitment to the merit principle, by the mid-1980s they had come to the conclusion that flexibility should be a core value of the personnel system.[19]

In 1986, Department of Employee Relations Commissioner

Nina Rothchild told the legislative committee that oversees the agency: "We recognize that we serve the public best by providing the best workers for the state, by serving applicants fairly and quickly, by maintaining good labor/management relations, and by helping state agencies to deliver successful programs." Employees in the central personnel agency had previously seen their job as requiring agencies to conform to a basic set of rules about staffing and were largely unconcerned about the day-to-day problems that line agencies faced.[20] Some staffing professionals specialized in recruiting and examining, while others specialized in classifying positions. Although this institutional arrangement was designed to generate production economies, "it became an unfortunately common occurrence for agency personnel officers to approach their assigned representative in the classification division and be told they had an exam problem, only in turn to be told by the assigned class representative in the exam division that their problem was due to an inappropriate classification."[21]

In 1985, the state legislature asked Admin's Management Analysis Division to study the hiring and firing processes in the Department of Employee Relations.[22] Through the leadership of Deputy Commissioner Elaine Johnson, department executives and managers saw the study as an opportunity to examine the wisdom of focusing attention on the technical quality of classification and examination work while reducing attention to solving staffing problems identified by managers and supervisors throughout state government. For their part, Admin executives saw the hiring/firing study as an opportunity to demonstrate the advantages of using the Management Analysis Division to produce change in state government. The previous role of Management Analysis, in contrast, had been to issue recommendations, usually accompanied with a diagnosis casting blame for unfortunate situations on particular employees and work units:

> Unlike previous studies, the Management Analysis study did little to compare Minnesota statistics with other states' in an effort to show that we were better or worse than others. They merely took at face value their own data and state managers' criticism that the system moved too slowly. They worked cooperatively with Employee Relations management and staff at ways things could

be improved. The results were the most positive of any study ever conducted of the hiring function. Recommendations were made which Employee Relations management supported and stood ready to implement—not to refute, as had often happened with previous studies.[23]

Admin's study, and the Department of Employee Relations reaction to it, proved to be the primary catalysts for change in the Staffing Division.[24] Once central staffing managers concluded that their unit's primary customers were line agency managers and supervisors, the personnel division created an agency services section. The section was divided into three teams, for social service agencies, scientific and technical agencies, and administrative agencies. Each agency services team became responsible for coordinating all personnel knowledge and actions necessary to resolve customers' problems within statewide staffing norms.[25]

The emergence of the new outlook and organizational structure in the staffing area constituted a breakthrough in several respects. It showed that ideas resembling those of marketplace dynamics could be applied to what had been viewed primarily as a technically oriented control activity. Similarly, the department's advocacy of this approach suggested to many observers that there was more to the story of trying to improve management in Minnesota state government than just a set of changes championed by Admin.[26]

PURCHASING BEGINS TO CHANGE

After much debate, purchasing identified line agencies as customers. Much effort was then devoted to learning about customer needs and clarifying how responsive this staff operation should be to its customers. Purchasing clarified its obligations to line agencies in the following words: "Our mission is to purchase products and services that best meet the necessary quality requirements for the needs of our customers, at the best possible prices, from responsible vendors, within the required time frame, in accordance with all applicable statutes and in an ethical and professional manner."[27]

This way of conceptualizing responsiveness to line agencies did not come naturally to many purchasing unit employees:

> The level of passion that existed [for the bureaucratic paradigm] can be seen in the debate over the inclusion of the words "quality requirements." For those on the committee who held to the old vision, the specter of line agencies purchasing Cadillacs flew in front of their eyes. Agencies [they argued] would surely over-specify their needs either because they were duped by some sharp salesman or because of a personal preference on their part.[28]

Most buyers warmly endorsed the view that they—unlike line agency personnel—had the expertise and responsibility to bring objectivity to bear in writing specifications and minimizing the price paid to vendors. Yet, according to buyer James Kinzie: "To those of us on the committee who saw the agencies as our customers and the services they deliver to the public as what government is all about, the inclusion of these words was a natural and necessary part of the mission."[29]

Kinzie and his like-minded peers often found themselves in conflict with their supervisor, although in concert with Admin executives: "Upper management expressed one vision while the division management didn't model that vision and at times even ridiculed it to the staff. This led to a period that was extremely stressful for the staff of the division. The process of change within the division could not start until there was a consistency of modeling throughout the management structure."[30]

To bring about such consistency, agency executives created a new Materials Management Division, whose work units included purchasing, the central supply store, resource recovery, and surplus property. After six months of recruiting and selecting candidates for the career position of division director, executives offered the job to a materials manager from Control Data Corporation, John Haggerty, who decided to take it: "Through the hiring process I became convinced that the concept of quality customer service was in fact a very strong vision and operating philosophy for those people who formed the top management within the Department of Administration. Convinced that public employees could provide quality customer service, I said yes to a new career in the public sector."[31]

The new director of materials management took on the day-to-day responsibility of helping his people to understand the implications of identifying line agencies as the division's principal customers. Moreover, purchasing officials knew that Haggerty, as a civil servant, would likely be in charge for more years than the department executives who had been championing the customer-service approach. Haggerty's change strategy included not only introducing concepts and practices of quality management but also asking veteran buyers who supported the new purchasing philosophy to take on substantial leadership roles. Meanwhile, the long-time director of purchasing, who had been unwilling to support the new mission and strategy, was removed from the chain of command and eventually left state service.

Thus, Admin executives could not persuade all employees of the merits of their arguments, even after three years of effort. Acceptance was strengthened by the appointment of a career manager (familiar with state-of-the art methods of materials management) to oversee purchasing, by promoting such individuals as Kinzie (who during fifteen years as a buyer had felt "something was very wrong") to head the purchasing unit, and by making use of the civil service system's limited flexibility to remove recalcitrants, such as the previous division chief, from positions of authority.

REORGANIZING INFORMATION MANAGEMENT

Identifying the Difficulties

Despite efforts to improve service to line agencies, Admin executives heard bitter complaints from line agency executives during the second round of agency relations meetings. Much of the criticism was directed at the Information Management Bureau (IMB). This bureau had been created and assigned to Admin in 1968, when Governor Harold LeVander issued a reorganization order that combined all data-processing capabilities in the executive branch. The action purposefully created a service *and* control organization to emphasize cost efficiencies.[32]

When line agencies used IMB's services, they paid for them out of their own appropriations, in the form of a transfer of funds to IMB's revolving fund account.[33] This financing arrangement gave line agencies some discretion over the volume and total cost of the computing services they consumed. But because IMB also had oversight responsibility for computer systems across state government, line agencies could buy neither computer equipment nor outside computing services without IMB's permission. Managers complained that all too often IMB balked at granting such permission. To them, IMB seemed to be using its oversight power to ensure that the volume of business it did with line agencies—and, therefore, the amount of funds transferred to its revolving fund account—was not affected by competitive pressures. As an additional irritant, the cost of IMB's oversight function was built into the rates the activity charged line agencies for using its services. Managers also criticized IMB's service quality: processing time was too long, they said, and the bureau was slow to make state-of-the-art services available to state agencies. They also complained that annual rate increases were substantial. In fact, rates were increasing much faster than the budgets of most line agencies.

Representative Phyllis Kahn, chair of the State Departments Division of the House Appropriations Committee, was concerned with state expenditures on information management. Representative Kahn and other committee members were particularly displeased with the substantial rate increases that IMB asked for because the committee was being pressured by other appropriations committee divisions to help keep the spending of line agencies under control. Moreover, she was committed to promoting the wise use of computer technology in state government. Among other issues, she was interested in expanding the use of non-mainframe computers in agencies and in ensuring that the state's data resources were shared among agencies.

From the legislative viewpoint, furthermore, IMB did not seem particularly accountable.[34] The State Departments Division did not actually make appropriations to the activity because IMB was financed by revolving funds. Committee members felt that this arrangement made IMB more inclined to listen to the opinions of line agencies than to the legislature. They suspected that, as a result, the resources dedicated to carrying out IMB's oversight and control responsibilities were systematically diminished in an effort to improve agency relations and to decrease the overhead costs that were otherwise built into the rising rates. For their part, managers felt powerless when attempting to influence the bureau's rates, service quality, or oversight decisions. From their perspective, IMB did not appear accountable to anyone.

Separating Service and Control

Thus, IMB posed a dilemma that arose again and again in Admin: how could an operating unit of the department succeed in providing services that line agencies valued, while performing oversight responsibilities on behalf of the legislature and governor? The IMB case focused agency executives' and key legislators' attention on the inherent rivalry between service and control responsibilities. The result, in this case, was an agreement to create an Information Policy Office (IPO) in Admin and to transfer IMB's control responsibilities to this new work unit. IPO, like IMB, was to be headed by an assistant commissioner, reporting to the department's deputy commissioner.

While IPO was to be exclusively in the business of winning agencies' compliance to norms set by overseers, IMB was to focus on meeting line agencies' needs for high-quality, cost-effective service. Similarly, whereas IMB was to be funded by charging its line agency customers for the services provided to them, IPO was to be funded by way of appropriations made by its customers: elected officials. Agencies, therefore, were no longer to bear the cost of being overseen, and the State Departments Division was to be assured that control activities would actually be performed. Executives and overseers believed, in sum, that the department as a whole would be much more capable of managing the service/control rivalry if each of its operating units was focused on one kind of activity and if each was funded by its customers. This experience provided an important context in which Admin executives and a number of overseers began to learn how a staff agency could help provide support for line agency operations and increased accountability in state government.

The state legislature and governor in 1987 gave the IPO an

ambitious mandate and substantial formal authority, as expressed in the following statutory language:

> The office must develop and establish a state information architecture to ensure that further state agency development and purchase of information systems equipment and software is directed in such a manner that individual agency information systems complement and do not needlessly duplicate or conflict with the systems of other agencies. The development of this information architecture must include the establishment of standards and guidelines to be followed by state agencies. . . . The office shall assist state agencies in the planning and management of information systems so that an individual information system reflects and supports the state agency's and the state's mission, requirements, and functions. The office must review and approve all agency requests for legislative appropriations for the development of information systems, equipment, or software. Requests may not be included in the governor's budget submitted to the legislature unless the office has approved the request.[35]

The IPO was thus invested with all the attributes of a powerful control agency. Its purpose was to make government operate efficiently and effectively by bringing a statewide view to bear on a subset of administrative decisions made by people in dozens of executive agencies. The individual selected to head the IPO, Larry Grant, had mostly recently served in product development and marketing at a major regional banking corporation.

Once the IMB shed its policy responsibilities, it changed its executive leadership, mission, ways of relating to line agency executives and managers, lines of activity, culture, and even its name. When the position of assistant commissioner and head of IMB opened up in 1987, Commissioner Hale appointed an individual with over a dozen years of management experience in line agencies, including the Department of Transportation. The new assistant commissioner, Judy Pinke, renamed IMB the InterTechnologies Group and described it as "a $50 million business inside government that provides data processing, telecommunications, and information services to executive branch agencies, the legislature and courts, city and county government, higher education, and public corporations."[36] She also worked with InterTech managers to revise IMB's mission, which had been "to provide centralized management of computer applications and facilities, telecommunications, and records for state agencies." InterTech's mission became "to achieve results from information assets that customers value."

PRESENTING THE
ENTERPRISE-MANAGEMENT STRATEGY

By 1986, even before the reorganization of information management, top executives at Admin were coming to see clearly how the diverse initiatives, all stimulated by specific problems and opportunities, reflected an overall strategy for managing this staff agency. Through the agency relations process, the experiments with marketplace dynamics, the development of the STEP program, the Management Analysis Division's cooperative approach to improving the staffing operation in employee relations, and the decision to separate service and control in information management, the department's executives learned a great deal about how a staff agency could improve its own performance as well as that of state government as a whole. However, most Admin managers could not see how the pieces fit together, and many worried that the commitment to improving service meant abandoning the agency's traditional oversight and control role. To build employees' commitment to the change process, department executives decided to articulate an overall strategy—subsequently labeled *enterprise management*—that showed how concepts such as service and control, marketplace dynamics, statewide leadership, managerial discretion, and accountability related to one another.[37]

Admin executives had in mind external audiences for this strategy as well. Commissioner Hale, in particular, wanted to demonstrate to the governor, business executives, legislators, counterparts in other agencies, and the media that the STEP program was only a part of the department's effort to make Minnesota the best-managed state in the nation. The deputy commissioner was eager to reach two key external audiences: the State Departments Division and the Department of Finance. Legislators had been infuriated by complaints from line agencies about IMB. In particular, rapidly rising computer rates seemed to imply that the subcommittee had allowed IMB's spending to get out of control. This concern exacerbated legislators' distrust of all financing mechanisms that provided agencies with a source of revenue other than appropriations.[38] Subcommittee members frequently remarked to Admin executives that they intended to fund more internal services with appropriations as a way to gain control.

The deputy commissioner confronted these concerns by arguing that revolving funds were a better tool for managing such activities because they offered the possibility of enlarging managerial discretion, holding managers accountable for results, and giving agencies an incentive to economize on the use of resources. The deputy commissioner also wished to respond to Department of Finance managers who were opposed to exposing some internal services to competition from private providers.

Formulating the Strategy

The strategy devised by Admin executives conceptualized how each of the department's numerous activities should be managed, overseen, and funded. In rough outline, the argument was as follows. Admin is in the business of both service and control, and each Admin activity should be in the business of either service or control. The customers of service activities are government agencies. These operations are accountable for meeting customer needs for high-quality, cost-effective services. State agencies should be accountable to overseers for properly or economically consuming the services offered by Admin or its competitors. The customers of control activities are the state's citizens collectively, represented by the governor and the legislature. Bringing a statewide perspective to bear in making particular administrative decisions and overseeing some administrative operations is a service that the department provides to overseers as customers. These activities, therefore, should be called statewide leadership and control services. Service activities should be financed by revolving funds whenever possible. Control activities should be financed by general fund appropriations.

Furthermore, when it is in the taxpayers' interest for individual state agencies to be required to utilize services from a single internal source, the service should be managed as a regulated utility, accountable to state agencies as a whole. Otherwise, the service should be managed as a competitive marketplace activity. In this event, each agency should be granted the flexibility either to purchase the service from the provider that offers the best value from its point of view or to provide the service itself. Customer panels should be created to hold utilities accountable for the quality and cost of services provided. Market forces offer an effective means to hold competitive marketplace activities accountable for the quality and cost of services provided. Marketplace activities should be given the high level of freedom and flexibility they need to compete effectively.

Finally, Admin can compete successfully in the marketplace only if it has a competitive advantage over alternative sources. To the extent that marketplace activities compete with private enterprise, this competition should be considered desirable because it saves the taxpayers money. State agencies will choose the government-provided activity over that of private providers only if the price and quality of service are the best.[39] Marketplace activities may not be competitive and may fail financially. The unit must then be allowed to go out of existence. If this is unacceptable, the service should be categorized as a utility.

In sum, Admin executives argued that activities should be placed in one of three categories—statewide leadership and control activities, utilities, and competitive marketplace activities—and then funded, managed, and overseen accordingly.[40] Appendix 1 reproduces the written report Admin submitted to the legislature, outlining the categories and assigning activities to them.

Defending the Strategy

Although members of the State Departments Division found the utility and competitive-enterprise concepts instructive, they were uneasy about a few key issues of oversight and policy. They wanted to think hard about how they could effectively oversee services financed by revolving funds, whether revolving fund financing would give services and line agencies too much discretion, why competitive marketplace services within government should seek to make a profit, and whether it was appropriate for state government to compete with the private sector.

Overseeing Revolving Funds.   Admin executives sought to answer these important questions by elaborating on the arguments underpinning the strategy. In particular, they argued that legislators could effectively oversee revolving funds by taking the time to review the financial and operating performance of services. In the case of competitive marketplace activities, legislators were asked to review net income and the use of retained earnings. When profits were earned, Admin executives suggested that legislators discuss when it was appropriate to transfer retained earnings to the general fund for use elsewhere in state government. When a pattern of losses arose, overseers were urged to discuss the desirability of closing down the service. In these ways, the legislature—according to executives—could ensure that Admin's marketplace activities met agency needs better than alternative providers and that control over the use of profits was in overseers' hands.

In the case of utilities, legislators were asked to review the rates charged by each activity as well as changes in retained earnings. As part of reviewing utilities, Admin executives suggested that legislators and their fiscal analysts examine whether rates were satisfactory to line agencies, whether rates were comparable to prices charged by private providers, whether retained earnings were being managed appropriately, and whether agencies were satisfied with service lines and quality. The executives promised that Admin would be responsive to overseers' concerns as they had been in the areas of information policy and management.[41]

Discretion and Accountability.   The response to the question about excessive discretion focused on the economic rationality of using rates—rather than quantitative limits—to control the amount of a resource consumed. Setting revolving fund rates informed line agencies about the costs of providing a unit of service, which is what they needed to know in order to decide how much of the service they should consume given their budgets and operating strategies. When the rates for a particular service increased, all things being equal, line agencies would face a precisely calibrated incentive to use less of it. Imposing quantitative limits on how much service is provided would thwart efforts by line managers to decide rationally how to adjust to the rate increase. If consumption of a particular service by a given line agency seemed excessive given the rates charged per unit of service, the subcommittees overseeing the line agency could take up the matter with its executive. In the absence of such concern, it would make practical sense to leave to line agency executives and managers decisions about how much of each internal service to consume in any particular rate environment.

The staff agency's discretion over revolving funds was similarly controlled, according to executives explaining the strategy. The policy of neither accumulating nor depleting retained earnings over any given medium-term horizon, they said, created a link between utilities' expenses and their revenues. Revenues, in turn, were driven by line agency consumption levels and rates. While consumption levels were determined by individual line agencies' operating decisions, rates had to meet with the approval of rate panels. In this context, the discretion given to staff agency executives and managers naturally involved delivering quality services to line agencies, satisfying rate panels, increasing revenues, and controlling costs. Thus, executives argued that overseers could productively grant specific kinds of discretion to executive branch officials by exercising control over rates.

Making Profits in Government. The argument for marketplace services also raised issues of control and discretion, but these were bound up with the question of whether such activities should seek to make a profit. In defense of this idea, executives reminded legislators that revenues are related positively to the amount of value created by an enterprise for its customers, while expenses reflect the cost of generating those revenues. Under certain conditions, the net income earned by an enterprise provides a rough indication of how much value it creates for its customers—net of cost—during a year. Why not, executives asked, take advantage of this unique situation in which a single measure—net income—provides good information about the extent to which an activity within government accomplishes its goals, in this case that of efficiently meeting line agencies' needs for inputs? Allowing line agencies choice over the source of services and focusing attention on the net income earned by Admin's marketplace activities, they argued, would motivate state employees to outperform other providers of the same or substitute services. This line of argument appeared especially persuasive to legislators familiar with the business world or economic principles.

Competing with Business. When legislators asked why state government should compete with private sector suppliers, executives responded that Admin's purpose in providing internal services is to serve the interests of taxpayers. Taxpayers benefit when Admin meets line agencies' needs for inputs more effectively and efficiently than do private suppliers. The best guarantee that internal services achieve this goal, furthermore, is to provide line agencies with choice over their source of supply (unless the services should be operated as utilities) and to avoid situations in which competitive marketplace activities operate at a loss in order to attract line agencies' business.[42]

Acceptance of the Strategy

Legislators' behavior after the strategy was presented in 1986 implies that many accepted these arguments or at least were unwilling to reject them. Legislators did not defend the position that suppliers' interests should take precedence over taxpayers' interests in deciding whether to operate internal service activities. Their behavior also included shifting the plant management, telecommunications, and management consulting operations—all categorized as service activities—to revolving fund financing.[43] The legislature also appropriated general funds to the newly created control activity responsible for information policy. In addition, legislators stopped threatening to place upper limits on spending by operations financed by revolving funds.[44] Finally, acceptance of Admin's enterprise-management strategy was also evident in the lack of opposition to managing some internal services as competitive marketplace activities.

CHAPTER FOUR

Reworking the Culture and Producing Results

SERVING STAFFING CUSTOMERS

After creating the Staffing Division, Department of Employee Relations executives and managers worked toward developing performance standards. As a first step, staffing managers conducted focus groups with state managers who were asked to present their images of the department. Among the images were: "the most bureaucratic agency in state government"; "anti-management, biased, unaware, uncaring, mechanical, disrespectful, and unfair"; "operates within difficult guidelines, but does not attempt to lessen the burden for themselves or their clients"; "big brother"; and "slow, rigid, directed to mediocrity, and incredibly frustrating."[1] One survey conducted for the Staffing Division showed that managers and supervisors felt "they must know the right people within the personnel system or invest inordinate amounts of their time and energy to insure prompt action on their hiring requests."[2]

Redesigning Work

In implementing their customer service strategy to change these images, department executives sought to empower their own employees. The new organizational structure—involving agency services teams—signaled the change in emphasis from perform-

58

ing a set of separate technical functions to providing a unified service to a segment of the customer base.[3] As part of the same strategy, operating-level staffing professionals were given the intellectual tools to respond proficiently to whatever problem customers brought to their attention. Through cross-training, for example, employees who had known only about position classification learned how to deal competently with recruiting and examining. Conversely, specialists in the hiring process learned how the system of position classification worked.

The initial impact of reorganization and work redesign was blunted by the prior beliefs of personnel professionals. Built into their work life had been the premise that they should defend the civil service system against the efforts of line agencies to undermine it.[4] In defending the system, personnel professionals had asserted their authority to make technical determinations of how the system's statutes and rules applied to the objective facts of the cases at hand.

As part of the empowerment strategy, staffing managers communicated a revised doctrine for personnel professionals and modeled the kinds of behaviors that were expected of agency services representatives and their team leaders. Their new doctrine stated that the commitment to serving line managers as customers meant that staffing should help them put the system's increased flexibility to the greatest practical use. More specifically, agency services team members were asked to size up each situation, to probe the manager's view of the problem, to take on the problem as their own, to present the entire range of technical options, to educate the customer about how statewide norms relate to both the situation and the options, to offer professional opinions about practical solutions to the problem, and to seek a consensus about what action to take. Thus, staffing professionals were challenged to help customers solve particular staffing-related operational problems in a timely fashion, and a good solution was conceptualized as a practical response to the situation at hand. The intended outcome of this process was staffing decisions that would be satisfactory to customers and consistent with the public policies and norms of the personnel system.

Refining the Doctrine

This new professional doctrine—which interwove concepts of problem solving and customer service—was gradually refined by staffing managers, partly in response to questions and concerns about what it meant to serve agency managers as customers.

Exercising Judgment.   Many employees were highly uncomfortable with the idea that they should exercise judgment rather than make purely technical decisions based on statutes and rules. Addressing these sentiments in a memo to agency services team leaders, Staffing Division manager Julie Vikmanis argued:

> The ultimate right answer [to a staffing issue] can never be provided. Even the ultimate approach cannot be provided. All of the questions can't even be assembled. (Or at least I don't know how to do it.) I do know, however, that given any set of facts, I can think of multiple considerations, analyze them and make a decision, which I can then defend to others and rationalize to myself. I'm not always comfortable with what I decide. But I can decide. If I can, team leaders can, too.[5]

The emphasis on judgment and problem solving was incorporated into the Staffing Division's training and coaching strategies. Training focused on understanding guidelines for exercising situational judgment rather than on rules and procedures. Agency services teams met frequently to learn how their members handled various problem situations. The idea was to build confidence in team members' ability to make judgments and to foster some degree of consistency among the different team members' interactive styles, reasoning, and decisions. In the words of the Staffing Division manager, to whom central personnel staff had previously referred all complex staffing decisions:

> The idea behind the reorganization is to share the knowledge, the philosophy, the authority, and the decisionmaking with a wider group of people in order to be able to deliver service-related decisions better and faster, while sacrificing a minimum of consistency. Will team leaders make different decisions given the same

set of facts than I might? Yes. Will they make different decisions among themselves given the same set of facts? Yes. Will there consistently be vastly different approaches and solutions among team leaders? No. That's what decision guidelines, team building, and open communications are all about.[6]

Exercising Authority. While urging staffing professionals to use a less judgmental voice in providing service to customers, the Staffing Division's managers also argued that the personnel system was designed, in part, to prevent certain kinds of actions or outcomes. When customers disagreed with staffing decisions, the front-line agency services representatives were urged to bring the issue to the attention of their team leaders, who were empowered to make final decisions on staffing matters.

Meeting Quality Standards. Quality service in the staffing area came to be defined as meeting standards for responding to fully documented customer requests. Standards included producing within one day lists of already certified candidates for an opening, providing copies of candidates' applications within three days, and assigning vacant positions to a class within two weeks. These standards were formulated by staffing employees in consultation with line agency managers, tested for several months, and subsequently publicized in a newsletter distributed to all state managers; production was then tracked to determine whether the standards were being met consistently. Quality performance was also conceptualized, in part, as demonstrating that the Staffing Division cared about customer needs, while fostering realistic and informed customer expectations about the services that staffing could deliver.

As part of the strategy of meeting quality standards, the Staffing Division attempted to streamline the hiring process. For example, when examinations were viewed as an impractical way to advance the merit principle, as in the case of routine service workers, this step in the hiring process was eliminated. As another example, staffing offered some exams to job applicants on a continuous rather than periodic basis, thereby reducing the time required to provide line managers with lists of eligible candidates for vacant positions. Also, authority for hiring applicants for certain positions (for example, clerk typists) on the basis of local job-service referrals was delegated to line agencies.[7]

Sharing Information with Customers. The first focus-group sessions had indicated that line managers learned about the personnel system through their encounters with personnel specialists. Because many specialists provided them with as little information as possible in an effort to safeguard autonomy and power, line managers' understanding tended to be incomplete and distorted. Staffing managers recognized that the strategy of helping agencies take advantage of the personnel system's flexibility could be crippled by line managers' confusion and agency personnel officers' power games. According to Deputy Commissioner for Personnel Elaine Johnson: "We decided that we needed a vehicle that would empower managers to interact differently with the agency personnel people. We then spent a lot of time figuring out what managers needed to know and how we could best share that information."[8]

Smart Staffing, a monthly newsletter, became the primary vehicle for communicating directly with line managers.[9] Each four-page issue contained nontechnical information about an aspect of the personnel system that, until then, had been known exclusively by Employee Relations and agency personnel specialists.[10] *Smart Staffing* released to managers information that had formed part of personnel specialists' power base. By the end of its first year, the publication had discussed ten hiring options, the selection process, interviewing, compensation, job classification, position descriptions, and job-related exams. One issue outlined the turnaround standards described previously. Customer satisfaction surveys and informal feedback indicated that this publication was extremely well received by line managers. (An issue of *Smart Staffing* appears as appendix 2.)

When the Staffing Division surveyed line agency managers in March 1988—less than two years after the initial focus groups were conducted—50 percent said they were satisfied with the department's efforts to "make the system understandable." In January 1989, 90 percent of those surveyed said they were satisfied with performance on this dimension. Line agency managers' satisfaction on the dimension of "helping to solve problems" reached 72 percent. According to the same survey, 74 percent of respondents reported satisfaction with the department's ability to "help managers to hire staff to serve the public."[11]

Bringing Partners Along. The concept used to describe the relationship between central staffing and their counterparts in line agencies was that of a partnership. The idea was that the two partners would jointly serve line managers as customers. In managing partnership relations, the central staffing managers had to rely largely on indirect management tools because the agency-based partners reported only to their agencies' executives.

Although one motivation for publishing *Smart Staffing* was to mobilize the customer base as a source of influence over agency personnel officers, another was to provide agency personnel officers with the tools to respond effectively to their better informed customers. Staffing managers therefore distributed a similar but more in-depth publication to agency personnel offices prior to mailing the newsletter to customers. The introduction to the guide accompanying the issue on hiring options stated that its purpose was "to help personnel officers understand the nuances involved in the use of the various hiring options, particularly where judgment calls must be made about how to interpret and apply provisions of more official documents including laws, rules, and administrative procedures."[12]

Staffing managers also reached out to agency personnel officers through regular meetings with personnel directors. At annual conferences for all members of the state personnel community, the strategy for staffing was explained and training in some of the new skills was provided.[13] In addition to communicating with customers and personnel officers, Deputy Commissioner Elaine Johnson met regularly with line agencies' assistant commissioners for administration—to whom many of their partners reported—in order to "assist them in visualizing and articulating what they wanted from their personnel function."[14] Agency executives were also encouraged to hold their personnel officers accountable for providing quality service to customers using methods similar to those employed in central staffing.

SERVING PURCHASING CUSTOMERS

As part of its organizational transformation, purchasing placed a high value on periodic face-to-face contacts with customers. The purchasing manager even made agency visits part of the buyers' position descriptions. These meetings provided valuable two-way communication about recurring problems and possible solutions, and they signaled to customers that the central staff employees cared about their concerns. In addition, these sessions facilitated subsequent information exchanges by telephone. According to the purchasing manager: "The practice of visiting agencies opened up the lines of communication between staff and customers, based on the trust one gains from seeing a face to go along with a voice."[15]

Purchasing managers argued that buyers should be like consultants who deliver advice to customers on how to use the purchasing process to find the best deal on the materials they need. Job qualifications were revised to include problem solving, negotiation, and communication skills. Training in customer service was provided.

Empowerment

Most buying decisions had to be approved serially by a half-dozen officials whose roles were distinguished by modest increments in signature authority.[16] One purchasing agent, reflecting on twenty years' experience, said he "saw two messages being sent to the staff in this process; you cannot be trusted to do things right and you do not have to take personal responsibility for your work because someone else [will] review and correct it."[17] Admin executives and managers sought to correct this problem by empowering buyers to become decisionmakers and problem solvers. Their method was to flatten the organizational hierarchy and delegate formal authority to approve contracts of any amount to buyer team leaders.

Buyers were urged to exercise judgment in order to create value for agencies. Most buyers had been unwilling to take into account quality, reliability, vendor ability to deliver, and the life-cycle costs of an item in addition to cost. Buyers had been convinced that "one of the principles of management was not to take risks"[18] and felt that buying from vendors other than the lowest bidder would have exposed them to the risk of vendor protests and even legal action. But Admin executives stood behind one buyer even when the state was sued by a disappointed vendor who questioned the objectivity of the process by which bids were evaluated. The out-of-court settlement of this case—which was highly favorable for the state—led numerous buyers to become proficient at the purchasing techniques designed to create value for agencies.[19] Later, Admin executives sought explicit statutory authorization to make purchasing decisions based on life-cycle costs.

Flexibility

The most significant measure introduced—with legislative authorization—to increase flexibility was delegating purchasing authority to line agencies for items costing less than $1,500. Purchasing managers further demonstrated the value they placed on flexibility by awarding some contracts to several vendors and then allowing agencies to determine which vendor met their needs best.

Speed

As part of the agency relations process, Admin learned that line agencies felt that central purchasing took too long to process their requests.[20] In implementing the customer service strategy, managers began to measure how well purchasing performed on this dimension of quality. Results showed that in 1986 only 22 percent of materials requisitions were processed in fewer than twenty-five days, and, on average, more than fifty days were required.

In less than three years, line agencies reported a great deal more satisfaction with the performance of the buyers during agency relations meetings. Data from 1989 substantiate why purchasing was succeeding in the eyes of its customers: on average, only twenty-one days were needed to process incoming requisitions fully. The number of requests sent to central purchasing declined by 27 percent in 1989, principally because of the use of expanded local purchasing authority by agencies, while average processing time was more than cut in half.[21]

Gains were achieved in part by tracking inflows and outflows, analyzing process flows carefully, eliminating unproductive tasks, measuring turnaround times at the individual and buying-team levels, improving coordination, delegating increased authority to line agencies, and making effective use of technology.[22] Purchasing also vastly expanded the use of competitively bid indefinite-quantity contracts, which enabled agencies to obtain the price advantages of volume purchases without having to wait for central purchasing to combine individual orders.

INVENTING THE LEADERSHIP MODEL OF CONTROL

In shaping the structure and operation of the Information Policy Office (IPO), Admin executives were determined to avoid reproducing the enforcement model of control in this new area of administrative policy. They asked themselves:

- What would happen if we based our actions on the premise that 95 percent of state employees would be willing to comply fully with norms if only they knew what was expected of them and why?

- Can we design a control system that does not shackle most employees, while making use of techniques that will be fruitful in dealing with the minority who are unwilling or unable to comply?

- Can we exercise control in ways that help managers succeed in fulfilling their agencies' missions?

IPO's Tasks

In answering these questions, Admin executives—including IPO Director Larry Grant—likened state government to a community whose members would adhere to consensual norms. This assumption suggested that information policy should be formulated by the community of agencies and that the authority to enforce the norms should derive principally from the community's support for them. The executives also believed that IPO should facilitate the process of articulating norms, the adherence to which would advance the community's interests and enable agencies to adapt to technological change. IPO's other major role, they reasoned, should be to win compliance to the norms by helping agencies become willing and able to apply them. In the minds of departmental executives, education, training, consulting, feedback, and incentives should be IPO's principal stocks in trade.

The key elements of IPO's strategy included the following:

- Working closely with over a dozen agency executives represented on an Information Policy Council to create a vision of information management in state government. The vision consisted of beliefs and values that were designed to help managers think about information as a resource and state government as a community.

- Educating managers and executives about the vision, standards, and guidelines supported by the Information Policy Council. IPO then offered coaching to agencies, which were responsible for applying the norms in their contexts. Above all, IPO resisted pressures to issue rules and regulations.

- Judging each agency's ability to manage information. These opinions accompanied the IPO's evaluations of agency funding requests for information systems, which were submitted to overseers during the budgeting and appropriations process. This evaluation method provided executives with incentives to become involved in planning their agencies' information systems.

By seeking to win compliance with the emerging norms of information management in the state, IPO served the needs of overseers, who made budgeting and appropriations decisions for state agencies. The technical complexity of information systems compounded the difficulties of reaching agreement on apportioning limited resources among competing agencies. Therefore, overseers needed assurance that expenditure on planned information systems was justified on two levels. Spending on these systems had to fit the individual agency's overall strategy for implementing public policy and delivering services as well as make sense within the context of what other agencies were doing. To help overseers make funding decisions, IPO developed a budget book containing plain language evaluations—each a single page—of the need for every funding proposal and of the agencies' ability to manage information in accordance with statewide norms. As a measure of overseers' satisfaction, few appropriations were made to agencies whose proposals IPO did not support. Overseers also praised IPO's role in the budget process during a performance appraisal session that the office organized in early 1990.

Thus, from the start, IPO's customers were the governor and the legislature. In meeting customer needs, IPO assumed responsibility for performing three critical tasks: making information policy, winning compliance to the norms, and assisting overseers' efforts to use the budget process as an instrument to improve governmental efficiency, effectiveness, and accountability.

IPO's Window of Opportunity

Several key features of IPO's operating environment and institutional design enabled the office to develop a distinctive strategy for control. First, information management was at once a highly technical area, a growing expenditure category, and critical to agency operations. These facts made IPO's efforts to facilitate information planning and accountability to overseers extremely valuable to its customers and other stakeholders.

Second, agencies' funding requests for information management, by statute, could not be incorporated into the governor's budget without IPO's approval, and agencies needed IPO's permission to spend appropriated funds on goods and services relating to information management. If IPO's influence came to parallel its formal authority, the office could therefore reward agencies for complying with information policy norms as well as enforce these norms.

Third, IPO could draw on the Information Policy Council, made up of executives from across state government, for political support. Many of these executives believed that the command and control approach to compliance was detrimental to achieving their agencies' missions, especially in the area of information management.

IPO's Strategy for Winning Compliance

Taking advantage of these favorable circumstances, Admin executives and IPO staff members developed what they called the leadership model of control. The intended outcomes of this strategy included satisfied customers, improved information planning, successful efforts to comply with norms, and acceptable compliance costs.

Negotiating Principles, Standards, and Guidelines.   IPO adopted as its own the norms agreed to by the Information Policy Council. The purpose of these norms was more to influence how officials conceived of their managerial responsibilities and approached the task of information management in state government than to dictate what agencies could or could not do. This purpose was clear from the preamble to the Council's statement of information management principles:

> Management of state government will be greatly enhanced with better management of its information. The gains will not only be in the efficiency of operation but also in taking fuller advantage of information when making critical decisions. This will be accomplished when we consider information as a state resource and cooperate toward a common direction for the state's information facilities, networks, and data. To that end, these general principles represent a foundation of understanding and agreement. These principles will assist agencies in accomplishing their legislatively mandated responsibilities while also contributing effectively to the collective needs of the state.[23]

Two principles expressed the belief that choices of information-processing technologies and methods of data collection, storage, and utilization are managerial decisions, for which agency managers and executives should be held accountable.[24]

The remaining principles offered a vision of how agencies should cooperate in the information management area. For example, a basic norm referred to as the data principle stated that "all data is owned by the state, not by the particular agency that collects or uses it." This principle was translated into specific expectations, including norms for interagency planning of data collection and storage, reciprocal access, and quality control. Similarly, the standards principle stated that "the components of information management—applications, data, and technology—must be integrated in a way that supports the necessary linkages among state agencies and between state and local government." In formulating the standards principle, Council members expected that specific norms would take the form of protocols and conventions as well as of approved technologies and applications.[25]

The practice of negotiating agreement on principles, standards, and guidelines, which extended to formulating IPO's methods for evaluating agency budget requests, contributed to agency executives' understanding and support for the norms. As a further consequence, Council members became increasingly effective in managing the implementation process in their respective agencies. They also supported IPO's overall efforts to win compliance as well as the office's utilization of its enforcement powers against noncompliers.

Influencing the Agency Planning Process.   IPO decided to review documents at various stages in the development of agency plans to modify their information systems rather than await the submission of final plans. Specifically, IPO required agencies over time to submit an organizational mission statement; an analysis of their information management goals and objectives; a conceptual scheme for using data, applications, and technology; and a tactical plan for implementing this scheme. By making these requirements and providing feedback at each stage, IPO intended to foster a culture of information management within each agency and to oversee the implementation of the statewide data and standards principles. In some cases, IPO Director Grant attended agency-level meetings to ascertain whether executives and specialists knew how to use information management to advance their agency's overall plans for managing resources and delivering services. By following this strategy, rather than focusing on the inspection of fully developed requests and plans, IPO expected to achieve more compliance with norms at lower cost.

Facilitating Understanding of Norms.   IPO focused on helping agencies understand what it expected of them. One means of setting expectations was to provide executives and managers with a nontechnical manual outlining strategic information planning methods. IPO also offered brief courses on the state's principles of information management for the many executives who were not members of the Council, and it trained agency personnel in life-cycle costing and other tools that the office expected agencies to utilize in planning new systems. In addition, IPO's staff coached individuals within agencies on how to comply with the state's principles, standards, and guidelines.

Streamlining the Process. IPO eliminated hurdles when it believed they were redundant. For example, if an agency's budget request received an extremely high evaluation by IPO, the office did not exercise its statutory authority to review purchase orders for equipment. IPO also authorized agencies to purchase microprocessing equipment from vendors who had been awarded indefinite-quantity contracts, which had previously been approved by IPO. This step avoided a bottleneck in the compliance process and permitted IPO to dedicate resources to helping agencies with strategic information planning.[26]

Creating Incentives. When agencies successfully complied with norms of information management, including those of strategic information planning, IPO was much more likely to support their funding requests than when they did not. For example, IPO recommended that overseers fund a request for $600,000 in appropriations for an information clearinghouse managed by the State Planning Agency. In this case, IPO told overseers that "this request has top management backing and supports the long-term vision of how the State Planning Agency provides services to clients. It also supports the way State Planning develops and maintains their information systems. This request makes sense in light of the changing role of the Land Management Information Center. In the past it has been applications oriented; now it has become a data collection, integration, and transfer service."[27]

In contrast, when agencies did not comply with norms of information management, IPO recommended against overseers' approval of funding requests. For example, after evaluating the Transportation Regulation Board's proposal to hire consulting services to study its functions and needs and to help it determine which software and hardware packages to buy and develop, IPO wrote: "Due to a complete lack of planning, we do not recommend funding at this time. . . . The Board has no strategic plan, mission statement, or information system plan. . . . There is no recognition of the possibility of sharing data, applications or technology resources with the Departments of Transportation, Public Safety, or the Public Utilities Commission."[28]

IPO's recommendations proved consequential. The 1989 legislature allocated over $37 million to support new and continued development for information systems, only $5 million of which had not received IPO support.[29] Moreover, IPO's recommendation against funding four projects proposed by the Department of Education was respected by the legislature despite the agency's concerted lobbying effort to receive funding anyway.[30]

Asking for Feedback.   In early 1990, IPO convened an annual stakeholders meeting. The purpose was not only to elicit comments and criticisms from key legislators and agencies but also to ensure that each stakeholder group was aware of the others' views. IPO received the most positive feedback for developing quality publications, creating a strategic information planning process, providing staff support to the Council, managing its role in the budget process, and balancing legislative and agency needs. IPO was criticized for responding slowly to the Council's recommendation to adopt a particular standard as an official norm and for paying inadequate attention to the tasks of reshaping current delivery systems and developing a statewide data architecture.[31]

SERVING INFORMATION MANAGEMENT CUSTOMERS

Cost Issues

Instability in rates Admin charged for data-processing services posed major difficulties for line agencies. Not only did rate instability make the task of formulating biennial budgets complex, it also sometimes led, in effect, to an across-the-board cut in the second year of the budget cycle. For these reasons, customers argued that rate stability was essential. Backed by line agency executives serving on the data-processing utility's rate panel, Admin executives eventually convinced reluctant Department of Finance executives to allow this activity's revolving fund to eliminate surpluses or recoup losses over a three-year period.

Rate performance improved markedly in the years after the information management service was separated from IMB, which had encompassed both service and control responsibilities. The weighted average of rate changes for the data-processing utility for the subsequent period changed as follows:[32]

Rate Changes for Computer Services

Fiscal Year	% Change
1987	+ 9.00
1988	+ 2.91
1989	− 4.71
1990	− 8.50
1991	− 4.75

This downward trend in rates, which was helped along by trends in demand and by technological change, also eliminated the problems generated by rate instability.

Service Quality

In a 1990 survey Admin's information management customers were asked to indicate on a scale from 1 to 7—from "not at all" to "a great deal"—the extent to which they perceived that the quality of information services had improved during the previous few years. The average response was 4.42 and the most frequent response was 5.[33] Customer comments about service quality included "good improvement in the data processing center," "better at meeting deadlines," "more open to explore alternative solutions," and "I am impressed with the improvement of staff I have dealt with." About 13 percent of respondents did not perceive an improvement in service quality.

Interagency Collaboration on Utility Policy

Utility rates specify how much customers will be charged per unit of service they consume. Choosing among alternative definitions of the unit of service was one of the most sensitive tasks in the rate-setting process. In coming to agreement on this issue, the line agency executives who represented customers' interests on the rate review panels of the information management operation confronted such questions as:

- Should the unit of service of the mainframe data-processing utility be central-processing-unit (CPU) seconds or an alternative that would be more meaningful to line agency managers?

- Should the unit of service of the voice-telecommunications utility be access to the network for one year, a one-minute call to any location in the state, or a combination of call duration and the distance over which the call travels?

Although the question of how to define a unit of service at first sounded like a technical one, line agency executives discovered that they were faced with discerning their agencies' individual and joint interests in the utilities' operations. Specifically, they had to reach collective agreement on which consumption patterns to encourage, how costs should be shared among agencies, and what level of associated administrative costs should be incurred. The rate-setting process required a judgment about how these considerations should be weighed. Interagency collaboration in governing Admin utilities was valued by those who participated. In the words of one deputy commissioner, "I developed a clearer understanding of the issues that affected each of us and I learned what good community decisions can do for all of us."[34]

MANAGING MARKETPLACE ENTERPRISES

Practices

To succeed, Admin's marketplace enterprises made routine use of many common business practices. Some examples are described here.

Market Research.   Motor-pool employees conducted surveys and focus groups to determine why many state employees preferred to be reimbursed for driving their own cars rather than rent less expensive state vehicles. The reason: motor-pool cars were considered uncomfortable and the rental procedure cumbersome. The central motor pool responded to these criticisms by upgrading and expanding the fleet by 25 percent between 1984 and 1987. Over the same period, central motor-pool rates barely increased.

Competitive Analysis. Managers in printing concluded that if they located high-speed equipment on customers' premises and offered multiple levels of service, their business unit could compete successfully with office copiers on the basis of cost and quality. Management consulting found that its staff's knowledge of how state government works offered it a competitive advantage over private consulting firms. The managers of the central supply store, in contrast, decided that their business unit could not compete with local vendors in supplying certain products to state field offices.

Executive Review of Plans. Managers of marketplace activities presented business plans periodically to Admin's top executives. Pricing, promotion, investment, service delivery, staffing, overhead, and other issues were discussed. Managers and executives negotiated net income targets. Business plans served as a key tool in holding operating managers accountable for results.

Cost Analysis. The central supply store found that the turnover of many items was too slow to merit stocking them.

Service Delivery Redesign. The central supply store streamlined processes so that orders could be filled quickly. The motor pool increased its locations in the capital city to make short-term rentals by agencies convenient.

Product Promotion. Printing provided attractive poster-sized calendars free of charge to its customers. The calendar displayed information about how to purchase services from printing.

Financial Reporting. All marketplace activities reported monthly on profits and losses and submitted quarterly financial statements.

Additional Requirements. In addition to focusing on customer satisfaction and financial performance, marketplace activities were expected to comply with the state's evolving norms for staffing, purchasing, information management, financial management, and the like.

Impediments

The main handicap facing marketplace activities proved to be divergences between the state's compensation system and the external market. Internal marketplace wages—established through collective bargaining between the state and three unions—were frequently out of line with those paid by its private sector competitors, in one direction or the other. As a result, marketplace activities either could not fill positions with qualified employees when wages were low or proved uncompetitive when wages were high. The difficulty of rewarding employees monetarily for extraordinary performance was also a concern.

The limited flexibility of the state's staffing process also worked to the disadvantage of marketplace activities. Market conditions seemed to change more quickly than the rate at which the staffing process could adapt.[35] These impediments remained a matter of concern, even though staffing made substantial efforts to respond to the needs of marketplace activities, within the constraints of the personnel system.

Results

Table 1 displays revenue, price, and retained earnings data for five marketplace activities: management analysis, central supply stores, printing, micrographics, and electronic-equipment rental. Each of these activities faced competition from other sources, although competition from private vendors was limited in some cases.[36]

Table One
Financial Data for Selected Marketplace Activities

Division	Revenue ($000)		Retained Earnings ($000)		Price per Unit Change (average annual %)[b]
	1983	1990	1983	1990	1987–90
Central stores	2,246	4,915	−113	265	−5.81
Printing	2,360	5,800	−129	296	1.72
Management analysis	0	571	8[a]	46	6.69
Micrographics	455	777	−20	46	2.27
Electronic-equipment rental	286	692	−180	228	−11.20

[a] For FY87, the first year for management analysis.
[b] The average annual percentage change in the consumer price index for 1987–90 was 3.91.

Entrepreneurial Spirit

In May 1990, Admin executives received a proposal from Mike Bodem, the manager responsible for the state's Records Center, asking that his service be financed by revolving funds:

> If the Records Center is set up on a revolving fund it is sure to grow in holdings because we have never advertised our services or existence. It also has not accepted certain types of records, such as permanent or short term records. If the Center were to be established as a revolving fund, it would accept any type of record an agency wished to store, charging a fee for each retrieval as well as storage, and would develop and implement a marketing strategy to increase holdings.[37]

Bodem planned to market the records storage and retrieval service by demonstrating that agencies that utilized it would operate more cost-effectively. Why would state agencies pay for this service when they could continue storing all their records in prime office space? Agencies had an incentive to economize on the use of space in state-owned buildings in the capitol area, Bodem pointed out, because they annually paid $11 per square foot into Admin's recently established plant management revolving fund. The reason the Records Center could charge attractive prices for storing documents was straightforward: across town, warehouse space could be leased for $3 per square foot. In the spirit of the enterprise-management strategy, Bodem reasoned that some agencies would take advantage of his unit's service in order to put their prime office space to better use, while other agencies would choose to reduce the amount of space they consumed. Bodem had thus spotted a cost-saving opportunity for state agencies and a market opportunity for the Records Center. When challenged to explain why the Records Center would be able to compete with hypothetical private providers of the same service, Bodem responded by identifying his operation's sources of competitive advantage. In particular, he mentioned the added security of keeping government control of documents as well as his employees' in-depth knowledge of official record retention schedules.

It is hard to imagine that a proposal like that of the Records Center would have emerged deep from within the Department of Administration had the enterprise-management strategy—and especially the concept of marketplace activities—not been well understood and supported. This strategy empowered middle managers like Bodem to use their knowledge of the workings of state government to create, market, and deliver services that could help line agencies make better use of scarce resources.

CHAPTER FIVE

Challenging Financial Paradigms

By the decade's end, the organizational strategies of the Department of Administration's control and service activities and of Employee Relations' staffing operations had been decisively altered. The results were a source of pride for the original champions of these strategies and for many who did the vital work of extending and implementing them. At the same time, the lack of congruence between these strategies and the routines followed by the Department of Finance's accounting and budgeting operations was a constant irritant. For example, the statewide accounting system did not provide Admin service operations with timely financial information, and conflict with budgeting officials over marketplace activities was regularly ignited. From the champions' standpoint, the troublesome consequences of a host of accounting and budgeting routines were problems and should have been solved years earlier.[1]

The Department of Finance remained impervious to the new thinking that was guiding changes in the missions, mandates, cultures, and routines elsewhere in state government. As heirs to the bureaucratic reform vision, Finance employees were convinced that they served the public interest by providing expert staff support to political overseers during the biennial budget process, by controlling budget execution, and by acting as the state's financial agent. No one found reason to charge that financial controls were lax, and the governor gave no indication that he was dissatisfied with the staff support he received from Finance. Finance commissioners serving during the 1980s maintained the culture and routines of this powerful and competent staff agency.[2]

As the final year of his second term began, Governor Perpich appointed a new finance commissioner to succeed a long-time aide who decided to leave his post for the private sector. The appointment was viewed by some champions as providing the best possible opportunity to apply to the Finance Department what they increasingly called "the new vision" of management in state government.[3] The reason was that the new commissioner, Peter Hutchinson, was predisposed to embrace some tenets of the new vision as a result of his public policy training, experience as public affairs vice-president of Dayton Hudson Corporation, and recent participation in Harvard Business School's advanced management program. Once in office, Hutchinson did not make any personnel changes in Finance but sought the counsel of known champions, including Babak Armajani, who was involved with statewide finance issues as a member of the governor's fiscal policy group.

The finance commissioner and his network of advisors from outside the department looked for ways to use financial systems to hold line agencies more accountable for serving their customers, managing resources, and complying with statewide norms. They were not short on ideas, some of which would have required years of organizational change effort. Hutchinson's inclination was to identify and manipulate a few levers of financial change during his first—and possibly last—year as commissioner of finance. During 1990, the commissioner therefore attempted to bring the new vision to bear by managing two high-level policy issues requiring his attention: bonding authority and the biennial budget.[4]

THE CAPITAL BUDGET

When Hutchinson arrived at Finance, state agencies, including the higher education systems, had already asked for $1 billion worth of capital projects to be financed by issuing state bonds.[5]

Given accepted limits on indebtedness and the governor's fiscal policies, the Finance Department faced the task of recommending a bonding bill of much smaller proportions. Budget officials proposed that Finance identify priority projects by requiring agencies to demonstrate health and safety benefits and then reviewing the justifications. The commissioner agreed to this approach. Agencies proved adept at adducing health and safety arguments for most projects, including new roofs and heating systems. In many instances, budget officials did not have the knowledge or analytical tools to determine whether such arguments were reasonable or spurious.

While the Finance staff applied the health and safety criterion to the mass of proposals already on the table, the commissioner looked for ways to suppress the tendency of state agencies to ask for much more bonding authority than could be approved. From the viewpoint of the new vision, the fact that agencies were not charged for debt service on the bonds financing their capital projects was one reason why agencies asked for so much capital spending authority. The funds used to service the state's debt were appropriated directly to the Finance Department for reasons that were presumably convincing to bureaucratic reformers.[6] Agencies, consequently, faced few disincentives to seek as much bonding authority as they could conceivably obtain or to undertake projects once authorized. As a way to decrease the demand for bonding authority in future years and to induce agencies to evaluate carefully whether authorized projects should be built, the finance commissioner fastened on the idea of requiring agencies to fund the costs of debt service out of their appropriations.

The commissioner's political strategy was to recommend that the governor adopt this approach and initially target the sector of state government making the largest share of capital requests: the higher education systems. The governor agreed to the bonding bill's provision for charging these state institutions for debt service on their new projects. In so doing, the governor incurred stiff criticism from higher education officials and their constituencies. Although most legislative leaders—similarly frustrated by the size of claims repeatedly made on state borrowing capacity by this sector of government—were sympathetic to the governor's proposal, some other legislators came to the defense of the higher education systems. A compromise was negotiated: higher education institutions were required under the new bonding authorization to cover one-third of debt service costs from their appropriations, while the remainder was still to be covered by Finance.[7] Hutchinson was reasonably pleased with the outcome of round one and hoped that future bonding authorizations would make all agencies financially responsible for their capital spending.

THE BIENNIAL BUDGET

After the legislature enacted the bonding bill and adjourned, the finance commissioner turned his attention to preparing the biennial budget for fiscal years 1992–93. Until then, the budget process was one in which agencies prepared justifications for proposed increases in spending and staffing levels and defended them before Finance and, ultimately, the legislature. Most deliberations concerned whether the agencies really "needed" to be funded and staffed at the proposed levels.

A standing criticism of the budget process among champions of the new vision was that it focused overseers' and managers' attention on inputs rather than on results. Time devoted to justifying increased spending and staffing levels was time not invested in improving the cost-effectiveness of ongoing programs or the performance of state employees. At Admin, champions had sought to shift the focus from inputs to results by purging activities financed by revolving funds of the general fund mentality. Later champions of the new vision leading the generally funded revenue department tried to bring about a similar shift in orientation, in part by requiring managers to fund new initiatives or investments in ongoing operations with savings they could generate from both controlling costs more rigorously and divesting low-priority activities.[8] Hutchinson was attracted to the idea of challenging the general fund mentality statewide.

Base Adjustments

The highly routinized budgeting process began when Finance issued budget instructions. The instructions invariably authorized state agencies to increase their base budgets to reflect their growing needs, defined as known prior commitments as well as anticipated increases in wages, salaries, and other costs of doing business. Budget officials came to the finance commissioner with recommendations to raise the base for all agencies by several percentage points. But the finance commissioner did not accept the premise that agencies' needs increase as prices of inputs rise and considered recommending that the governor issue budget instructions making no provision for base increases except as required by law.

When Hutchinson discussed his position on base-level increases with the governor's fiscal policy group, all members except two revenue department executives attempted to dissuade him. One objection was that services would deteriorate. The finance commissioner made known that he was unwilling to accept the implied assumption that agencies could not improve their productivity to compensate for rising prices and salaries. He argued that if the budget instructions and reviews focused attention on improving results while holding base-level spending constant—as was his plan—agency managers would find myriad ways to deliver services to their customers more cost-effectively. A second objection was that this proposal would be viewed as an across-the-board budget cut and that the governor should not be seen to support such a move during an election year. The finance commissioner responded to this second objection by arguing that the public did not want to fund costs (or so-called needs) but rather counted on overseers to purchase results on their behalf. The only way to purchase results, he claimed, was to give agencies responsibility for identifying the outcomes they expected to produce for the price the public was willing to pay. The best information about the public's willingness to pay available at the initial stages of the budget process was the amount of the current base plus increases required by law. A third objection was that the unions representing state employees would oppose the commissioner's budget strategy, since traditionally the base-level increase roughly indicated the amount of the state's initial offer in upcoming collective bargaining negotiations. The finance commissioner promised to persuade union leaders that the state's bargaining strategy would not be affected by this change in the budget process. Despite Hutchinson's responses to this series of objections, his skeptical colleagues on the fiscal policy group remained concerned that agencies' needs would be underfunded and that the governor would suffer politically from following this budget strategy. The open question was what the governor himself would decide.

No Change Requests

The commissioner believed, in principle, that the budget process should begin by discerning not the anticipated costs of providing government services but rather the public's overall demand for those services as measured by projected revenues. Based on a March 1990 forecast, revenues for fiscal years 1992–93 were expected to be approximately equal to the amount spent by state government during the 1991 fiscal year. The policy question facing the commissioner was whether to apply the general principle by informing agencies that requests for increased spending beyond the base level (so-called change requests) would be unwelcome. As a practical matter, Hutchinson thought that letting agencies know the bad news at the outset of the budget process would allow managerial time to be devoted to improving the use of resources presumably available and avoid the disappointment that would accompany the likely rejection of most change requests at a later stage in the budget process. The political danger of this policy, according to fiscal policy colleagues, was that many constituencies would become disenchanted with an incumbent governor whose administration was unwilling to entertain arguments for new programs and spending until after the election.

Support from Overseers

Over the objections of some of his long-time advisors, Governor Perpich gave his support to Hutchinson's budget strategy. The governor is said to have liked the opportunity to argue that his policies were fiscally conservative when challenged by Republican contenders for his job. He also wanted to avoid a situation in which he began a third term facing a state budget deficit. The governor also appeared to understand how the proposed budget strategy extended the new vision of state management that had developed during his two consecutive terms in office.

Once he secured the governor's support, the finance commissioner began to consult legislative leaders. According to Hutchinson:

> Most of the leaders agreed with the overall approach. Most appealing to them was the argument that the traditional approach would result, as it always had in the past, in a major conflict between the "needs" for greater spending and the real limits on revenue growth. Thus, most of the legislature's time in the traditional budget process was spent cutting agencies' proposed budgets and services. For the leaders, that often meant building support for "tough" votes on budget matters. The alternative we proposed had the benefit of reducing unfundable requests and unwarranted expectations. Much of the winnowing out would take place in the agencies as would the thinking on how to maintain services within the state's resource limits.[9]

Disseminating the Budget Instructions

In August 1990, state agencies received the governor's budget instructions (excerpts reproduced as appendix 3). In addition to stating the governor's policies on base-level adjustments and change requests, the instructions directed agencies to use discretion, flexibility, and creativity in defining programs and designing service delivery mechanisms. To focus attention on results, the instructions did not ask agencies to provide much of the usual detailed information about costs.

Arrival of the budget instructions created a furor in state government. Agency executives, like most of the commissioner's fiscal policy colleagues, claimed that Finance should increase their base-level budgets to reflect their needs. In a series of meetings, the finance commissioner assured agency executives that he recognized that their costs were rising. He added, however, that the governor's new budgetary policy was to start with the price the public appeared willing to pay for state government in the form of taxes and other revenues and then to use those limited resources to fund the results he wished to purchase from agencies on behalf of the public. As a matter of policy, then, needs or costs were not to be the starting point or focus of budgeting. These arguments fell, to a large extent, on uncomprehending ears—not only in the agencies but among budget professionals in Finance as well. Much confusion therefore surrounded the task of following the budget instructions.

The clash of budgetary paradigms—funding costs versus purchasing results—was not to be resolved under Governor Perpich, who lost the November 1990 election. (The Republican candidate was forced to drop out less than two weeks before Election Day because of a character issue. He was substituted by the second-place finisher in the Republican primary, Arnie Carlson, whose late start turned out to be an advantage in an election year marked by anti-incumbent sentiment.) With the impending departure of the Perpich administration, including Hutchinson, many career managers expected reasonable budget instructions to be forthcoming. Much to their surprise, the governor-elect announced shortly after the election that he planned to adopt the unconventional budget instructions as his own.

PART THREE

Generalizations

CHAPTER SIX

More Problems, Fewer Conditions

Does the information presented in part 2 prove that any or all of the troubling situations along the staff/line frontier are problems everywhere and at each level of government? The answer to this question is no, and it would be negative even if every state in the nation were exactly like Minnesota. A situation cannot be proven to be a problem; it can only be judged to be a problem. To make the point forcefully: we cannot as a logical matter even prove that the troubles along the staff/line frontier were problems in Minnesota itself.

Can the experiences described here enable government officials and others to improve their judgments about whether any or all of the troubling situations in their environments can and should be improved on through intentional problem solving? The answer to this question is yes; information about these experiences can make a good case for categorizing unsatisfactory situations as problems. The objective of this chapter is to raise the likelihood that possibilist-minded officials and citizens everywhere and at all levels of government will contribute to deliberation by making good arguments for the claim that any and all of the difficulties along the staff/line frontier in their setting are problems.[1]

Possibilists should prepare to encounter deliberators who think like Defender and Social Scientist, whom we met in chapter 2. A robust strategy for persuading each to accept the possibilist position is to help them envision cases in which troubling situations are defined as problems, solutions are tried, and the results prove encouraging.[2] The main idea would be to show that staff/line troubles are susceptible to effective problem solving, just as troubles along the frontier between line agencies and the public sometimes are.[3]

A CONTINGENCY APPROACH

Some deliberators who think like Defender and Social Scientist may easily envision a local scenario of effective problem solving as soon as they learn that such a case has already occurred along the staff/line frontier somewhere in the United States.[4] If possibilists believe their fellow deliberators are so inclined, all they have to do is relate the stories told in part 2. Possibilists pursuing this strategy would sensibly organize this information around concepts that people in government ordinarily use to describe problem solving, such as defining problems, altering routines, cultivating political support, and assessing feedback.

But what should possibilists do if their fellow deliberators regard Minnesota as so different from their locale that information drawn from part 2 has no more relevance for them than would a story about effective problem solving in, say, Sweden? This possibility must be taken seriously because most Americans consider Minnesota peculiarly well endowed in problem-solving capacities, and they often attribute this endowment to the Nordic origins of an unusually high proportion of Minnesotans.[5] Three ways of dealing with protestations of irrelevance are:

- To demand that deliberators offer a rigorous defense of the claim that aspects of Minnesota government, politics, or society explain why effective problem solving took place there, and then to raise questions about the validity of the presumptions that underlie that defense. Because most deliberators are not necessarily committed to norms of professional social inquiry, this approach does not appear promising.

- To argue that even if Minnesota were somehow uniquely capable of inventing strategies to solve problems along the staff/line frontier, it is not necessary to be like Minnesota to make use of the same strategies. The problem with this approach is that deliberators may not accept the claim that conditions enabling invention are different from those conducive to replication and adaptation.

- To cast about for information about effective problem solving along the staff/line frontier in what deliberators perceive to be less unusual settings. The risk of this approach is that dissimilarities between any two settings can always be found.

The common liability of these approaches is that they misdiagnose the problem. When deliberators are local rather than cosmopolitan in their orientation, they are unlikely to be persuaded that other states' experience is relevant.[6] What possibilists need to do in such circumstances is to ground their arguments in some facet of local experience.[7] Surely one way to proceed is to call attention to a familiar local instance of improved governmental performance and to describe that experience as a general problem-solving scenario. Then possibilists can describe a hypothetical case of problem solving along the staff/line frontier whose main elements resemble those of the positive local experience. Possibilists can fill in enough detail so that the scenario is vivid, thereby adding to its plausibility. Here, the Minnesota experience would serve as an aid to the possibilist imagination but would not enter into the argument explicitly.

Whichever approach is deemed suitable, possibilists should be prepared to argue that most if not all troubles along the staff/line frontier are more likely to derive from malleable organizational cultures, constraints, incentives, and routines than from seemingly immutable factors such as human nature or individual personality traits. In this way, deliberation can focus on solving problems rather than on lamenting conditions. In addition, possibilists should be prepared to distinguish among the kinds of problems that deserve solution and to identify some concepts that can guide problem-solving efforts.

CATEGORIZING PROBLEMS AS FAILURES
OF ACCOUNTABILITY

The range of possible ways to define problems along the staff/line frontier is enormous. One approach is to offer an ad hoc, highly contextual definition of the problem posed by each of a long series of troubling situations. At the other extreme, a possibilist could say that the persistent bureaucratic paradigm is the underlying problem. Depending on the audience and the set·ting, an intermediate approach may be attractive: defining the problem in terms that apply to a variety of staff functions but not at such a high level of generality that specific troubles disappear from view. Minnesota's staff agency executives pursued this middle way after discerning patterns in the function-specific problems they were trying to solve.[8] In retrospect, staff agency executives categorized problems as three distinct failures of accountability.[9] Whether using information about the Minnesota experience directly or indirectly, possibilists may wish to categorize problems similarly. In some cases, the problem was that staff agencies were not sufficiently accountable to key stakeholders. In others, the problem lay in what staff agencies were accountable for rather than in the degree to which they were accountable to stakeholders.

Weak Accountability

Three different kinds of cases of weak accountability received attention. First, staff agencies in some cases were not sufficiently accountable to overseers. For example, a few state legislators were extremely concerned that the Information Management Bureau (IMB) was not performing its oversight responsibilities when financed by revolving funds rather than appropriations. Second, some staff operations were not sufficiently accountable to the line agencies utilizing their services. For instance, line agencies complained about poor service and rising costs; neither utilizing an alternative provider nor withholding their consent for rate increases was an available remedy. As another example, neither the centralized personnel operation responsible for recruiting and examining nor the one responsible for position classification was accountable for resolving line agency managers' staffing problems. Third, agency-level staff personnel were insufficiently accountable to the line executives to whom they reported; nor were they accountable to their counterparts in central staff agencies for their overall performance. Neither line agency executives nor the Department of Employee Relations, for example, had developed adequate tools to hold line agency personnel officers accountable.

Misplaced Accountability

Principal responsibility for economizing on the use of inputs was unnecessarily absorbed in many cases by the central staff and the overseers they supported. First, some internal services believed that they—rather than users—were accountable for choosing the appropriate level of utilization of their services. The motor pool did so by operating a relatively small, low-quality fleet of vehicles, despite the fact that demand could not be met and employees could be reimbursed for driving their own cars on state business. Second, some staff agencies did not give line agencies an incentive to economize on the utilization of their services. For example, telecommunications did not charge for use of the statewide voice network, and training did not charge for its services. Similarly, the Finance Department did not charge line agencies for their share of the interest expense incurred by the state in financing capital projects. Third, the budget function invited line agencies to add up and then defend the operating costs they would like to incur. It then became the responsibility of the budget examiners, Finance Department executives, the governor, and the legislature to decide how line agencies should economize. As a result, line agencies did not take responsibility for improving the costs per unit of service or commit to achieving success on other dimensions of performance in exchange for funding.

Misguided Accountability

In some cases, staff agencies' conception of what they were accountable for was narrow. For example, central purchasing minimized the price paid for commodities, but optimizing and balancing such factors as purchase price, life-cycle costs, quality, vendor reliability, and timeliness of delivery would have been more reasonable. Front-line officials in central personnel believed they were accountable principally for saying no to inappropriate line agency requests when it would have been more reasonable to seek ways to optimize and balance such factors as timeliness, flexibility, and fairness and to help line agencies solve their personnel problems. Some control-oriented activities believed they were accountable for enforcing rules and regulations when it would have been more valuable to win compliance to norms and analyze the costs and benefits of administrative policies.

In other cases, staff agencies operated with a misguided sense of what they should hold others accountable for. The Finance Department, for example, believed that line agencies and internal services should be accountable for competent planning. In practice, agencies were regarded as competent in planning when they spent every dollar that had been allocated to their general fund accounts. Spending less than was allocated was punished, not rewarded. Similarly, the Finance Department criticized activities financed by revolving funds when they happened to close out the year with positive net income; to avoid such criticism, revolving fund activities increased their costs in order to offset unanticipated revenues.

SOLVING ACCOUNTABILITY PROBLEMS

The main idea for solving these problems was to develop and implement improved organizational strategies for the centralized staff operations. In each case, steps were taken to give staff agencies increased reasons, incentives, and opportunities to meet the needs of their identified customers. Putting the new strategies into practice generally altered organizational routines in such areas as production, marketing, human-resource management, financial management, executive leadership, and political oversight. In some instances, the strategies were supported by readjusting formal organizational structures and by changes in statutory authorization.[10]

The remainder of this chapter links key elements of some of these organizational strategies to specific accountability problems.

Measures to Strengthen Accountability

Accountability to Overseers.   Separating service and control activities within the Department of Administration was an essential part of the solution to one instance of weak accountability to overseers. Admin executives backed by a few legislative leaders and a governor's blue-ribbon panel decided to focus the IMB on providing services to line agencies and to create the separate Information Policy Office (IPO), financed by general fund appropriations, to serve overseers as customers. These customers needed assurance that each agency's information management decisions made sense from a statewide perspective; they also needed help evaluating budget requests for information systems. What made IPO accountable to overseers were mainly its organizational mission, mandate, and culture. Among the mechanisms reinforcing IPO's accountability to overseers was the budget and appropriations process.

Staff agencies needed to be accountable to overseers even when line agencies were customers. Admin executives persuaded legislative overseers that they could achieve greater accountability by making internal services more accountable to line agencies and by analyzing and reviewing the financial performance of revolving funds than they could by scrutinizing overall performance every other year during the appropriations process.

Accountability to Line Agencies.   The prerequisite for holding internal service activities accountable to their customers was to finance them with revolving funds. Line agencies began paying for the services they received from several activities, including plant management and management analysis. This funding arrangement made it possible for internal services to respond to customer demand. Incremental demand translated into incremental revenues and thus the ability to fund expansion. Likewise, falling demand translated into fewer available resources for the internal service activity. This structural possibility also reinforced Admin executives' message that the mission and mandate of internal services was to meet line agency needs for high-quality and cost-effective services. Not only did the exchange relationship between providers and customers support the idea that internal services were accountable to line agencies, but revolving funds also brought into everyday use a variety of indicators of operational and financial results, including costs, revenues, expenses, net income, retained earnings, and return on investment.

To enhance accountability to line agency customers, some constraints had to be removed. For example, the motor pool was no longer instructed to maintain a fleet of fewer than 800 stripped-down cars but rather was encouraged to build market share relative to the more expensive alternative of private vehicle reimbursements. As another example, the constraint that revolving fund activities had to plan neither to accumulate nor to deplete retained earnings was relaxed in order to meet customer needs for rate stability. In addition, the constraint that internal services would not be permitted to fail and be closed down was removed.

The complementary strategy was to allow for increased customer choice. These measures unleashed competitive pressures from substitutes and alternative suppliers. Printing, for example, lost its power to veto line agency purchases of a highly competitive substitute: office copiers. The mainframe-oriented computer operation lost its authority to regulate line agency purchases of microcomputers. In several cases, including typewriter-repair services, line agencies were permitted to purchase the same service from an external source or to provide it in-house. Among the consequences, typewriter repair proved uncompetitive and was shut down, and the Revenue Department began to provide its own data-entry services. Remaining limitations on line agency choice were imposed either by control activities or by collective bodies representing line agencies. When the centralized internal service was the sole provider, the amount it charged per unit of service was reviewed by rate panels composed of customers. This process provided the opportunity for line agencies to ensure that investments and overhead expenses, for example, made sense from the customer viewpoint.

These methods were not used to hold purchasing and staffing accountable to their line agency customers. Both continued to be financed through general fund appropriations. The principal methods employed in these cases included reorienting the organizational culture, redesigning routines, and empowering front-line employees to solve customer problems.

Accountability of Staff in Line Agencies.   Much administrative work was carried out by operations within the line agencies.

In many instances, line agency executives were more familiar with substantive issues than with administration. They did not know how to hold their staff accountable for good performance. In attempting to solve this problem, the deputy commissioner of employee relations worked to provide executives with the tools they needed to manage their staff. Similarly, the director of the IPO helped line executives oversee the information-resource managers in their organizations.

Measures to Redirect Accountability

Admin, Employee Relations, and Finance executives eventually recognized that the system of staff/line/overseer relations was poorly set up given the immense complexity of late-twentieth-century state government. The staff agencies, in particular, had been expected to absorb too much responsibility for good administrative decision making. In case after case, it appeared that state government could come closer to satisfying public needs only if line agencies were accountable for the economic and other consequences of their administrative decisions. This stance had repercussions for the organizational strategies of staff agencies' service and control activities. In principle, these repercussions should have occurred simultaneously because the strategy of holding service activities accountable to line agencies as customers was premised on the notion that line agencies would be held accountable for making good management decisions by overseers assisted by staff agency control activities. As it happened, the process was sequential rather than simultaneous, with the new service strategies taking hold several years before the new control strategies did.[11]

Service Activities.   Measures designed to hold service activities more accountable to line agencies also made line agencies more accountable for their administrative decisions. First, placing nearly all internal services on revolving funds created an incentive to economize. The consequences of consuming more space in buildings operated by Admin, for example, included having fewer budget dollars to spend on other inputs. Second, the strategy of financing service activities with revolving funds and giving them the mandate of serving their customers helped translate such incentives into attractive choices. For example, one Admin activity developed and marketed a comparatively inexpensive off-site records storage and retrieval service that, if utilized by line agency customers, enabled them to economize on the use of costly prime office space. Third, line agencies continually received the message that Admin trusted their judgments about how to accomplish their missions within the funding constraints imposed on them by the budget and appropriations process. This message was designed to increase line agency managers' psychological accountability for making good resource-utilization decisions.

Control Activities. The IPO recognized that information management decisions were powerful levers for transforming pressures for better line agency performance into improved operating routines. To realize this potential, IPO decided to hold line agency executives rather than specialists accountable for information management. As an inducement to learn how to manage information as a resource, line agency executives were advised that IPO's evaluations of their budget requests for information systems would take into account their demonstrated ability to manage information strategically. IPO then coached line executives on how to ensure that program managers were making the most of the expertise of information management specialists. In addition to individualized coaching, IPO produced guidelines for leading an organization through the process of strategic information planning. IPO was reticent to second-guess decisions produced by what it considered good strategic information planning processes; overseers, in turn, tended to support IPO's strategy and its evaluations of information-related budget requests.

Line agencies were also held accountable by IPO for devising and implementing strategic information management plans that were consistent with statewide information policies. To enhance accountability, IPO aimed to promote psychological ownership of the constraints within which line agency executives planned. IPO's method was to empower a collective body of line agency executives to stipulate statewide principles of information management and to pass judgment in hard cases on whether individual line agency plans violated these norms.

The idea of holding line agencies accountable for making good administrative decisions eventually spread to the budget process. The fact that agencies faced no incentive to economize on capital spending was recognized as a major problem by the governor and legislative leaders, who repeatedly endured the unenviable political task of paring down line agencies' wish lists. An incremental solution to this problem was to require the state agencies that requested the largest authorizations to cover a significant portion of the interest costs of the state bonds floated to finance their capital projects.

During the same period, the finance commissioner convinced the governor that the budget process did not press agencies to assume responsibility for improving their productivity or overall performance. The process instead focused line agency efforts on defending anticipated or desired operating costs. The finance commissioner advised the chief executive to instruct agency heads to show how they could achieve better results without increasing spending, rather than detail how they could spend more. The result was an innovative set of budget instructions issued just over two months before the Democratic governor was defeated in the 1990 election. The incoming Republican governor then adopted his predecessor's budget instructions.

Measures to Expand Accountability:
From Guardianship to Problem Solving

Staff agency executives sought to rework the missions, mandates, and routines of central personnel and purchasing. The new mission of personnel was to enable line agencies to operate successfully while complying with evolving norms designed to implement such policies as selection on the basis of merit, collective bargaining, and affirmative action. The new mandate of the reorganized staffing operation was to serve line managers as customers by enabling them to participate effectively in identifying and solving personnel-related problems. The new mission and mandate translated into new routines. For example, to em-

Table Two
Differences in Organizational Culture

New Culture	Old Culture
Focus on the way things should and could be	Focus on the way things have been
Focus on helping customers and/or compliers solve their problems	Focus on operating the system and preparing to say no
Caring about customers and public policy	Caring about current rules and technical expertise
Focus on producing value net of cost	Focus on the volume and cost of inputs
Caring about people and working relationships	Caring about roles and responsibilities

power line managers in their relations with line agency personnel specialists, the Department of Employee Relations published in serial fashion a guide to the personnel system for line managers. Members of newly created agency services teams within the Staffing Division, furthermore, routinely tested their arguments for particular resolutions of hard cases in group review sessions with one another and senior managers.

The old mission of purchasing was to save taxpayers' money and to be fair to vendors. After a long series of deliberations, the mission became "to purchase products and services that best meet the necessary quality requirements for the needs of our customers, at the best possible price, from responsible vendors, within the required time frame, in accordance with all applicable statutes and in an ethical and professional manner."[12] Among the key operative concepts in the new mission statement were customers' quality and time-frame requirements. Complementing the new mission was a revised mandate for central purchasing. A core idea of the new mandate was to optimize and balance—within the expanding limits of statutory authority and legal precedent—such factors as product quality, vendor reliability, initial purchase price, maintenance costs, and delivery schedules; the previous mandate had been to minimize the initial purchase price and avoid risks. Another core idea of the new mandate was to specialize in operations requiring the statewide scope and concentrated expertise of central purchasing. To carry out the new mission and mandate, routines were drastically changed. Line agencies made small dollar purchases on their own using local purchasing authority; commodity buyers made routine visits to their customer agencies; life-cycle costing was regularly employed; and indefinite-quantity contracts were utilized to purchase nontraditional commodities, like microcomputers.

Changing the Culture

Perhaps every change in constraints, incentives, and routines made some mark on the organizational cultures of the staff agencies and their components. Not only did such changes alter everyday work activities, they also influenced patterns of thought. Every change was accompanied by some form of argumentation, and most arguments made innovative use of familiar concepts such as customer service, marketing, leadership, and competition. The usual way some executives, managers, operators, and overseers reasoned about staff/line/overseers relations was notably different by the late 1980s.[13] Table 2 highlights a few differences between the organizational culture that was gradually being created and the one slowly being left behind.

CHAPTER SEVEN

Managing Customer-Focused Staff Agencies

Once audiences find persuasive Possibilist's argument that recurring troubles along the staff/line frontier are problems, they may challenge him to answer the question "What is to be done?" In this event, Possibilist should probe whether his audiences are more likely to engage in effective problem solving if he tells them what to do or if he instead suggests that they first reconsider their beliefs about how staff agencies can contribute to the implementation of public policies. If Possibilist decides that the second leadership strategy is more promising, he might choose to help his audiences deliberate about the meaning and usefulness of post-bureaucratic principles of staff agency management.[1]

PRINCIPLES FOR MANAGING STAFF AGENCIES

1: Spread Responsibility for Economizing and Compliance

Economizing. Think of all the inputs that are utilized to get the work of government done. Employees' work effort, clean and maintained office space, work stations, training, travel, printed documents, office supplies, filing cabinets, management consulting, computer programming, data processing, database management, voice and data telecommunications, and electronic mail are some of them. As the number of tools needed to manage complex organizations increases, the list of inputs gets longer.

Who should be responsible for economizing on the use of inputs like these? One option is to assign responsibility to a central planner. Not in the United States, you say? Listen to how in the early 1940s Leslie Gravlin, Minnesota's founding commissioner of administration, described how he was to make state government run economically and efficiently:

> The commissioner of administration has charge of all the budget activities, the operation of the quarterly allotment system, the purchasing of supplies and equipment and services, supervision of all power plants, and the revision of all departmental public reports. He also supervises the design, construction, and repair of all public buildings, and improvements. He signs all contracts and prepares rules and regulations concerning travel expenses. He is also responsible for the maintenance of all capitol buildings and grounds; is custodian of all state equipment and must maintain a perpetual inventory of all state property; and operates a central mimeograph, store, and mailing service. . . . In practical effect the commissioner of administration is the business manager of the state.[2]

This job description sounds quaint not only because it is no longer customary—except in legal matters—to attribute a whole agency's activities to its head but also because Gravlin's arguments for giving such wide-ranging and detailed control to a state business manager—when made explicit—would not even receive a sympathetic hearing in Moscow.[3] The leaders of the former Soviet Union have decided that their political-economic system should be transformed to accommodate the reality that productive systems tend to create more value net of cost when every work unit, rather than a central planner, bears responsibility for economizing.[4] It is not too much to suggest that Americans accept the same reality and follow the same principle. The responsibility for economizing should not be given to staff agencies alone but rather to all work units in government including line agencies.[5]

Compliance. As an empirical fact, the compliance process in complex organizations like government entails people at all levels making frequent and consequential choices about how to respond to multiple controls. For example, line managers need to decide what the chief executive's budget instructions, standard accounting rules, and principles of information policy mean in their particular contexts. Whom should overseers hold accountable for making good choices among alternative ways of bringing government's heterogeneous operations into compliance with administrative policies? One possibility is to hold contemporary state business managers—staff agencies such as departments of finance and administration—accountable. But staff agencies are in a poor position to make judgments about how line agencies should best comply with administrative policies for the same reasons that they are in a poor position to make judgments about how much of any single input line agencies should consume in a given year. Like good resource consumption decisions, good compliance decisions require refined and informed judgments about the consequences of alternative courses of action in particular circumstances.[6] Unless staff agencies were to become as large and complex as all the line agencies—a situation that is considered intolerable—staff agencies will lack a comparative advantage in making these judgments.[7] A more attractive possibility—once overseers and others stop denying the reality that innumerable choices are made in the compliance process—is therefore to assign the responsibility for compliance along with the responsibility for economizing to all work units in government including those operating under the leadership and authority of line agency executives.

Implication for Staff Agency Mandates

In effect, bureaucratic reformers gave staff agencies the following mission and mandate:[8] Solve the highly interrelated problems of inefficiency, incompetence, and corruption in government. Attack these problems by exercising your authority over all aspects of administration. Specifically, administer the budgeting, accounting, procurement, and personnel systems in an impersonal and responsible fashion, and, to the degree possible, monopolize the production of all inputs other than those purchased from vendors. Justify your role and specific actions with arguments referring to fact, law, expertise, policy, and the public interest.

This generic mission and mandate was inspired not only by industrial age beliefs in the efficiency of centralization but also by the progressive era belief that to solve a problem or a set of highly interrelated problems it is necessary to assign a single authority the responsibility for doing so. From a contemporary vantage point, mandates premised on these beliefs are suspect.[9] Making economically efficient use of scarce resources and bringing operations into compliance with norms are functions that cannot be effectively performed by staff agencies alone. Nor can these functions be performed—as is often supposed—by subjecting line agencies to unilateral control by staff agencies. For these critical functions to be performed tolerably well, staff and line agencies need to engage in mutual adjustment, not unilateral adjustment. The basic mission and mandate for staff agencies therefore should be: Participate usefully in the various disjointed, interactive decision-making and production processes through which outcomes of government operations—such as customer satisfaction with public services, cost per unit of service, and satisfaction with the governance process—are determined. The intended consequences of your actions should be improvements in these outcomes. Justify your actions with arguments about how best to implement the whole array of substantive and administrative policies that are supposed to guide government operations.

How should central staff operations carry out this mission and mandate? The following principles can be used to structure deliberation about this pressing question.

2: Conceptualize Work as Providing Services

In carrying out the bureaucratic reformers' mandate, staff agency executives, managers, and operators have conventionally defined their work as exercising authority, following rules, executing budgets, and competently performing tasks. This definition of work has been meaningful to those engaged in combating such legacies of the nineteenth-century United States as administrative disorganization, arbitrariness, and mismanagement.

But defining work according to rules, tasks, authority, and budgets has many negative consequences.[10] First, when attention is focused on the means by which an organizational unit performs its presumed useful functions, for all practical purposes the means become the ends. When an organization's ends and means come to have the same content, moreover, its members tend to lose the will and capacity to identify and evaluate ideas for improving their performance. A second consequence is that focusing on exercising authority and performing tasks leads to unilateral adjustment and work specialization. The importance of working interactively and cooperatively in the problem-solving process is therefore downplayed. A third consequence is that when status and satisfaction are derived from having control over budgetary and human resources, efforts to economize on the use of resources are not intrinsically rewarding. Fourth, in a society that increasingly questions the value of work described in bureaucratic terms, the self-image of staff agency employees as protectors of the public interest is less validated than it once was. The predictable result is declining morale, commitment, and performance.

There are two main reasons to conceptualize the work of staff agencies as providing services. First, outcomes become meaningful. When work is defined as providing a service as opposed to performing tasks, exercising authority, and spending money, employees and overseers can conceptualize the proximate outcomes of staff agencies' work effort. The proximate outcome of such work is the delivery and consumption of an intangible product by users. To a degree, these outcomes can be measured and analyzed, using such concepts as units of service delivered, level of service provided, perceived service quality, and the value of a unit of service net of cost. Once employees understand their work as producing outcomes, they can examine critically the otherwise presumed usefulness of their current ways of doing business.

Second, mutual adjustment becomes valued. Who produces a service? Whenever users fill out a form, wait in line, or engage in a service encounter, they are just as involved in the production process as the ostensible service providers. Once employees are conscious that they and the users are engaged in coproduction, attention can focus on optimizing their interactive working relationship in the production process. As a further consequence, improving working relationships and optimizing mutual adjustment processes can come to be valued by staff agency employees, substituting for the value conventionally placed on delineating roles and responsibilities and on the unilateral adjustment of line agencies to staff agencies.

3: Identify Customers with Care

Some users of services provided by staff agencies are not customers. The most important provider/user relationship that should not be categorized as a customer relationship arises in connection with compliance organizations such as Minnesota's Information Policy Office (IPO). Although the users of IPO's training and consulting services are line agency executives and managers, to identify them as customers would unnecessarily strain the meaning of the term *customer* as well as Admin's working relations with legislative overseers. IPO's purpose in providing services to line agencies is to facilitate compliance with statewide principles of information management and to provide overseers with the information they need in order to hold individual line agencies accountable for managing information efficiently and effectively from a statewide perspective. IPO is engaged in a customer relationship with overseers and a complier relationship with line agencies. In general, because the purpose of having control activities provide services to line agencies is to help these users comply with norms or meet overseers' demands for accountability, overseers should be identified as the customers and line agencies should be identified as compliers.

Unfortunately, the people and organizations we identify as compliers—such as individual taxpayers—are often referred to as customers. The potential consequences of identifying as customers the people obligated to comply with norms include misstating the principal purposes of compliance organizations and dissipating the conceptual force of the term *customer* when used appropriately. The frequency with which well-intentioned public officials violate principle 3 can be explained by the fact that most have yet to make the conceptual distinction between a service-oriented approach to production (for example, applying principles of service management to the compliance process) and defining organizational purpose as serving the needs of customers (for example, the intended beneficiaries of a well-managed compliance process). This conceptual distinction probably remains obscure because of the understandable reticence of those who train public managers in quality management and customer service to raise for deliberation the hoary question of what makes government different from the private sector. Downplaying public/private differences can be reasonably defended for some defined purposes. However, neither trainers nor their audiences should ignore compliance activities' inherently distinctive purposes and working relationships. (More generally, both groups should be more creative than they are in putting concepts from exemplary private sector manufacturing and service enterprises to work in government.)

As a rule, staff operations should decide whether their customers are overseers or line agencies.[11] Some choices are likely to be easy once the customer concept—properly understood—is considered a valuable management tool. Arguments for identifying overseers as the customers of central budgeting, auditing, treasury, policy planning, and information policy are likely to be much stronger than arguments for identifying line agencies as the customers. Arguments for identifying line agencies as the customers of input-producing and input-supplying activities, like telecommunications and data processing, are likely to be similarly persuasive. In numerous cases, however, deciding whether overseers or line agencies are the customers requires careful argumentation and deliberation.

Consider the case of the Management Analysis Division.[12] Conventionally, the division was called in by overseers to study poorly performing agencies and to recommend remedial actions; the unofficial mandate from legislators often included casting blame and knocking heads.[13] The argument for identifying overseers as the customers was therefore powerful. But this argument was opposed by another—namely, that the division could contribute to public policy implementation by providing high-quality consulting services to line agencies on a voluntary basis. This argument, which drew on evidence that many line agencies preferred to work with the Management Analysis Division rather than with consulting firms, suggested that line agencies should be identified as customers. In this case, the conflict between the arguments could be resolved by using the customer concept at the level of the major unit of service: a study. In this way, an exception to the rule that a staff agency should identify either overseers or line agencies as customers—but not both—was safely made. The division's customers were identified as either overseers or line agencies, depending on the source of the request.

Purchasing and staffing are intermediate cases along the continuum of control and service activities, which runs, say, from auditing to typewriter repair. Both have enormous influence over two key categories of productive inputs—materials and labor—but neither produces them. The main argument for identifying overseers as the customers of purchasing and staffing is that these agencies are expected to play an important role in the process by which line agencies comply with statewide norms in these two areas. Historically, their role was preeminent. The main argument for identifying line agencies as customers is that the principal purpose of government operations should be to serve the individual and collective customers of line agencies and that line agencies should be empowered to solve *their* purchasing and staffing problems in accordance with the norms. The key empirical question is whether identifying line agencies as customers sets up a working relationship between these staff operations and line agencies that produces satisfactory solutions to agencies' purchasing and staffing problems. Although the scientific evidence is weak, the Minnesota experience suggests that such solutions are more likely to be produced when line agencies rather than overseers are identified as the customers of purchasing and staffing.[14]

4: Be Accountable to Customers

Once a staff agency's customers are carefully identified, agency executives, managers, and operators along with overseers and customers should deliberate about what they think the provider/customer relationship ought to entail. Such deliberations are likely to be more fruitful if the participants share a common definition of a customer relationship than if they do not.[15] A customer relationship is a mutually adjustive working relationship in which a provider's main purpose is to meet users' needs.[16] In a typical customer relationship, users believe that providers should be accountable to them (and perhaps to other parties) for fulfilling this purpose, and providers recognize that they ought to be so accountable. Built into the definition of a customer relationship is an additional key presumption: as a rule, customers' informed and reflective judgments about how well a service meets their needs are accurate.[17] Therefore the most relevant information and evidence for judging how well a provider fulfills the main purpose of providing a service are users' evaluations of service quality and value, however expressed.[18]

When a staff operation identifies line agencies or overseers as customers, its employees should be accountable to them as customers. This statement does not mean that staff agencies should live by the proverb that "the customer is always right." It does mean that a staff agency's work should be based on the essential presumptions of a customer relationship stated above, unless persuasive arguments for suspending or adding to these presumptions are made. When a staff agency is truly accountable to its customers, its employees are emotionally invested in these presumptions and the reasons for them. As a result, user evaluations of a staff agency's activities become intrinsically important to them. When customer feedback is positive, a truly accountable provider experiences success; when feedback is negative, he or she feels an intense need to improve users' evaluations.[19]

Collective Customers.   The customers of control activities include legislators, who are customers only insofar as they speak for the collegial body of which they are members. Hence, the challenge of being accountable to a collective customer, in this case the legislature, is to discern whether the feedback offered by an individual member of the collective body constitutes customer feedback. The name of the work required to meet this challenge is political management.[20]

The concept of a collective customer may also be valuable in delineating aspects of the relationship between some staff agency operations and line agencies. For example, services governed as utilities might say that they are accountable to the collegial body of line agency executives that reviews their rates, investments, overhead spending, and financial plans. The argument for identifying this collective body as a customer is to highlight the need for utility managers and staff agency executives to help integrate and balance the often divergent interests of the individual line agency customers. The counterargument is that utility employees, including operating-level staff, may feel justified in downgrading customer feedback provided by individual users of their services.

Other Stakeholders. The message that a particular staff operation is accountable to line agencies or overseers as customers should not imply that its employees are not accountable to anyone else.[21] Indeed, staff agencies are accountable in some specialized sense to every stakeholder. Internal services, for instance, are accountable to legislatures as overseers.[22] To avoid misunderstandings, staff agency executives and managers should devote time to carefully identifying and precisely communicating in what respects their units are accountable to stakeholders other than their customers. (In making this point, we surely do not want to be heard by our readers as saying that less care should be given to defining what it means to be accountable to the customers.)

5: Reorganize to Separate Service from Control

Rival responsibilities for service and control are frequently assigned to the same work group within centralized staff operations and agencies. A problem with this organizational structure is that the value system that orients human action in a control relationship undercuts the value system that orients work in a service relationship. When an organizational culture incorporates rival value systems, employees are likely to be terribly confused about the nature and purpose of their work. Because of these motivational and performance problems, no work group as a rule should be designed to serve both line agencies and overseers as customers.

In applying this rule to information management, for example, Admin executives and their legislative overseers agreed to create the separate IPO, to which the IMB's control responsibilities were reassigned. In applying this rule to central purchasing, it would have been appropriate to create a separate work unit whose mission was to win line agencies' compliance to statewide norms when they exercised their local purchasing authority.

An interesting question is what this rule implies for the organizational structure of whole staff agencies or even the executive branch. Some may argue that an agency head, like the commissioner of administration, should not be responsible for both service and control activities. This argument stretches the rule out of proportion. High-level executives are in a better position to juggle, balance, and integrate rival purposes than are front-line employees. Arguments for separating service and control responsibilities at such high levels should not be made on the basis of this rule but rather on a more contextual interpretation of principle 5.

6: Let the Customer Fund the Providers

The general argument for this principle is that customers are more empowered to hold providers accountable for meeting their needs if their relationship involves some kind of payment for services rendered. The psychological and incentive effects of customer empowerment on both providers and users are often impressive—partly because of cultural understandings of what an exchange relationship entails and partly because of the establishment of resource dependence. The determination to create value for customers by serving them well may be substantially enhanced by having customers pay a provider even when the staff agency activity faces no direct competition. Paying customers can affect a provider's financial resources simply by making increased use of substitute ways to meet the same need or otherwise changing their level of demand. Line agencies can exert this kind of influence with every consumption decision, and overseers can do so directly through budget allocations and appropriations. Therefore, as a rule, control activities should be financed by general funds and service activities should be financed by revenues earned by selling services to line agency customers.

An acceptable exception to this rule was made when Admin executives decided to finance employee assistance services, whose customers were individual state employees, with general funds. The main reason was to encourage users to take advantage of this resource rather than to economize on its utilization.[23]

Ruling Out Exceptions.   Another exception to the rule that staff functions should be funded by their customers was the financing of the centralized training activity with general fund appropriations. The commissioner of employee relations argued that if this activity were funded by revolving funds, internally provided training services would be allocated on the basis of ability to pay rather than need. The resulting disparities in training among agencies, she argued, would be unacceptable.

This argument is unpersuasive. First, the commissioner's presupposition that Employee Relations could make better judgments than line agencies about the amount of training that should be provided from a centralized source within state government is suspect. In principle, line agencies' effective demand for Employee Relations' training services when provided on a fee-for-service basis would be a less imperfect measure of the statewide need for training services than the size of Employee Relations' budget allocation for training. The commissioner's defense of general fund financing of training therefore violates principle 1. Second, on the dubious assumption that overseers valued some kind of distributive equity in the utilization of internally provided training activities, such purposes could have been served without violating the principle that staff functions should be funded by their customers (for example, through a consumption-subsidy scheme).[24]

As an empirical matter, line agencies had made it known that they wanted to utilize more internally provided training services than Employee Relations could deliver using only the general funds allocated to this activity, and the customers were prepared to bear the incremental cost. Given principle 1, this information represented good evidence that investing in training was a cost-effective way for line agencies to carry out their missions and mandates. Moreover, because line agencies could purchase training services externally, this information indicated that Employee Relations possessed a competitive advantage in providing such services. Who benefited from Employee Relations' violation of the rule? Vendors of training services. Not line agencies. Not their customers. Not taxpayers. The argument for making an exception to the rule in the case of an internal training activity is, on inspection, untenable, as has been recognized in other settings.[25]

CHAPTER EIGHT

The Post-Bureaucratic Paradigm in Historical Perspective

The increasingly common use of such terms as *customers, quality, service, value, incentives, innovation, empowerment,* and *flexibility* by people trying to improve government operations indicates that the bureaucratic paradigm is no longer the only major source of ideas and argumentation about public management in the United States.[1] In the search for better performance, some argue for deregulating government.[2] Others make the case for reinventing government, a concept that encourages Americans to take note of marked changes in operating practices taking place in an array of public activities.[3] As a challenge to conventional thinking, many government agencies are investing millions of dollars in training programs structured by a conceptual system that includes customers, quality, value, process control, and employee involvement.[4] To increase flexibility and financial responsibility, some advocate a vast expansion of exchange and payment relationships in place of general fund financing; many also argue for utilizing competition as a device for holding operating units of government accountable to their customers.[5] Among the programmatic concepts that have arisen from studied criticism of the ways in which the bureaucratic reform vision and bureaucratic paradigm have played out in compliance and service organizations are market-based incentives in environmental regulation,[6] promoting voluntary compliance in tax administration, community policing,[7] social service integration,[8] the one-day or one-trial jury system,[9] school-based management,[10] and school choice.[11]

Is there a single core idea—perhaps reducible to a sound bite—behind this ferment in thinking and practice? Some readers will respond that the core idea is service. Or customer focus. Or quality. Or incentives. Or creating value. Or empowerment. But the major concepts of emerging practice are not organized hierarchically, with one master idea at the top. As an indication, the concept of incentives does not subsume the equally useful idea of empowerment, which can be defined as a state of affairs in which individuals and groups feel psychologically responsible for the outcomes of their work. Since emerging argumentation and practice are structured by a paradigm rather than by any single core idea, those who want to make the most of the new conceptual resources should understand how various components of the system are related to one another.[12]

To understand the structure and workings of the newer paradigm well enough to improve public management requires attention and thoughtfulness but not the honed skills of an analytic philosopher or social linguist. The new paradigm, we suggest, can readily be understood by working with the metaphor of an extended family of ideas. The image of an extended family is helpful because it indicates that each idea is somehow related to every other, and it implies that some concentration is required to identify just how. The same metaphor can be pushed much further.[13] Think of the new paradigm, as well as the bureaucratic one, as a generation within an extended family. Although the members of each generation may not enjoy equal standing, their relationships—like those between concepts in either paradigm—are not hierarchical. All the cousins may be compatible in many situations, but their personalities—much like the entailments of the concepts of incentives and empowerment—are likely to differ markedly. Furthermore, just as siblings and cousins seek to prove that they are individually and collectively different from their parents' generation, self-definitions of the new paradigm emphasize divergences from the bureaucratic paradigm. Generational differences in extended families and paradigms also reflect changes in the social, economic, and political environments in which they have lived. To pursue the metaphor one more step, just as the siblings and cousins are influenced more by the preceding generation than they care to see or admit, concepts in the new paradigm are deeply conditioned by their lineal relationships to concepts in the bureaucratic predecessor.

The most appropriate term for the new generation of the extended family of ideas about how to make government operations productive and accountable is the *post-bureaucratic paradigm*. This term implies that the post-bureaucratic paradigm is as multifaceted as its predecessor. An unrelated name would hide the fact that as a historical matter, the younger generation of ideas has evolved from the bureaucratic paradigm.

Table 3 depicts this evolution. This framework guides the effort to identify the post-bureaucratic paradigm and to place it in historical perspective.

SHIFTING PARADIGMS

From the Public Interest to Results Citizens Value

The purpose of the bureaucratic reforms was to enable government to serve the public interest.[14] Government would serve the public interest, reformers argued, if it were honest and efficient. By honest, they meant a government cleansed of particularism, featherbedding, and outright stealing of public funds. By efficient, they meant a government that improved urban infrastructure, provided education, and promoted public health.[15]

In time, the reformers' strategy for serving the public interest came to define the public interest. A central element of that strategy was to recruit, develop, and retain experts in such fields as accounting, engineering, and social work. This strategy was designed not only to achieve results, but also to use expertise as a way to legitimate the actions of unelected officials in an administrative state. As an unintended but unsurprising consequence, these officials came to presume that the public interest was served whenever they applied their various bodies of knowledge and professional standards to questions within their respective domains of authority.

In the age of bureaucratic reform, when the effective demand

Table Three
Comparing the Paradigms

Bureaucratic Paradigm	Post-Bureaucratic Paradigm
Public interest	Results citizens value
Efficiency	Quality and value
Administration	Production
Control	Winning adherence to norms
Specify functions, authority, and structure	Identify mission, services, customers, and outcomes
Justify costs	Deliver value
Enforce responsibility	Build accountability Strengthen working relation-ships
Follow rules and proce-dures	Understand and apply norms Identify and solve problems Continuously improve processes
Operate administrative systems	Separate service from control Build support for norms Expand customer choice Encourage collective action Provide incentives Measure and analyze results Enrich feedback

for combating disease, building civil works, and accounting for public funds had just become significant, the presumption that decisions made in accord with professional standards were congruent with citizens' collective needs and requirements was reasonably defensible. This presumption is no longer reasonable to make. Government often fails to produce desired results from the standpoint of citizens when each professional community within government is certain that its standards define the public interest.

To stimulate more inquiry and better deliberation about how the work of government actually bears on citizens' volitions, the post-bureaucratic paradigm suggests that the specific rhetorical phrase "the public interest" should be confined to books on the history of American politics and administration. A desirable substitute expression is "results citizens value." Compared with its predecessor, the newer expression can be used to motivate more inquiry, clearer argumentation, and more productive deliberation about what results citizens collectively value. This rhetorical construction also conjures up the network of ideas about customer-focused organizations, emphasizes results over inputs and process, and implies that what citizens value cannot be presumed by professional communities in government.[16]

From Efficiency to Quality and Value

Leaders of the scientific management movement in the early twentieth century crafted and popularized a commonsense theory about the causes, nature, and significance of efficiency.[17] This commonsense theory rang true because it explained the industrial progress that characterized the age and because information about the workings of modern factories was widely known. It is a small step to infer that reformers used their knowledge of efficient industrial administration to inform their conception of efficient public administration.[18]

What did reformers know about factory administration? They knew that an efficient factory system succeeded in producing ever-increasing quantities of goods while reducing the cost of production.[19] They also knew recipes for achieving such success. In factories, managers controlled production in great detail through hierarchical supervisory structures. They knew that production and administrative systems were designed and operated by experts, who staffed offices responsible for personnel, accounting, inspection, power and works, engineering, product design, methods, production efficiency, and orders.[20] Bureaucratic reformers also knew that factory managers and experts applied their authority and expertise to industrial administration without partisan political interference.

Thus, industry was not just a source of rhetoric about efficient government; reformers' understanding of the main ingredients of efficient government—reorganization, accounting systems, expertise, and cost control—was rooted in their knowledge about industry.[21] Reformers elaborated some ingredients into specific processes and techniques, such as careful delineation of roles and responsibilities, centralized scrutiny of budget estimates, centralized purchasing, work programming, reporting systems, and methods analysis. However, one key concept—the product—did not make the journey from industry to government.[22]

Since it excluded the concept of product, reformers' influential conception of efficient government was trouble waiting to happen. It encouraged the notorious bureaucratic focus on inputs to flourish and it permitted specialized functions to become worlds unto themselves. More specifically, an increase in efficiency could be claimed in government whenever spending on inputs was reduced, whereas it was much easier to argue in an industrial setting that cost reduction improved efficiency only when it led to a reduction in the cost per unit of output. Industrial managers may not have had an easy time keeping every specialized member of the organization focused on the product, but in this concept—embodied in the goods moving through the production stream and out the door—they at least had a way to think precisely and meaningfully about how integration of differentiated functions could achieve efficiency. For reasons discussed above, the concept of the public interest did not possess the product concept's powers of integration; indeed, the strategy of sharply delineating roles and responsibilities and exalting specialized expertise cut in the other direction.[23] The bottom line—illustrated by the horror stories told in chapter 2—is that the pursuit of efficiency without adequate tendencies toward functional integration was a sham.[24]

Efficiency should be dropped from the lexicon of public administration, as it has from sophisticated practical theories of manufacturing and service enterprise management.[25] Public officials, like their counterparts in nongovernmental organizations, instead should make use of such interrelated concepts as product or service, quality, and value when deliberating about the nature and worth of government activities. The claim is that deliberation in these terms is as useful in the public sector as elsewhere.[26]

The post-bureaucratic paradigm does not try to settle most of the controversies about the general definitions of the concepts of product or service, quality, and value.[27] Legislating the precise definition of such rhetorical and analytical categories is probably futile; in any event, what is important for our purposes here is how well people in practice make use of such concepts in formulating and deliberating over made-to-measure or ad hoc arguments about how the performance of particular organizations should be evaluated and improved.[28]

To make the most of such deliberation efforts, some minimal agreement on terms is necessary. First, the appropriate perspective from which these concepts should be defined is that of the customer. By this rule, the recurring definition of quality as conformance to customer requirements is acceptable. Second, net value should be distinguished from value by taking costs into account. By this rule, the claim that reducing expenditures is desirable needs to be scrutinized in terms of the effect on the cost *and* value of products and services. Third, the nonpecuniary costs borne by customers when coproducing services or complying with norms should be taken into account. By this rule, costs measured by conventional accounting systems should be adjusted in service or compliance contexts.

From Administration to Production

The bureaucratic reformers had a theory of how individual public servants contributed to efficient administration. The theory claimed that the purpose of administration was to solve public problems by implementing laws efficiently. Agencies performed their functions by subdividing responsibilities and assigning them to positions. Public servants, assigned to positions on the basis of merit, performed their responsibilities competently by applying their expertise.[29] This theory promised order and rationality in that new domain of public affairs denominated as administration[30] and nicely combined a political argument about administrative legitimacy with an organizational argument about efficiency. The theory also provided a reason to believe that the work of public servants served the public interest.

To some degree, this theory of work in the administrative branch of government lives on. Ask public servants to describe their work and many will relate facts about their organization's functions and their own responsibilities. In order to communicate what the incumbent of a position does, some agencies compose titles mimicking the chain of command. For example, one senior manager in the Veterans Administration carried the title of Assistant Associate Deputy Chief Medical Director.

This strategy of defining work is failing to satisfy public servants.[31] Younger members of the workforce are less willing to accept close supervision.[32] It is a reasonable inference that specifying organizational positions is an unsatisfactory way to characterize their identity and purpose at work. Another problem with the standard account is that citizens are skeptical about the value of work public servants do—and public servants know it.[33] The bureaucratic paradigm offers late-twentieth-century public servants few tools for explaining to themselves and others why their work counts.

The accumulating evidence that production is a powerful alternative to the idea of administration comes from the total quality management (TQM) movement. TQM provides employees with methods—such as process flow analysis—for identifying and improving production processes.[34] Most government employees whose experience with TQM concepts and methods has been positive are deeply committed to the idea of process analysis and control.[35]

Why is production a powerful idea? One reason is that operating-level employees are typically involved in decision making, another is that formalized methods of reasoning are considered—often for the first time—in deliberations about how the production process should be organized. Both employee involvement and objective analysis mitigate the sense of powerlessness among employees in organizational hierarchies.[36] Furthermore, by using methods of process analysis, employees can develop a shared visual representation of the organization without making any reference to its hierarchical structure or boundaries. What is more important is that through process analysis, individual employees can visualize and describe for others how their work leads to the delivery of a valuable service or product. And coworkers develop an understanding of—and appreciation for—the work each does.[37]

To guard against mistaken analogies between production in government and manufacturing, the post-bureaucratic paradigm suggests that the concept of production be rendered as service delivery.[38] This terminology reminds public servants of the complex and intimate relationship between process and product in service delivery: whereas the production of goods is a separate process from distribution and consumption, many services are produced, delivered, and consumed in the same process, often with customers participating as coproducers.[39]

From Control to Winning Adherence to Norms

Within the bureaucratic reformers' vision of government, control was the lifeblood of efficient administration. Control was considered to be so vital that the intention to strengthen it served as an effective major premise in arguments supporting a wide array of practices that deepened and extended the bureaucratic reforms. These practices included accounting systems, budgetary freezes, reorganizations, reporting requirements, and countless measures to reduce the exercise of discretion by most public servants.

Why did such a cold, mechanical idea become revered by advocates of efficient administration? The answer lies in the fact that control was an important concept in each of the several lines of thought that became interwoven in the bureaucratic reform vision.[40] Control was essential to realize the aim of a unified executive branch. Control needed to be exercised to purge administrative decisions of particularistic influences. Control was the basis for the efficient operation of large-scale organizations.[41] And control assured the public that someone, namely the chief executive, was in charge of administration.

Influenced by ideas of rational-legal bureaucracy and industrial practice, the formulators of the bureaucratic paradigm pursued the aims of order, rationality, impersonal administration, efficiency, and political accountability by instituting centrally controlled systems of rules. The focus on rules, commitment to centralization, and emphasis on enforcement spawned worrisome consequences, which have tended to make bureaucracy a pejorative rather than a descriptive term.

Rules.   The bureaucratic paradigm encouraged control activities to develop ever-denser networks of rules in response to changing circumstances or new problems.[42] When rule systems became extremely complex, staff operations of substantial size—located in both staff and line agencies—were needed to understand, administer, and update them.

Centralization.   The bureaucratic paradigm urged overseers to centralize responsibility and authority for making administrative decisions in the hands of staff agencies. Centralized staff operations generally lacked the capacity to process incoming requests quickly, either because their power in the budget process was slight or because they were committed to the idea of saving taxpayers money. As a further consequence, decisions made centrally did not take into account the complexity and variability of the situations confronted by line agencies.

Enforcement.   Staff agencies focused on enforcement were typically blind to opportunities to correct problems at their source.[43] For instance, agencies were often unable to comply with norms because their employees did not know how to apply them to specific situations. Many such compliance problems could have been solved by providing education and specific advice about how to improve administrative or production processes; however, compliance organizations stressing enforcement tended to underinvest in problem solving. Furthermore, an emphasis on enforcement unnecessarily set up adversarial relationships between control activities and compliers. This kind of relationship discouraged efforts to comply voluntarily with norms.[44]

In our view, after more than a half-century of use, the concept of control is so bound up with the obsolete focus on rules, centralization, and enforcement that continued use of the term is an obstacle to innovative thinking about how to achieve results citizens value. Alternative terms currently in use, such as *delegation, decentralization, streamlining, incentive-based regulation,* and *voluntary compliance* are not wholly adequate as substitutes. Whatever term comes to structure post-bureaucratic thinking, the concept should serve to (1) illuminate means other than rules, such as principles, to frame and communicate the norms to which agencies should adhere; (2) recognize the complexity and ambiguity of the choice situations faced by compliers; and (3) underscore the role that rewards and positive working relationships can play in motivating compliers to make good decisions. The term *winning adherence to norms* is designed to fulfill this function. This concept indicates several lines of post-bureaucratic thinking about organizational strategies of compliance activities—one of which deserves to be highlighted here.

Since achieving adherence to norms requires people to make choices among alternatives under conditions of complexity and ambiguity, compliance strategies should empower compliers to apply norms to their particular circumstances. Compliers become empowered, by definition, when they feel personally responsible for adhering to the norms and are psychologically invested in the task of finding the best way to comply. Taking personal responsibility for results is as crucial to making good compliance decisions as to delivering quality goods and services.

As analysts have discovered in studying the sources of productivity and quality in organizations, taking personal responsibility is substantially influenced by the work setting. In particular, researchers argue that employees are most likely to take personal responsibility at work when they receive clear direction about purposes and desired outcomes, education, coaching, material resources, feedback, and recognition.[45] These findings suggest that taking personal responsibility for adhering to norms is likely to be enhanced when compliers understand the purpose of the norms, obtain education and coaching about how to apply the norms to the situations they face, receive timely and useful information about the extent to which compliance is being achieved, and are recognized for their accomplishments.

The willingness to take personal responsibility for complying with norms also depends on several other factors, including the extent to which the community of compliers supports the norms; whether other members of the community are assuming their obligations; whether compliance organizations seek to streamline the compliance process; and whether the capacity to enforce the norms upon those who fail to live by them is apparent.[46] The post-bureaucratic paradigm recognizes that some people may not respond adequately to efforts to win their compliance. For this reason, enforcement remains an indispensable function even when the focus is on winning adherence to norms.[47] These factors are increasingly recognized by tax administrations and other agencies that rely for their success principally on the willingness and ability of people and organizations to bring themselves into compliance with norms.[48]

Beyond Functions, Authority, and Structure

The bureaucratic paradigm defined organizations in terms of their assigned functions, delegated authority, and formal structure. Functions were abstract categories of work to be performed within the larger organizational machinery of government. Authority was the right to make decisions and demand obedience from subordinates on matters related to the grant of authority. Formal structure referred to the system of superior-subordinate relationships, which matched delegated authority with subdivided functions ultimately to the level of individual positions.

The critiques of this outlook are legendary. The focus on functions made organizations seem like technical instruments rather than institutions whose members are committed to achieving purposes.[49] The focus on authority concealed the power of other methods of social calculation and control, including persuasion and exchange.[50] The focus on formal structure put the cart of organizational means before the horse of organizational purpose and strategy.[51]

From a post-bureaucratic perspective, the central challenge of organizations is to channel human energies into thinking about and doing socially useful work. Public servants need better categories than functions, authority, and structure to meet this challenge. The concepts of mission, services, customers, and outcomes are valuable because they help public servants articulate their purposes and deliberate about how to adapt work to achieve them.[52] Missions are claims about the distinctive contribution an organization makes to the public good.[53] Services are the organization's products.[54] Customers are individuals or collective bodies—whether internal or external to the organization—to whom employees are accountable as parties to customer relationships.[55] Outcomes are precisely defined states of affairs that the organization intends to bring about through its activities.[56]

From Enforcing Responsibility to Building Accountability

According to the bureaucratic paradigm, a key role of administrators was to use their authority to enforce responsibility upon their subordinates.[57] As a mandate for managing people in organizations, this formalistic, hierarchical, and remedial conception of accountability left much to be desired. Formalism neglected the roles that emotions, commitments, and peer group norms play in shaping intrinsic motivation and behavior. The focus on hierarchy steered attention away from managing the network of interdependencies between subordinates and employees reporting to different superiors. And the notion of enforcing responsibility gave accountability a retrospective and defect-finding cast.

From a post-bureaucratic perspective, the most effective way to hold employees accountable is to make them feel accountable.[58] This route to accountability is attractive, in part, because employees want to be accountable. They want to be accountable because it is the only way for them, as for us all, to be important. According to a noted contemporary philosopher:

Importance has two aspects. The first involves having external impact or effect, being the causal source of external effects, a place from which effects flow so that other people or things are affected by your actions. The second aspect of importance involves having to be taken account of, counting. If the first aspect of importance involves being a causal source from which effects flow, the second involves being a place toward which responses flow, responses to your actions, traits, or presence. In some way they pay attention to you and take you into account. Simply being paid attention to is something we want.[59]

Psychologists specializing in the study of work argue that employees feel accountable when they believe intended work outcomes are consequential for other people, receive information about outcomes, and can attribute outcomes to their own efforts, initiatives, and decisions.[60] Informed by this kind of argument, the post-bureaucratic paradigm values efforts by public managers and their overseers to bring about states of affairs in which public servants feel accountable for achieving desired results.

As a way to overcome the hierarchical and remedial thrust of accountability in the bureaucratic paradigm, attention should focus on the spectrum of working relationships, including the customer relationship, through which public servants create results citizens value. (Table 4 shows a classification scheme of working relationships.) From a post-bureaucratic perspective, accountability between the parties engaged in such working relationships should be a two-way street. For example, providers should be accountable to customers for meeting their needs for quality and value, while customers should be accountable to providers for clarifying their own needs and for giving feedback. More generally, in thinking and deliberating about accountability to customers and others, public managers should call to mind all the ingredients of well-functioning relationships: a consistent understanding of the purpose and character of the relationship; a detailed understanding of what behaviors and results the parties believe would be satisfactory; the provision of feedback about how well the parties are performing and how they could make improvements; responsiveness to feedback; and reconsi-

Table Four
Working Relationships

CUSTOMER RELATIONSHIPS
Individual or organizational customers
  • within the organization
  • within government
  • outside government

Collective customers
  • within the organization
  • within government
  • outside government

PRODUCTION RELATIONSHIPS
Coproduction relationships with customers

Complier relationships
  • within government
  • between government and the public

Relationships with providers
  • within government
  • vendors

Team relationships
  • between individuals
  • between task groups
  • between functions

Partner relationships
  • within government
  • between public and private sectors

OVERSIGHT RELATIONSHIPS
Relationships with executive branch leadership and their staffs
Relationships with legislative bodies, legislators, and staff
Relationships with courts

MEMBERSHIP RELATIONSHIPS
Employment relationships
  • between employees and their organizational leaders
  • between employees and their immediate superiors
  • between employees and the employer

Communitywide relationships
  • among agencies
  • among public servants

Peer group relationships
  • among executives
  • among members of a professional specialty

deration of the working relationship in light of changing circumstances and cumulative experience.

From Justifying Costs to Delivering Value

Budgeting, according to the bureaucratic paradigm, was a process of arriving at annual spending plans. As part of the budgeting process, administrators were charged with the task of developing estimates of their organization's needs.[61] In practice, administrators assumed the task of developing convincing arguments that their needs in the upcoming budget year were greater than in the current one. The major categories of acceptable evidence for arguments about needs included current spending, expected increases in the cost of doing business, and the estimated cost of expanding the organization's level of activity. Upon receiving estimates of needs, central budget offices built arguments for the claim that the agency's costs were less than the estimated ones as part of an effort to judge whose claims for resources were most justified.[62]

The bureaucratic paradigm of budgeting was congruent with its many other aspects. For example, the rhetoric of need was consistent with reformers' idea that government was supposed to satisfy citizens' wants without wasting taxpayers' dollars. It was also consistent with the belief that the responsibility for making government efficient should be vested primarily in the hands of overseers and their budget staffs. And the task of making government efficient meant scrutinizing costs.

Some advocates of the post-bureaucratic paradigm raise provocative questions about this conception.[63] They speculate that citizens are much more interested in the quality and value of public services than they are in costs; hence, it is mistaken for overseers to scrutinize costs during budget deliberations. They envision a world in which budget deliberations enable overseers to make informed purchases of services from agencies on behalf of the public. They further contend that improving the quality and value of public services can be achieved on a routine basis if agencies are expected to track changes in customer requirements and to improve productivity through better management of production processes; they point out that budget processes under the bureaucratic paradigm instead motivate public managers to spend their limited time justifying costs. From a post-bureaucratic perspective, it is urgent to work out the implications of these claims and speculations in theory and practice.

Beyond Rules and Procedures

The premise of countless arguments made from the bureaucratic paradigm is that the proposed course of action (or inaction) is consistent with existing rules and procedures. The prior discussions of the concepts of efficiency, administration, and control explain why such arguments were generally persuasive.

From a post-bureaucratic angle, arguments premised on existing rules and procedures should be greeted with a reasonable degree of skepticism. Arguments premised on rules should be challenged and the issue reframed in terms of achieving the best possible outcome, taking into account the intention behind the rules, the complexity and ambiguity of the situation, and the ability to secure support from those who would enforce the norms. In this way, problem solving rather than following bureaucratic routines can become the dominant metaphor for work. Similarly, arguments premised on current procedures should be countered by instigating deliberation about how process improvements could enhance service quality and value.

Beyond Operating Administrative Systems

Centralized staff agencies were institutional embodiments of the bureaucratic reform vision. By operating administrative systems, these organizations put into practice the concepts of efficiency, administration, and control. Their cultures and routines spawned many of the constraints and incentives facing line agencies, which from a post-bureaucratic vantage point now detract from government's ability to deliver results citizens value.

If the time has come to break through bureaucracy, centralized staff operations must be part of the process. In serving this purpose, centralized staff operations need to transform their organizational strategies. Just like line agencies, they can benefit from using the concepts of mission, services, customers, quality, value, production, winning adherence to norms, building accountability, and strengthening working relationships. More specifically, central staff operations should separate service from control, build support for norms, expand customer choice, encourage collective action, provide incentives, measure and analyze results, and enrich feedback in the context of all working relationships. What this extended family of concepts means in practice should constantly evolve through deliberation and incremental innovation. A starting point for both processes is the information and argumentation contained in this book.

ROLE OF PUBLIC MANAGERS

The bureaucratic paradigm informed public administrators that their responsibilities included planning, organizing, directing, and coordinating. Planning meant looking beyond the day-to-day operations of each function in order to determine how the work of the organization as a whole should evolve. Organizing meant dividing work responsibilities and delegating to each position requisite authority over people and subject matter. Directing meant informing subordinates of their respective roles in implementing plans and ensuring that they carried out their roles in accordance with standards. Coordinating meant harmonizing efforts and relations among subordinates.[64] The deficiencies of this role conception have been amply and ably catalogued by management writers for more than forty years.

The post-bureaucratic paradigm values argumentation and deliberation about how the roles of public managers should be framed. Informed public managers today understand and appreciate such varied role concepts as exercising leadership, creating an uplifting mission and organizational culture, strategic planning, managing without direct authority, pathfinding, problem setting, identifying customers, groping along, reflecting-in-action, coaching, structuring incentives, championing products, instilling a commitment to quality, creating a climate for innovation, building teams, redesigning work, investing in people, negotiating mandates, and managing by walking around.[65] As a contribution to current deliberation, we suggest that breaking through bureaucracy is a useful supplement to this stock of ideas. This concept alerts public managers to the need to take seriously the profound influence of the bureaucratic paradigm on standard practices, modes of argumentation, and the way public servants derive meaning from their work.

Historically aware public managers, committed to breaking through bureaucracy, will help coworkers understand that the bureaucratic paradigm mistakenly tended to define organizational purpose as doing assigned work. They will argue that a crucial challenge facing all organizations is to imbue work effort with purpose while thwarting the tendency to presume that current practices deliver as much value as possible. They will build capacity within and around organizations to deliberate about the relationship between results citizens value and the work done.

Public managers guided by the idea of breaking through bureaucracy should employ not only a combination of historical knowledge and post-bureaucratic ideas as tools to diagnose unsatisfactory situations and to spot inadequacies in arguments rooted in the bureaucratic paradigm, but should also deal creatively with the fact that many public servants are emotionally invested in the bureaucratic paradigm. Public servants, in our experience, are generally willing to move on to a newer way of thinking and practicing public management if they are convinced that the efforts they expended in past years will not become depreciated by the move. An effective way to overcome resistance to change stemming from this source is to make an informed argument that the presuppositions of the bureaucratic paradigm as played out in the organization's particular field of action were reasonable during most of the twentieth century, but that times have changed.[66]

Appendix One:
Department of Administration
Strategy (1986)

A STRATEGY FOR FUNDING AND MANAGING DOA ACTIVITIES

DEPARTMENT OF ADMINISTRATION

The Department of Administration (DOA) provides services to the Governor, Legislature, state agencies and local units of government that are funded either through a general fund appropriation or a revolving fund.

The department's purpose in undertaking its base level review is to formulate a strategy for funding and managing the finances of DOA activities. In particular, the review seeks to strengthen *accountability* for DOA activities both to the Legislature and to client agencies.

This approach to a base level review differs substantially from those of other departments. By mutual agreement, the departments of Administration and Finance determined that addressing the issues of funding base and accountability to the Legislature for revolving funds are of paramount importance.

Recommendations at the conclusion of this report apply this strategy to the F.Y. 1988–89 DOA biennial budget.

EXECUTIVE SUMMARY

PURPOSE

The Department of Administration (DOA) undertook its base level review in order to determine the best funding base and management strategy for each of the services provided by the department.

BACKGROUND

Over the years, the Legislature has used both revolving and general funds to finance Department of Administration activities. At various times, shifts in the funding sources have occurred.

In addition, the Legislature has expressed concern about its role in *overseeing revolving funds*. In the past, the biennial budget process has not provided the Legislature with the tools it needs in this regard.

This document outlines a strategy for choosing the most appropriate funding source, general fund or revolving funds. Further, it suggests an important distinc-

137

tion between *two types of revolving funds*—those which give agencies a *free choice* in the source of the service, and those for which use of the DOA-provided service is *mandated*. These three types of funds must be managed *differently*.

GOALS

The service management strategy seeks to meet the following goals:

o To use the most *efficient* approach to providing a particular service.

o To provide for *greater accountability* and control of these activities.

o To provide *incentives for the appropriate level of use* of DOA services by consumers.

o To provide activity managers with *flexibility* to best meet client needs.

Details on the Background and Goals can be found in Part 1.

SERVICE MANAGEMENT MATRIX

General funds and two types of revolving funds create three distinct approaches to funding and managing DOA services.

TYPE I: STATEWIDE LEADERSHIP AND CONTROL services should be funded via a *general appropriation* from the Legislature because they serve a statewide, rather than agency perspective. This approach is characterized by the following features:

o The taxpayers, Legislature, and the Governor are the primary customers.

o Affected agencies have no choice in deciding the source and amount of service rendered.

o The Legislature, via an appropriation, determines the amount of funding for the service.

o Unspent funds are reverted to the general fund.

o Productivity investment decisions are determined by the Governor and the Legislature.

o The Governor and Legislature oversee and control through the budget process.

TYPE II: UTILITY services are funded through an *internal service revolving fund*. These are DOA monopolies because economies of scale make a centrally managed service most efficient. This approach is characterized by the following features:

o State agencies and local governments are the customers.

o Customers have a choice over the amount of service utilized, but not the source.

○ The rates for the service are determined through a cost allocation based on the benefit derived.

○ Rates are designed to break even; any excess revenue can be returned to the customers in the form of lower rates or used for productivity investments.

○ A customer service panel should be established to advise on productivity investments and rates.

○ Ultimate responsibility for developing rates rests with the departments of Administration and Finance with legislative review.

○ The Legislature controls spending through its appropriations to customers of the service.

TYPE III: COMPETITIVE MARKETPLACE services should be funded through *enterprise revolving funds*. DOA provides these services because it has some sort of competitive advantage over other providers. This approach is characterized by the following features:

○ The customers have free choice in both the source of the service and how much they consume.

○ Fees charged for the service are determined by the marketplace.

○ The marketplace controls spending. When revenues are reduced, spending must be reduced accordingly.

○ Business plans are developed and approved by the department and reviewed by the Legislature.

○ Profits are returned to the general fund or used to make new productivity investments.

○ Activities that are not profitable will face the same fate as any marketplace enterprise—it goes out of business.

Details on the Service Management Matrix can be found in Part 2.

RECOMMENDATIONS

Based upon the above strategy, the department makes the following recommendations:

○ Some activities should be moved from revolving funds to the general fund.

○ Some activities should be moved from the general fund to revolving funds.

○ Some services, not currently provided by the department however, because of their critical nature, should be given consideration for general fund appropriations.

○ A number of management changes, including better tools for accounting to the Legislature, should be implemented.

Details on the Recommendations can be found in Part 3.

PART I

INTRODUCTION

In order to develop a strategy for funding and managing DOA activities, it is essential to distinguish between the general fund and revolving funds in state government. The general fund is well understood. It is financed by general state-wide taxes, primarily income and sales taxes, and it is used to fund most of the general operations of state government. The Legislature appropriates the general fund's revenues to state agencies for specific purposes.

Revolving funds are less well understood because the concept behind them is entirely different. Revolving funds do not receive general tax revenues, and they are not appropriated by the Legislature.

Revolving funds are established when there are benefits to government by providing a statewide service from a centralized source. The use of the centralized service by another state agency may be mandated or optional. In either case, the customer agency is *charged* for the use of the centralized service.

Charges are based on pre-established *rates*. The providing agency must charge a rate that, given an assumed volume of business, will generate sufficient revenue to fund the costs of providing the service. If the revenue exceeds operating costs, those *earnings may be retained* for future investment and for *reducing rates* in the future. If revenues fall short of needs, activity managers must *respond by reducing costs,* increasing business, raising rates, or carrying forward an operating loss. Operating losses that are carried forward must be recovered. The financial accounting for the activity is based on Generally Accepted Accounting Principles (GAAP) and uses techniques such as accrual accounting and depreciation of assets in preparing profit and loss statements and in determining fund equity.

All in all, revolving funds operate like a business. Their success depends on customer demand and good management techniques. Revolving fund activities should be reviewed differently than general fund activities. *Reviewing rates and earnings* is particularly important for evaluating revolving funds. Reviewing expenditure levels is not as important as in general fund activities because the size of the activity depends on customer demand. As a result, revolving fund expenditures are not dependent upon appropriations; they are dependent upon customer demand and revenues.

There are two kinds of revolving funds. *Internal service funds* sell services to other state agencies. *Enterprise funds* have most of their customers outside of state government. Enterprise funds set their own prices and rates while internal service funds submit their rates to the Commissioner of Finance for approval. Other than these two differences, internal service funds and enterprise funds operate similarly and like businesses. Together they are coloquially referred to as revolving funds.

Because of these differences between the general fund and revolving funds, it is important to identify the advantages and disadvantages of each. Each fund has its benefits. Some activities are more appropriately funded out of the general fund and other activities are more appropriately provided out of revolving funds. It is the purpose of this paper to provide a policy framework for the use of the general fund and revolving funds in the Department of Administration. Recommendations based on the new policy framework are also identified.

REVOLVING FUND

The primary advantage of a revolving fund is that it provides optimal allocation of scarce public resources. Other *advantages* are:

○ Marketplace factors such as consumer need, and the price and quality of the service provide a direct relationship between the decision to use or not use a specific service.

○ The use or nonuse of a service provides managers and policy makers with valuable information as to the value of the service which can be used to determine if the service should continue to be provided by DOA.

○ Revolving funds are *responsive to changes* in customer needs. Government is justifiably criticized for being slow to respond to the changing needs of society. A revolving fund operating on marketplace principles must be responsive to the changing needs of the consumers of their services or cease to operate.

○ Consumers of the revolving-funded services will be *more cost-conscious* because savings can be used to improve the service and to lower rates.

○ Providers of the services have *incentives to be more efficient* when their revenues depend on voluntary consumer transactions rather than appropriations.

○ Activity managers are more *accountable to the cost,* quality, supply and timeliness needs of their customers.

○ Provides for *investment planning* that will enable the provider of the service to make capital investments based on the *return* of the investment to the activity manager's account.

○ Causes the activity manager to consider the future service needs of the customer.

Aggressive use of revolving fund mechanisms may cause policy makers to require activities that are not appropriately financed through a revolving fund mechanism to be financed with revolving funds. This phenomenon may cause activities that serve the broad public purpose to be underfunded or not funded at all. Other *disadvantages* are:

○ The Legislature spends less time reviewing revolving funds because there are *no appropriations* to be made. This leads to a feeling that there is less legislative control over revolving fund activities. However, there is sufficient information for legislators to review agency consumption and revolving fund performance.

○ The cost of purchasing some services may cause agencies to *not utilize* a service even though it may be essential to its operations. For example, there is the fear that if the AG's Office were to charge for its services, in order to save money, agencies might attempt to act without legal advice.

○ Cash flow needs can be difficult to manage since revolving funds cannot use the state's general cash resources.

GENERAL FUNDS

The establishment and use of a revolving fund is not appropriate for all activities. The department provides a wide array of services to other state departments and local units of government that are not suited to revolving fund financing. These services have distinct characteristics that make a general fund appropriation the most appropriate funding mechanism. Some *advantages* are:

○ General funds serve a broad public policy purpose. For example, the department has a legal responsibility to assure that goods and services are purchased from third party vendors at the lowest possible cost. The enormous purchasing power of the state would be lost if each state agency were left to purchase goods and services independently.

○ The direct beneficiaries of some services cannot readily be identified. The department provides services that benefit more than one agency and in some cases the general public.

○ The benefits of the activity accrue as much or more to the state as a whole as to the agencies who receive them. These statewide benefits may be due to the need for centralized information or for control and oversight over the use of the service.

○ Recipients of the service are determined by need rather than by the ability of the agency to pay.

o The total level of service is not determined by need or demand; appropriations control the level of service.

o Funding is reviewed by the Legislature through the appropriations process. New investments and levels of service are dependent upon appropriations.

Disadvantages are:

o Unspent appropriations cancel back to the general fund. This acts as an incentive for spending and discourages saving.

o Since the service is free to the customer, the service may be used without critical review of the need for the usage.

o Longer-term thinking is discouraged by the inability to carry forward savings.

REVOLVING FUND OR GENERAL FUND

There are several issues or questions that must be addressed before a decision to finance a department activity via revolving fund or general fund mechanisms is made. The answers to the following questions help determine the decision:

o Are there broad public policy considerations that require consistency among all customers offered the service?

o Are there legal requirements (laws, court orders, data privacy issues) that require state agencies to use the department's services?

o Is the department the only possible provider of the service?

o Is there a single identifiable customer or are there multiple users of the services?

o Is the delivery of the service or product measurable or are the services of such a nature that they cannot be measured in finite segments, thus making the cost of receipt of the services difficult to assess?

o Can the charges for the service be attributed directly to the demand and use of the service?

o Are all of the charges for the service affordable by the customer?

DEPARTMENT METHODOLOGY FOR DETERMINING CATEGORY OF SERVICE ACTIVITY

The department, in its efforts to address the issues raised in this review, undertook the following:

o Conducted group interviews with a selected group of non-Department of Administration managers that are familiar with the services provided by the department to provide data regarding the department's base level review effort.

o Sought feedback and advice from the department's managers regarding the review effort, particularly the review of the three major categories used in the analysis to determine what department activities fit into each category.

o Reviewed the criteria employed in categorizing the department's activities.

o Applied the criteria to each of the department's current activities in order to place each activity in one of the three major categories.

o Interviewed and briefed some state legislators and legislative staff.

o Developed strategies for funding and managing the department's activities.

PART 2

DEPARTMENT OF ADMINISTRATION
SERVICE MANAGEMENT MATRIX

Based on the issues discussed in the introductory portion of this report, our challenge is to determine the best funding base and management strategy for each of the services provided by the Department of Administration (DOA). In order to accomplish this task, the authors of this report in conjunction with the Department of Finance, managers from other state agencies, and managers of DOA activities have developed a service management matrix for presentation to the Legislature.

PERSPECTIVES OF THE KEY ACTORS

In developing this strategy, DOA sought advice and counsel from each of the segments of the state government community which have important stakes in the outcome. Summarized below are the principal concerns voiced by each group. Our overall strategy is designed to accommodate these perspectives to the maximum extent possible.

1. Overseers of DOA activities including Legislators, the Governor, Department of Finance and DOA leadership.
   This perspective desires a strategy which emphasizes:

   o From a statewide perspective, the optimal solution for providing administrative services.

   o Statewide efficiency.

○ Spending control both within the DOA activity and in terms of consumption by customers of the DOA service.

○ Accountability.

2. Consumers of DOA services including legislators, the Governor, state agencies, and units of local government.
This perspective desires a strategy which emphasizes:

○ Clear expectations of what a client can expect from a DOA service—standards of quality and service.

○ The lowest possible cost for the service—value emphasis.

○ Service from DOA which supports management goals.

3. Managers of the DOA activities providing various administrative services.
This perspective desires a strategy which emphasizes:

○ Efficiency—the ability to provide services at the lowest possible cost.

○ Client satisfaction.

○ Flexibility—the ability to take advantage of opportunities which allow DOA activities to better serve their clientele.

GOALS

Based on these perspectives, the service planning strategy is designed to meet the following goals:

1. To use the most efficient approach to providing a particular service.
2. To provide for greater accountability and control of these activities.
3. To provide incentives for the appropriate level of use of DOA services by consumers.
4. To provide activity managers with flexibility to best meet client needs.

The matrix, which is described in more detail in the following pages, delineates a clear strategy for funding and managing three distinctly different types of DOA services.

TYPE I: STATEWIDE LEADERSHIP AND CONTROL SERVICES

First, DOA provides many services which demand a *statewide, broad-based perspective* on various management issues. Purchasing services provided by the Division of Materials Management, space planning provided by the Real Estate Management Division, or statewide information planning provided by the Information Management Bureau (IMB) are examples of services in this category. Often these activities involve legislative mandates for DOA to provide *oversight* and *control* over other state agencies. Such services should be funded by the *general fund* since their primary purpose is to provide a statewide benefit rather than a benefit to an individual agency.

DOA also provides other statewide services which are appropriately funded by general fund appropriations. Such services provide significant statewide benefits as well as benefits to specific agencies; however, charging agencies for the service would be a *disincentive* for its use. Funding the activity out of the general fund allows agencies to use the service as much as they need to the extent funding allows. Examples of such statewide services are the Employee Assistance Program, consulting on building problems by the Division of State Building Construction, and review of construction plans for conformance with the State Building Code.

TYPE II: UTILITY SERVICES

Second, some services are most efficiently provided through a *centrally managed resource*. Examples of DOA activities which fall in this category include space management in the Capitol complex, utilization of the statewide data and voice communications network, and the use of the mainframe computer. These services are currently funded through internal service revolving funds. Since it is in the taxpayers' interest for state agencies to be required to consume these services from the centrally managed resource, a *monopolistic* condition exists. We refer to services in this category as *utilities* since the strategy for funding and managing these activities is similar to the approach the state takes toward public utilities.

TYPE III: COMPETITIVE MARKETPLACE SERVICES

Third, DOA provides some services because it has some sort of competitive advantage over other providers of the same service. Agencies have full freedom of choice in whether to choose DOA for these *competitive marketplace* services. Some examples include computer programming services, micrographics production, data entry, and materials transfer. In providing these services, DOA competes with services provided internally by state agencies, other community resources, and the private sector. The theory of this category is that *free market competition* provides state agencies, and ultimately the taxpayers, with the most cost-effective alternative.

SERVICE MANAGEMENT MATRIX

The service management matrix provides an overview of DOA's proposed strategy for funding and managing three different categories of services. In the following pages, each of the categories is described in much greater detail.

TYPE I: STATEWIDE LEADERSHIP AND CONTROL SERVICES

Services: These are services which are primarily designed to meet a statewide rather than individual agency need. For example, in taking advantage of statewide commodity contracts, DOA may require that state agencies use products which meet certain standard specifications. Although an agency may have opted for a particular product which better met their *individual* needs, a greater *statewide* need for efficiency is met through the provision of a standard commodity contract.

Many of these activities also meet specific executive branch or legislative requirements to have DOA provide oversight and control over other state agencies. For example, the Governor and Legislature have mandated DOA to provide administrative controls in such areas as the *purchase* of data processing equipment, copy machines, professional and technical consulting contracts, space utilization, etc.

Also included in this category are services provided by the Department of Administration for the benefit of the state as a whole rather than specifically for any given agency. The Employee Assistance Program, ceremonial space, and Capitol grounds maintained by DOA are all examples of such services.

Customer: Customers of these services are the taxpayers as represented by the Legislature and the Governor. DOA should be held directly accountable to the Governor and Legislature for these services. Therefore, *general funding is most appropriate.*

Customer Choice: Although DOA strives to provide these services in a way which best supports individual agency management, there is no agency choice in the amount or nature of these services. Those decisions are made by the Governor and the Legislature.

Pricing: Clients do not pay for these services, rather funding for the services is through legislative appropriation to DOA.

Spending Control: The Legislature, Governor, Finance Department and DOA executive leadership exert spending control over these functions through the normal budget development and budget management processes.

Oversight: The Governor, Legislature, and DOA executive leadership directly oversee these activities. Full budget review and appropriations control allow the Legislature to actively participate in setting the direction for these services.

Unspent Monies: Like other generally funded services, unspent monies in these activities are cancelled and returned to the general fund at the end of each fiscal year. Unlike categories II and III, activity managers for these services have *no incentive* to reduce costs, and typically therefore, spend an amount close to the original appropriation.

Productivity Investments: Investments are treated as CHANGE requests in the budgetary process and require approval of the Governor and the Legislature.

ISSUES. There are two issues concerning oversight and control activities which require the attention of managers and legislators. For the most part, state agencies are remarkably accepting of the need for control and oversight exercised by DOA. However, there is tension between what managers in state agencies perceive to be appropriate services in this category and what DOA, the Governor, and the Legislature might deem appropriate. Since circumstances are constantly changing, the Legislature and executive branch need to be in frequent dialogue about the efficacy of various DOA-provided control and oversight services.

Second, most services in this category are provided because they result in an ultimate savings to the taxpayer. The proposition that the *savings produced* through the oversight are greater than the *cost of providing the oversight* needs to be constantly reexamined, however. For instance, statutes require DOA to preapprove purchases of convenience copying equipment. This was a sensible approach to controlling the proliferation of convenience copying equipment. However, changes in copier technology, the dramatic increase in the use of DOA copy centers (a competitive marketplace service providing high-speed, very low cost duplication services), and the development of standard commodity contracts for copying equipment all raise serious questions about whether the state saves more money through the control of copier acquisition than the cost of providing that control.

DEPARTMENT OF ADMINISTRATION
Statewide Leadership and Control
(Category I)

Current Statewide Leadership and Control Activities

Risk Management Consulting
Small Business Set-Aside Program
Central Purchasing
Statewide Fixed Asset Inventory
Contract Management
Central Mail
Employee Assistance Counseling, Training, and Workshops
Advocating Volunteerism and Public/Private Partnerships
Office Automation Consulting, Technical Assistance, and Standards
Forms and Record Systems Activity
State Telephone Switchboard and Phone Directory
Phone System Design and Consulting
911 Emergency Telephone System
Data Privacy Act Administration
Building Code Plan Review, Consulting, and Certification
Space Leasing, Space Planning
Land Acquisition and Sale

Energy Conservation Programs
Construction Project Management and Design

Proposed Statewide Leadership and Control Activities

Resource Recovery (Recycling) Consulting and Technical Assistance
Information System Architecture, Standards, Contracts, and Enterprise Analysis
Local Government Records Management Program
Disaster Recovery Planning for Critical Information Systems
Upgrading of Critical Statewide Information Systems
Ceremonial Space Maintenance

TYPE II: UTILITY SERVICES

Services: There are many administrative services which can be provided most
efficiently to state agencies through a *centrally managed resource.* Economies of scale make it most practical for these services to be centralized rather
than having state agencies provide themselves with these services individually. Examples of such services include the statewide telecommunications
network, central mainframe computer, and the provision of office space in the
Capitol complex.

Customer: These services are provided to support management of individual
state agencies and units of local government rather than serving only a statewide need. Therefore, state agencies and units of local government are the
"customers" of these services. These services are funded through an internal
service revolving fund so that each customer pays its appropriate share of the
total cost of providing the service.

Customer Choice: Since by definition utility services are best provided from a
central resource, customers have no choice in the source of the service. It
would be inefficient, for example, to allow a state agency to construct its own
statewide telecommunications network or to allow a state agency to choose
to lease space in downtown St. Paul leaving state-owned buildings empty.
Therefore, customers of utilities have but one choice as a *source* for the service.

Customers do, however, have a choice over the *amount* of the service they
consume. Therefore, it is wise for these services to be funded through revolving funds. Requiring customers to pay their fair share for the service encourages prudent use of those services.

Since DOA has a *captive market* for these utility services, it is important that
customers have a clear expectation about exactly what services they can
expect from the utility. These are specified through *service-level contracts*
with each customer. Similarly, it is essential for DOA to estimate each year
the volume of service which is demanded by its customers collectively so that

rates can be established which will just cover the cost of providing those services. Therefore, in the service-level contracts, customers need to provide fairly accurate estimates of their planned consumption for the rate period.

Pricing: Rates for utility services are established using fairly detailed cost-accounting methods. To the maximum extent possible, customers are charged for utility services on the basis of the benefit they derive from those services. DOA regularly *compares rates* for these services *with those charged by the private sector* or alternative public resources to ensure that these *rates are competitive.*

Spending Control: Because these services are provided in a monopolistic environment, tight *control of the rates* is required. Controlling rates is *much more powerful than* controlling expenditures. Rates identify the *cost per unit of output*—the ultimate bottom-line cost to the taxpayer. Activity managers need to closely monitor and control both revenues and expenditures in order to keep rates down. But executives and legislators overseeing these utilities, should focus on control of the rates which represent bottom-line costs to taxpayers.

Oversight: Three dimensions of utility services require careful oversight.

First, the *rates* themselves need to be kept as low as possible while providing customers with appropriate levels of service. Second, the *nature and extent of services* provided by the utility needs to be carefully overseen. Third, proposed *investments* which would enhance existing services and/or provide additional services should be carefully overseen.

Beyond the activity managers themselves, there are four other groups who each have a unique role in the oversight of utility services:

1. *DOA executive leadership* carefully reviews both the revenue and expenditure plans, sets rate goals, controls the activity to meet those goals, translates legislative, gubernatorial, and customer expectations into concrete action, and reviews financial statements to assure the fiscal stability of the fund.

2. *A panel representing customers* advises the commissioners of Finance and Administration on the types of services to be provided by the utility, service levels required, investment proposals, and rate proposals.

3. *The Governor,* represented by the Finance Department, assures that the utility provides a statewide optimum solution to provision of administrative services, reviews and controls rates, and approves investment proposals.

4. *The Legislature* ultimately provides overall direction to the provision of these services. It decides what services should be funded in this manner, and annually reviews rates and financial statements. Most importantly, the Legislature controls expenditures through its appropriations to various state agencies who consume utility services.

There are two key vehicles for exercising oversight of utility services. First, the *annual rate packages* proposed by the activity managers delineate all of the key factors requiring oversight—revenue assumptions, spending plans, service levels, proposed investments, adjustments to retained earnings, and most importantly, the bottom-line which are the proposed rates. Second, the fiscal status of each fund is monitored through a *quarterly financial statement.* Unlike general fund financial reports which monitor only expenditures relative to budget, revolving fund financial statements provide a complete picture of the business. A financial statement includes a balance sheet listing assets and liabilities (including contributions to and from the general fund), a profit-and-loss statement showing a detailed picture of revenues and expenses, and data on cash flow which compares financial activities of the fund with working capital available.

Unspent Monies: At the end of each fiscal year, unspent monies, which are expressed in terms of retained earnings, are *used to lower the rates* for the subsequent year or for prudent investments which will lower costs and/or improve service. Through the annual rate proposals, activity managers propose methods for redistributing profits and/or making up losses. These are reviewed by a customer panel and must be approved by DOA executive leadership and the Finance Department.

Managers of utility activities strive to *set rates so that the fund breaks even* at the end of the fiscal year. However, managers are *strongly encouraged to find ways to spend less money than they take in.* They are rewarded for so doing. This is accomplished by finding ways to cut costs, increase productivity, take advantage of one-time, cost-saving opportunities, or increase revenues—particularly through marketplace expansion. For example, when use of the statewide telecommunications network is made available to units of local government, local governments can significantly reduce some of their telecommunications costs. At the same time, the substantial fixed costs of maintaining a telecommunications network are spread out over a larger customer base, thereby reducing everyone's rates.

Productivity Investments: From time to time, activity managers see opportunities to make an investment which will result in reduced costs, improved service, or both. For example, by upgrading the central processor of the mainframe computer, customer transactions can be completed using about half the computer resources previously required. This significantly reduces customer costs and broadens the capacity of the mainframe to meet ever-increasing customer needs.

Such investments are judged on two factors:

a) What is the expected financial return on the investment? and

b) Is the service enhancement represented by the investment necessary? Investment proposals are described in the annual rate packages and therefore require the full scrutiny of those who oversee rates as described above.

ISSUES. Several issues regarding the utility services require the attention of managers and legislators.

First, since DOA has a *monopoly* in the markets for these services, the utilities must be *carefully regulated.* This regulation, however, must not mitigate advantages of revolving funds over general funds. These advantages include:

o Incentives for customers to control consumption.

o Flexibility in altering service to meet customer needs.

o Incentives for activity managers to reduce costs.

o Accrual accounting.

o Long-term management consideration in making investments.

The best way to maintain these advantages and bring about greater accountability at the same time is to *control rates rather than spending.* This requires that rate packages and financial statements be reviewed carefully by the Legislature.

Second, customers of utilities are captive. Therefore, they need a mechanism such as the customer panel (see recommendations) to provide input.

Third, by definition agencies are required to purchase a utility service from DOA. Should centralized service usage be mandated for benefits of control and economies of scale? Or, should flexibility be granted to agencies to purchase the goods or service through the purchasing or contract process? This question should be asked of all activities to determine whether it is a monopolistic or a marketplace activity.

Fourth, are agencies willing to commit themselves to certain levels of business in order to ensure stable funding for the utility? Adopting service contracts between DOA utilities and its customers will help to provide stability in rates and service.

DEPARTMENT OF ADMINISTRATION
Utilities
(Category II)

Current Utility Activities

State Register
Vehicle Rental
Mainframe Computer Operations
In-WATS
Telecommunications Network
Capitol Complex Buildings and Grounds

Proposed Utilities

Occupational Health Services

State Records Center

TYPE III: COMPETITIVE MARKETPLACE SERVICES

Services: These services cover a variety of activities in which state agencies have a free choice about whether to obtain the service from DOA, to provide it internally, or to choose another outside provider. DOA *competes in this marketplace* because, for one reason or another, it has a *competitive advantage* over other alternatives.

For example, DOA provides microfilming services to state agencies. By microfilming important but infrequently used records and documents, agencies can significantly reduce their document storage costs. In addition to DOA, there are private sector vendors which meet state standards and specifications for microfilming public documents. DOA wins a healthy share of this market not only because its *prices are competitive with other providers,* but *also* because DOA provides larger measures of security for confidential data, convenient accessibility to customers, and a familiarity with state agency operations which allows it to efficiently meet agency needs.

Customer: Customers of DOA competitive marketplace services are primarily state agencies. For some services units of local government, private nonprofit corporations, and the general public are also customers. For example, the Federal Surplus Property Enterprise Fund, the Documents Center, and the State Register all have markets beyond state agencies.

Customer Choice: Customers of DOA competitive marketplace services have *full choice* both over the *source* of the service and of the *amount* they consume. Agencies, therefore, shop for the best price and value that they can achieve. If state agencies or other customers of DOA competitive marketplace services choose alternative sources of the service, the DOA activity must reduce its expenditures accordingly. Ultimately, if the activity is not providing an appropriate quality service at a competitive price, it will go out of business.

Prices: Prices for competitive marketplace services are set by activity managers based on a number of factors—the cost of providing the service, trends in the marketplace, development of market incentives, and customer resources. In sharp contrast to utilities, *prices are not solely based on an allocation of costs.* For instance, in submitting a bid to a state agency for computer programming services, the activity manager would not only consider the cost of providing that service, but also availability of staff, prospects of other business opportunities, and the extent to which this particular job fits the skills and background of the staff may also influence the bid.

Spending Control: Spending for DOA marketplace services is primarily controlled by the Governor and Legislature overseeing the budgets of state agencies who consume marketplace services. In addition, DOA activity managers, executive leadership, and the Department of Finance carefully monitor each activity's financial performance. *Annual business plans* project sales, expenditures, and prices. In addition, the plans identify new market development and productivity investment opportunities.

Since the marketplace effectively controls the bottom-line—the value which consumers of the services receive—direct oversight of activity expenditures by persons beyond activity managers is neither desirable nor productive.

Monthly financial reports allow activity managers to monitor revenues. Spending adjustments are made accordingly.

Oversight: Activity managers strive to offer value products and services to their customers and to do so profitably. DOA executive leadership oversees these activities by carefully reviewing and approving annual business plans which project revenues, expenses, and profit as well as identifying investment and market growth opportunities. DOA executive leadership also reviews monthly financial reports and quarterly financial statements. The latter are also reviewed and approved by DOF which ensures the fiscal stability of the fund.

Ultimately, the Legislature will oversee the activity by reviewing annual business plans and annual financial performance. While the Legislature seeks to reward profitability in the funds (which is in the interest of the taxpayers), it also holds state agencies accountable for expenditures they make toward the funds.

The marketplace provides the best control of these activities. Overcontrol only serves to interfere with market forces. Therefore, managers of these activities are given the high level of freedom and flexibility they need to effectively compete. They are also held accountable for the profitable operation of their activities—ultimately, through the threat of extinction.

Unspent Monies: Managers of these activities are encouraged to operate profitably. To the extent that the fund is able to accumulate profits, these retained earnings should be periodically returned to the general fund. Returns to the general fund take place biannually, and should be anticipated in the fund's business plan. The targeted amount for return to the general fund is negotiated with and approved by the Department of Finance.

Not all competitive marketplace activities will be able to accumulate retained earnings. Nor should they be expected to. As long as the activity provides a cost-effective alternative to its customers, it is serving the taxpayers well. For instance, an activity in the Materials Management Division takes surplus property from the federal government and makes it available to local governments and nonprofit groups. The fund is barely profitable because it needs to keep prices at rock-bottom levels. That's O.K. The Documents Center, on the other hand, sells publications and other material to the general public. Though its prices are fair and competitive, it is expected to make small profits. (Last year the fund returned $125,000 of accumulated retained earnings to the general fund.)

Productivity Investments: Investments in competitive marketplace services are based on anticipated return. Activity managers risk investments based on reasonable probabilities that those investments will allow them to compete more effectively in the marketplace. Since market forces are a very effective control of the activity, activity managers make primary decisions about investments. Cash for investments comes either from retained earnings or from loans from the Finance Department. Retained earnings are also used to make biennial returns of profit to the general fund. Therefore, investment decisions, which are outlined in the annual business plans, need to be negotiated with the Department of Finance.

ISSUES. There are several issues regarding marketplace activities.

1. There are trade-offs involved in accepting the marketplace environment as appropriate for state government. On the one hand, operating in a competitive environment provides an incentive to be as efficient and as low cost as possible. On the other hand, marketplace activities must be *given a freer hand* to determine investments, rates, and earnings.

2. For the competitive marketplace activity to work, activity managers need flexibility to *respond to changes* in their competitive environment. In order to allow this to occur, it will be important for legislators and others with oversight responsibilities to keep confidence and trust in activity managers. This can best be accomplished by having a thorough understanding of the principles underlying the marketplace approach.

3. Externally mandated activities and expenses cannot be required of a marketplace activity since this may make them uncompetitive. The activity itself must be free to determine how to invest its resources. It must also be free to determine its rates and rate structures. It must be acceptable for a marketplace activity to retain earnings for future investment and to take short-term losses in order to produce a longer-term gain.

4. State agencies must be trusted to choose the most cost-effective method for purchasing goods or services. Agencies want to maximize the dollars available for their program operations and will naturally minimize administrative support costs by choosing the cheapest and most effective source.

5. A risk involved in placing an activity in the marketplace category is that the activity may not be competitive and may fail financially. The activity must then

be allowed to go out of existence. If it is unacceptable to allow an activity to go out of existence, it has been improperly categorized within the marketplace. It should then be viewed as a utility or as a statewide need because there are overriding statewide benefits that require the activity to be retained. Thus, it is important to correctly categorize all activities.

6. To the extent that marketplace activities are seen as competing with private enterprise, this competition should be seen as desirable because it *saves the taxpayers money*. State agencies would only choose the government-supported activity over a private competition if the price and quality of service were best.

DEPARTMENT OF ADMINISTRATION
Marketplace
(Category III)

Current Marketplace Activities

Cooperative Purchasing
Central Stores
Sale of Recyclable Goods
Federal Surplus Property Sales
State Documents Sales and Distribution
Addressing and Inserting
Electronic Equipment Rental
Copy Centers
Data Entry
Computer Programming
Micrographics Products and Services
Voice Mail
Electronic Mail
Materials Transfer
Management Analysis Consulting

Proposed Marketplace Activities

Fixed Asset Records Management Systems
Printing In-House Production
Special Projects and Training on Using Volunteers
Office Automation Training and Support
Record Systems Consulting and Education
Telecommunications Services to Local Government

PART 3

RECOMMENDATIONS

Last year the Legislature took an important step toward implementing this strategy by establishing the Plant Management Division as a *utility* rather than financing the activity from the general fund.

We recommend additional changes during this session. Some activities which are currently funded through revolving funds should be financed by the general fund. Conversely, we are also recommending that some general fund activities be changed to utilities or competitive marketplace activities. In addition, we are making a number of recommendations which will improve the management of Department of Administration (DOA) services.

These activities should be moved from revolving funds to the general fund:

1. <u>Planning of statewide information management</u> activities should be funded by the general fund. Currently, these activities, to the extent that they are performed, are funded as overhead charges that are added to IMB computer services rates. However, these activities are Type I in nature. Information management at the statewide level will *control the sprawling growth in computer development according to a plan.* Overseeing the plan is not a direct service for which agencies are willing to pay. Rather, DOA should be directly accountable to the Governor and Legislature for statewide planning and control according to published policies, standards and guidelines. Statewide information management is minimally performed now since adequate funding would drive other computer rates too high. The *growth in decentralized mini and micro processor computing* over the last few years requires that action be taken to establish this function now.

2. Costs of *ceremonial space and statutorily free space* in the Capitol complex should be funded by the general fund rather than by state agency rent payments. The costs associated with maintaining these spaces should be borne by those who benefit from the space and who are responsible for creating the costs. Ceremonial space in the Capitol complex is provided for the public and is for their direct benefit. It is symbolic as well as necessary for conducting business in the public domain. Capitol complex space that is provided free of charge according to mandates of the statutes is part of the state's sound policy and benefits society as a whole. As a result, both of these activities should be funded by the general fund.

3. *Resource Recovery* should be partially funded by the general fund because it provides general statewide efficiency and environmental benefits. Currently, the total benefits of the Resource Recovery Program are not capturable in its enterprise fund. As a result, the program is not being advocated

and is in serious financial difficulty. The general management and environmental benefits of this activity currently do not accrue to the benefit of the fund. For example, the state *avoids* over $40,000 worth of hauling and land fill costs through paper recycling. But the fund receives no financial benefit for this cost avoidance. These general benefits should be recognized by *partially* funding the activity from the general fund.

4. The *Intergovernmental Information Systems Advisory Council* (IISAC) should be funded from the general fund rather than from fees. The purpose of IISAC is to promote the development of *standards* for local government systems and to improve the *interchange* of data between state and local government. It doesn't provide services to state agencies or local units of government for which they are expected to pay. In order for the Council to meet its purposes, the staff should be paid out of a direct appropriation.

5. The *Local Government Records Management Program* provides a statewide direction and coordination and should be funded by the general fund. The program develops records management and records retention standards and assists and encourages local government entities with the implementation of these statewide standards. This benefits both the individual local government, the Legislature, and those state agencies that interface with local government. A general fund appropriation is needed to continue this program.

These activities should be moved from the general fund to revolving funds:

6. The *Minnesota Office on Volunteer Services* should evolve into a program funded partially by donations and fees rather than being totally reliant upon the general fund. MOVS provides benefits to local units of government, non-profit organizations, profit seeking firms, and individuals. It seeks to form public-private partnerships. As such, it can *expect to receive occasional donations from firms and foundations,* and it can expect to *recover some costs by charging fees for its services.* A significant effort toward this end is planned for the upcoming biennium.

7. The *Fixed Asset Records Management System (FARMS)* has elements of both a Type I and a Type II activity and should be *funded by charges to customers* as well as by general fund appropriations. It is currently totally funded by the general fund. FARMS provides control and oversight of the state's assets and provides essential data for the state's Annual Financial Report. On the other hand, it provides a service to agencies that agencies demand and would be willing to pay for if it were not already paid for them. Some information contained on FARMS is strictly for the benefit of agencies and provided at agency choice. To the extent that FARMS provides direct benefits to agencies and services that are optional for agencies, the system should be funded by charging the consumer. Various alternatives for implementing a charge-back alternative are being reviewed.

8. The Legislature should give consideration to changing the funding base of the *Materials Management Division*. The entire process of managing materials from cradle to grave has elements of being both a *leadership and control* activity and a *utility* with economies of scale and direct benefit to customers. Materials Management provides centralized information and assurance of least cost purchasing and, as such, it should continue as a general-funded activity. On the other hand, many parts of Materials Management have the characteristics of a utility. Use of the services in Materials Management is mandated. The customers' use of the services is quantifiable. As a result, costs of agency use of the Materials Management activities can be allocated and billed. Alternative mechanisms for making certain Materials Management activities into the utility category are being reviewed.

These important activities are not being done by DOA utilities, but need to be addressed immediately. They should be considered for funding from the general fund:

9. The *upgrading of critical statewide information systems* should be viewed as a general statewide benefit and funded by the general fund. When agencies continue to use old technology on the statewide network, there are general costs on the entire system that everyone must pay. Eliminating old technologies from the statewide network will be of benefit to everyone and, therefore, should be funded by the general fund.

10. Having a *disaster recovery plan* for the state's critical information systems is of general benefit to state government and should be funded by the general fund. There is currently no disaster recovery plan that defines the resources necessary to operate critical state systems in the event of a physical disaster. If such a plan must be funded out of overhead on computer services rates, the plan is not likely to be completed. State government and the public are dependent upon the information contained in and the continued operation of certain of the state's information systems. Therefore, it will be of general benefit to all of state government to have a disaster recovery plan.

The following management tools are recommended for better implementation of the service management matrix.

1. *Service contracts* should be developed between DOA utilities and state agency customers. The contracts should guarantee a level of service from the DOA activity and, in return, DOA should receive a commitment to a level of business and dollar volume for that period of time. This should provide greater stability in rates and service and greater accountability to state agencies.

2. DOA revolving fund structure should be reorganized so that marketplace activities are placed in an *enterprise fund* and utility activities are placed in *internal service funds*. This would clarify which activities provide which type

of service and would allow for the differing management principles to be properly implemented. Internal service funds are appropriate for utility activities because they are set up to account for the financing of goods or services provided by one agency (DOA) to another agency or governmental unit on a cost-reimbursement basis. Enterprise funds are appropriate for marketplace activities because they account for operations that are financed and operated in a manner similar to a private business in the competitive marketplace.

3. *Customer panels* should be created to oversee each utility. The customer panel should review the quality of service provided, rates, investments, and other topics of mutual interest. It should be advisory to the departments of Finance and Administration. Utility activities should be held accountable by their customers for the quality and cost of services provided.

4. An improved *accounting system for revolving funds* needs to be developed. The Statewide Accounting System (SWA) is not adequate for revolving funds which use accrual accounting methods. Currently, SWA does not provide for depreciating assets, handling inventories, accounting for "work in progress" or accounting for revenues. As a result, accurate and timely information needed to effectively manage these businesses is not readily available. An accounting system that fits revolving funds would provide better information for the oversight and management of utility and marketplace activities.

5. The *consumption pattern of state agencies* who use utility and marketplace services should be *reported on a regular basis to the Legislature*. This will allow the Legislature as well as the Governor and the Department of Finance to review state agency levels of activity in these activity areas and to place accountability for such consumption upon the purchasing agencies.

6. Flexibility necessary to compete effectively must be given to *marketplace activity managers*. As these activities are identified, recommendations will be made to the Governor and Legislature on any necessary changes.

7. Reporting to the Legislature about revolving funds can be greatly improved. Financial data in the biennial budget document should be improved by providing a combination of data from the funds' balance sheets and profit-and-loss statements. Quarterly financial statements and annual rate packages should be presented to the Legislature rather than just made available to legislative staff. Business plans for marketplace activities should also be presented to the Legislature for its review.

Appendix Two:
Smart Staffing Newsletter

Smart Staffing

Turnaround Times
July 1988

an information series for managers and supervisors

Staffing requests at DOER: How long do they really take?

When Dan learned that he would receive the funding he had requested from the legislature, he was elated! Now he could hire those six employees he needed to get his program off the ground!

He wasn't sure how long it would take to hire six people or where to begin, but it was only May and the funds weren't available until July 1st anyway. He still had time to think about it.

In the meantime, he asked around and got a variety of responses:

"I got the names of people to interview within a couple of days."

"I had to wait months before I could even interview."

"I hired people off the street. It only took a week."

After spending the past month and a half lobbying at the Capitol, Dan had a lot of catching up to do at the office. Then new problems cropped up, demanding his attention. In the back of his mind, he thought about his new program. And so the time passed.

On June 15, Dan met with his personnel director and was told he would have to wait three months before he could even begin interviewing. He couldn't believe his ears! "Three months! I can't afford to wait that

long!" he sputtered angrily, "All I want to do is hire six employees! Why does it take so long?"

Sound familiar? Like Dan, you may be frustrated by the amount of time hiring takes or even by the lack of information about how long it will take. It might help you to remember that the state personnel system is set up to ensure public access to state jobs. That means giving all applicants a fair chance for hire and using objective selection standards. The merit system, collective bargaining, and affirmative action are all public policies designed to provide fair employment. Putting them into practice takes time.

"Sure, I want things to be fair. Who doesn't?" you're probably thinking. "But I would like to see things happen faster. Or at least know how much time they will require."

Take heart: improvement is on the way. The Staffing Division is taking steps to make their services more efficient. For example, they've set turnaround times for all staffing services. A chart of these turnaround times appears on page three. Use it to determine how much time your requests will take.

Knowing what to expect would have saved Dan time and frustration. And it can help you, too. ∎

Inside:

- *"Turnaround times for DOER's services" (p. 3)*

- *"Making the system work for you" (p. 2)*

163

Making the system work for you

Are you frustrated by the lack of control you seem to have over the staffing process? Keep in mind that you are the one who sets the game in motion. In tennis terms, you serve. When you serve in a tennis match, you determine how much spin the ball has, how low it travels over the net, and where it lands by the way you prepare for and execute your swing. In staffing as in tennis, there are many things you can do to make the ball go where you want it to go.

The five-step method:
1. *Plan ahead.*
2. *Talk to Personnel.*
3. *Write the position description.*
4. *Prioritize your requests.*
5. *Document your requests.*

1. Plan ahead.
Timing is everything. Keep an eye on your staffing picture:
• Is someone about to retire?
• Does anyone want to make a career change?
• Do you expect to receive funding from the legislature for new positions?

Use the chart on page three to find out how long it takes DOER to screen candidates using written exams. Add the time you and your agency personnel office need to develop the request and count back from the date you want to hire. That's when you need to begin your request.

Every year, the 37-member Staffing Division processes:
• over 60,000 applications
• 3,000 audit requests
• 600 exams

2. Talk to Personnel.
Nobody knows what you want better than you do. Your personnel office can guide you through the system. Ask them the following questions:
• Is there a class?
• Is there a list?
• Is there a test?
• Are there other options?
• What do we need to do?

Compare it to house-hunting: you are the buyer and Personnel is the realtor. You tell the realtor what you want and how much you are willing to pay for it. Both realtors and personnel experts can help you refine your needs, expand your options, and guide you through an unfamiliar system. Talking with the experts early on improves your chances of getting what you want, when you want it.

3. Write the position description.
Describing the job accurately is essential to job classification and candidate selection. Only you can design the job. Even if there already is a position description, you should review it to be sure that it reflects what you want to be done. A well-written position description gives personnel specialists the facts they need to determine:
• how to classify a job.
• what the job is and what skills are needed.
• what the salary range is.

4. Prioritize your requests.
The Staffing Division and your personnel office receive a barrage of staffing requests along with yours. They cannot always respond to your request as quickly as they would like. But you can improve your chances of getting a quick response by prioritizing your requests. List your needs in order of importance. Then set a realistic schedule with your personnel office for getting them met.

5. Document your requests.
Working with your personnel office, make sure that:
• the position description accurately describes the work and the skills required.
• the organization chart shows the relationship of the position to others in your department.
• the cover memo describes your rationale for the position and the class you are requesting.
• you complete a supervisory questionnaire, if the position is supervisory. ∎

Turnaround times for DOER's services

Service provided	Time required
• Produce certified lists of candidates	1 day
• Provide copies of candidates' applications	3 days
• Assign vacant positions to a class	2 weeks
• Reclassify occupied positions	6 weeks
• Recruit and screen candidates through:	
Experience & training evaluations	3 months
Written exams	4 months
Multi-part exams	exam specific

The turnaround time clock starts running on the day your fully documented request arrives at DOER.

Where does the time go?

• **Produce certified lists: one day**
Seven out of ten times, there is a pool of candidates who have already passed the required exam. A certified list is created from this pool of candidates. This list contains the names of candidates with the highest scores plus those names which would help you meet affirmative action goals. Your personnel office can access certified lists from the computer one day after DOER receives your request.

• **Provide copies of candidates' applications: three days**
Since certified lists contain only names, addresses and phone numbers, you may want to have copies of the candidates' applications sent to you. Allow three days for this step.

• **Assign vacant positions to a class: two weeks**
All positions must be assigned to a class which accurately and fairly reflects the work to be done. Staffing Division Specialists review the position description you submit to determine if the job fits into an existing class or if a new class needs to be created. If an appropriate class already exists, it should take no more than two weeks for a position to be assigned to a class.

• **Reclassify an occupied position: six weeks**
Reclassifying an existing position doesn't take any longer than classifying a new one. However, vacant positions get first priority because:
  • It is logical to fill jobs which are not getting done at all before fine-tuning those which are already being performed.
  • When an occupied position is moved to a higher class, it is possible to compensate the employee at the higher salary from the date of a fully documented request. The longer time (six weeks) doesn't harm the incumbent.

• **Recruit and screen candidates: three or four months**
Three times out of ten, the Staffing Division needs to create a certified list from scratch. Producing a list of candidates for you to choose from requires conducting an exam. Some of the steps involved in the exam process include:
  • Deciding whether an old exam will produce the best candidates or if a new one needs to be developed
  • Designing the exam
  • Printing the exam announcement in the state bulletin
  • Allowing time for applicants to respond, two weeks or longer, as determined by the manager
  • Scoring the exams
Screening candidates and developing certified lists using detailed job applications (experience and training evaluations) takes three months. Written exams take four months because of the need to schedule applicants and administer tests statewide. ∎

3

Smart Staffing

When could turnaround times be longer?

Ninety-five percent of the time, DOER's services will be completed within the turnaround times listed on the chart. However, unusual situations can extend turnaround times. Here are a few examples:

• **Placement of positions in bargaining units**
If there is a question about which bargaining unit a new or reclassified position should be assigned to, the Bureau of Mediation Services will need to decide where to place it.

• **Lack of consensus**
If you disagree with the way Staffing Division specialists classify a position, you may want to give more information to support your request.

• **Establishment of a new class**
If a position does not fit into any existing class, a new class may be created using the Hay evaluation process. This requires scheduling and conducting a panel review of the job. ■

What are your personnel office's internal times?

Your personnel office needs time to act on your request, too. For some classes, they may have delegated authority to act in place of DOER. Ask them to help you calculate the total amount of time you will need to allow for a request. ■

What should you do if you really can't wait?

Talk with your personnel office. Explain the whole problem and ask them to tell you what options may be available. ■

The Department of Employee Relations

Commissioner ....Nina Rothchild

Deputy Commissioner:
   Personnel ....Elaine Johnson
   Labor Relations ....Lance Teachworth

Smart Staffing, an information series for managers and supervisors, is published by the Department of Employee Relations Staffing Division, in partnership with agency personnel offices.

Editor ....Penny Hinke (296-1694)

Contributing author:
   Joe Kurcinka
      Staffing Division,
      DOER
Reviewers:
   Craig Johnson
      Human Services
   Ed Jones
      Staffing Division,
      DOER
   Cindy Valentine
      Staffing Division,
      DOER

Our thanks to the Departments of Human Services and Revenue for making this publication possible.

Appendix Three:
Fiscal 1992-93 Budget
Instructions (1990)

RUDY PERPICH
GOVERNOR

August 14, 1990

To: All Agency Heads

Fr: RUDY PERPICH
        Governor

As we prepare for the 1992–93 biennial budget, Minnesota's financial position continues to be sound and manageable. Although we can all be proud of the distinction that Financial World magazine afforded our state this year, we should strive to improve our position even further. This is accomplished not just by balancing our revenues and expenditures, but more importantly by the ways in which we spend our tax dollars and the choices that they represent. Our goal is to build a high quality of life for all our citizens and invest wisely in our future and that of our children.

Our challenge in the months ahead is to live within our resources. State revenues are projected to grow slightly above 5% each of the next two years. As we indicated last April when the Legislature concluded their session, these revenues are closely balanced with projected "baseline" expenditures.

As a result, I'm asking each of you to undertake an aggressive effort within your agencies to review the results of your agency's programs in the past and chart a course for improved results in the future. Our final recommendations will reflect your best thinking about what is possible with the resources we have available.

I appreciate your work and dedication. It's very important to our future and the citizens of Minnesota.

1992–93 Biennial
Budget Instructions

I. OVERVIEW OF BUDGET PROCESS

In the 1992–93 biennial budget process we will continue to shift from the traditional view of budgeting which focused on incremental changes toward an approach that emphasizes strategic planning, priority setting, realignment of base resources, and results. Cumulative changes in the expectations for state services and the financial outlook for the next several years provide an opportunity to update the manner in which resource decisions are presented and considered.

The 1992–93 budget process will emphasize management planning, priority setting and linking decisions to results. The goal is to convert state management planning efforts into concrete results-oriented decision-making through the budget process. Many state agencies have individually undertaken innovative planning efforts with a focus on substantive results. The 1992–93 budget process will require linking resource allocation decisions to planned results and implementation strategies throughout state government.

The purpose and benefits of program budgeting in Minnesota have to be reviewed and improved. Decision-making in the budget process has often been frustrated by consideration of two-digit inputs and incremental changes rather than the results to be achieved. The sheer volume of paper and documents is excessive and further frustrates the process. Changes in the 1992–93 budget process seek to reverse these trends. . . .

II. NEW CONCEPTS AND CHANGES

There are several key requirements and guidelines that each agency head should consider when preparing the agency's budget request for F.Y. 1992–93. These represent significant changes from past practice.

1. Base Level Budgets—Managing within Our Means

Agencies should prepare and submit budget plans which manage solely within their BASE level funding for F.Y. 1992–93. Each agency head must prepare a budget plan that meets the challenges facing their department without relying upon the traditional CHANGE request. The budget process for agencies will not support development of agency CHANGE level requests.

Agency budgets must present an effective response to the financial outlook and what it indicates for managing state operations. Funding for new initiatives must be generated by accompanying reductions in current spending. Further, inflation guidelines require that all potential increases in costs expected for the next biennium be managed within BASE level funding by redesign of agency services or programs.

2. Managing within Base Level Funding

Responsibility rests with agency management to make significant strategic decisions on the amount of spending and the scope, direction, and quality of state programs. The emphasis on two-digit object codes, headcounts, and levels of detail will be minimized in the budget presentation and decision process to provide agencies maximum management flexibility to plan services and programs in the most effective fashion. . . .

Required changes in regulations, statutes, or program administration which affect management ability to effectively structure services must be examined. Agencies must identify statutory requirements which should be eliminated or modified to effect their plan and develop complementary legislative proposals which would reduce the continuing costs of doing the state's business.

State agencies must remain cost conscious and take management action to control costs as a part of their response to base level budgeting requirements. The emphasis in developing budget requests must be to formulate value-added strategies which respond to needs. Any new commitments must be funded within the base level.

3. BASE Level Budget Justification

The focus of executive review of the budget will concentrate on the results produced by BASE level spending proposals. It is likely that BASE level plans that produce no definable results, or which fall below a line of "necessary and desirable," will not be recommended.

Consequently, agencies are expected to subject current operations to the detailed analysis and justification usually reserved for new program initiatives. The budget documents will be used to highlight the choices and decisions made by agency management. Agencies must be prepared to propose alternative funding levels for existing and requested programs. Past experience has taught us that trade-offs will be required to maintain fiscal stability.

4. Linking Resources to Results

The key to success in this budget process is the ability of each agency to link resource allocation decisions to specific results or outcomes.

A clear statement of both short and long term objectives associated with agency base level plans is required, as well as key indicators by which effective success can be measured. The agency's mission, program structure and budget narrative information must assure that budget decisions are linked to results which serve as the basis for resource allocations. Agency objectives, performance measures, and results provide the filter for making both intra- and interdepartmental trade-offs.

An agency's ability to retain even BASE level funding will depend upon the adequacy of this information. Budget formats will be changed to highlight information which ties together resource allocation decisions and their intended results. The results-orientation and the change in the format of the budget documents will require that agencies submit their budgets in a form to permit examination and discussion of the intended impact of agency decisions.

5. Budget Workgroups

As part of the 1992–93 budget process, the Governor will designate several work groups involving department heads and the Department of Finance. While each agency has responsibility to prepare an agency BASE level plan for the next two years, these groups will be organized around major program areas and will be asked to review priorities and identify opportunities within their joint funding base. These groups will be convened in August and will provide recommendations at the time of the November forecast. Each may consider and develop a wide range of policy options and recommendations on program funding choices and identify alternatives for the Governor's consideration. . . .

One of the primary purposes of these work groups is to ensure that all perspectives are considered in determining priorities and that the same standards of planning, priority setting and results are applied to *all* major state programs.

6. Four Year Planning Horizon

Continuing the practice initiated last legislative session, the Department of Finance will present and "track" the budget using a four-year planning horizon. This will ensure that all costs are considered when new appropriations are proposed and that all obligations created for future biennia are identified.

Agencies should include in their narrative for each program, the costs of any agency decisions that would significantly impact the 1994–95 biennium. These will be projected forward to ensure that expenditures remain in balance with revenues for the succeeding biennia.

Agencies' program narratives should describe the likely financial impact in 1994–95 of current and proposed programs where the growth is driven by factors other than inflation. This information will be used by the Department of Finance when the 1994–95 baseline is established for tracking purposes.

7. Assistance to Agencies

Support in orienting staff to the budget guidelines, changes in the budget process and identification of individual program results will be available from executive budget officers. As in past budgets, executive budget officers will provide technical orientation to the budget forms, format, and Biennial Budget System (BBS). . . .

IV. BASE LEVEL FUNDING: MANAGING INFLATION

Determining the F.Y. 1992–93 BASE Level

Agencies will develop their 1992–93 budget plans within determined BASE level funding. The BASE level for 1992–93 will be more restrictive than in the past and will be essentially consistent with the definition used in preparing the baseline estimate of general fund revenues and expenditures. In general, the reductions to agency budgets enacted in the 1990 session are assumed to be permanent reductions as reflected in agencies' F.Y. 1991 spending plans. . . .

Managing Budgets within BASE Level Funding

BASE level adjustments for F.Y. 1992–93 will *not* restore reductions or shortfalls in the current year enacted by the 1990 legislative session.

Base adjustments for F.Y. 1992–93 will *not* provide additional funding for general adjustments for increased costs. The funding decisions for the costs of salary increases will be reviewed after the November forecast. In preparing their budget submissions, agencies are expected to manage *all* anticipated cost increases within their base. . . .

It is expected that agencies will draft F.Y. 1992–93 plans which will manage within BASE level funding by reallocating existing funding and redefining priorities—as well as by considering changes designed to manage underlying costs within available funding. This may occur as redesign of services or programs, changes in the level of purchasing of goods and services, or reallocation of resources to the highest priority activities. . . .

Notes

FOREWORD

1. John Maynard Keynes, *The General Theory of Employment, Interest, and Money* (1936); quoted here from *Bartlett's Familiar Quotations*, 14th ed. (Boston: Little, Brown, 1968), 977.

2. This is, of course, quite commonly the way innovation proceeds. See Robert D. Behn, "Management by Groping Along," *Journal of Policy Analysis and Management* (Fall 1988): 643–63.

PREFACE

1. See, for example, Fred Jordan, *Innovating America* (New York: Ford Foundation, 1990).

2. Gordon Chase and Elizabeth C. Reveal, *How to Manage in the Public Sector* (Reading, Mass.: Addison-Wesley, 1983), 64–75.

3. The State of Minnesota was a recipient of a 1986 award from the Ford Foundation program on Innovations in State and Local Government for its program known as STEP (Striving Toward Excellence in Performance). For background, see "Striving towards Excellence in the State of Minnesota," John F. Kennedy School of Government case C16-87-737; "Denise Fleury and the Minnesota Office of State Claims," John F. Kennedy School of Government case C15-87-744; Michael Barzelay and Robert A. Leone, "Creating an Innovative Managerial Culture: The Minnesota 'STEP' Strategy," *Journal of State Government* (July-August 1987): 166–70; Alan Altshuler and Marc Zegans, "Innovation and Creativity: Comparisons Between Public Management and Private Enterprise," *Cities* (February 1990): 23; and Sandra J. Hale and Mary Williams, eds., *Managing Change: A Guide to Producing Innovation from Within* (Washington, D.C.:

Urban Institute Press, 1989). The state was also a finalist in the 1989 Ford Foundation awards competition for the staff agency management strategy known as enterprise management. Another John F. Kennedy School case focused on the origins of this strategy: "Introducing Marketplace Dynamics in Minnesota State Government," C16-88-826. Analysis of this experience was earlier presented in Michael Barzelay and Babak J. Armajani, "Managing State Government Operations: Changing Visions of Staff Agencies," *Journal of Policy Analysis and Management* (Summer 1990): 307–38. The Minnesota experience with enterprise management attracted the attention of contributors to practitioner-oriented publications: for example, Ron Zemke, "Putting Service Back Into Public Service," *Training* (November 1989): 42–49; David Osborne, "Ten Ways to Turn D.C. Around," *Washington Post Magazine*, December 9, 1990, 19–42; and Barbara Bordelon and Elizabeth Clemmer, "Customer Service, Partnership, Leadership: Three Strategies That Work," *GAO Journal* (Winter 1990/91): 36–43. This experience was also presented at the U.S. Office of Personnel Management's Research Conference on Service Management, Arlington, Virginia, November 1990, by Michael Barzelay, Jeff Zlonis, and Elaine Johnson.

CHAPTER ONE

BEYOND THE BUREAUCRATIC PARADIGM

1. William F. Willoughby, *The Movement for Budgetary Reform in the States* (New York: D. Appleton, 1918); Leonard D. White, *Trends in Public Administration* (New York: McGraw-Hill, 1933); Lloyd M. Short and Carl W. Tiller, *The Minnesota Commission on Administration and Finance, 1925–39: An Administrative History* (Minneapolis: University of Minnesota Press, 1942); Fritz Morstein Marx, ed., *Elements of Public Administration*, 2d ed. (Englewood Cliffs, N.J.: Prentice-Hall, 1959); Barry Dean Karl, *Executive Reorganization and Reform in the New Deal* (Cambridge, Mass.: Harvard University Press, 1963); Aaron Wildavsky, *The New Politics of the Budgetary Process* (Glenview, Ill.: Scott, Foresman, 1988), 53–63.

2. Stephen Skowronek, *Building a New American State: The Expansion of National Administrative Capacities, 1877–1920* (Cambridge, England: Cambridge University Press, 1982).

3. See, generally, Jack H. Knott and Gary J. Miller, *Reforming Bureaucracy: The Politics of Institutional Choice* (Englewood Cliffs, N.J.: Prentice-Hall, 1987), and Robert B. Reich, *The Next American Frontier* (New York: Times Books, 1983). According to Yale sociologist Charles Perrow, "The founders of organizations of all types and reformers of those that existed repeatedly held the industrial organization model—factories, by and large—as the important social innovation of the time. And it truly was." "A Society of Organizations," *Estudios del Instituto Juan March de Estudios e Investigaciones* (Madrid) (October 1990): 33.

4. In the words of historian Barry Dean Karl, these movements' beliefs and actions (as well as those of many New Dealers) were "in many respects a consequence of both industrialism and nationalism. The chief value of centralization rested on the increase in efficiency which it invariably seemed to bring to the growing urban and industrial chaos. But efficiency could also become identified with national purpose. The idea that human effort could be wasted when undirected and uncontrolled . . . was central to the growing concern with efficiency, leadership, and planning." *Executive Reorganization and Reform*, 182–83.

5. An excellent contemporary restatement of this outlook is contained in Jerry L. Mashaw, *Bureaucratic Justice: Managing Social Security Disability Claims* (New Haven, Conn.: Yale University Press, 1983). For a discussion of the concept of impersonal administration from a sociological and historical perspective, see Charles Perrow, *Complex Organizations: A Critical Essay*, 3d ed. (New York: Random House, 1986), 1–29.

6. See Woodrow Wilson, "The Study of Public Administration," *Political Science Quarterly* (June 1887): 197–202. See also Skowronek, *Building a New American State*, 47–84.

7. See Steven Kelman, *Procurement and Public Management: The Fear of Discretion and the Quality of Government Performance* (Washington, D.C.: American Enterprise Institute, 1990), 11–15.

8. Other key legacies are institutional arrangements, including hierarchical executive branches and staff agencies, and or-

ganizational routines. These arrangements, agencies, and routines embed certain habits of thought into people who work in
government.

9. A definition of paradigm that fits this usage is "the basic
way of perceiving, thinking, valuing, and doing associated with
a particular vision of reality. A dominant paradigm is seldom if
ever stated explicitly; it exists as unquestioned, tacit understanding that is transmitted through culture and in succeeding
generations through direct experience rather than being taught."
Willis Harmon, *An Incomplete Guide to the Future* (New York:
Norton, 1970), quoted in Joel Arthur Barker, *Discovering the Future: The Business of Paradigms* (St. Paul, Minn.: ILI Press, 1985),
13–14. A similar locution can be found in the literature on public administration: "Each of us lives with several paradigms at
any given time. . . . As it appears appropriate, each of us moves
in and out of paradigms throughout any work day, and with
scarcely a thought about the belief and values systems that un-
dergird them." Yvonna S. Lincoln, "Introduction," in *Organizational Theory and Inquiry: The Paradigm Revolution*, ed. Yvonna
S. Lincoln (Beverly Hills, Calif.: Sage, 1985), 30. The word *paradigm* began to be used in natural scientific and social scientific
communities after publication of Thomas S. Kuhn's *Structure of
Scientific Revolutions* (Chicago: University of Chicago Press, 1962).

10. Institute of Government Research, "A Proposal for a National Service of General Administration" (Washington, D.C.,
1929). See also Short and Tiller, *Minnesota Commission on Administration and Finance*. See discussion of administrative management in Karl, *Executive Reorganization and Reform*, 195–210.

11. For a summary of this literature, see Perrow, *Complex Organizations*, 62–118.

12. Mary Parker Follett, "The Process of Control," in *Papers
on the Science of Administration*, ed. L. Gulick and L. Urwick
(New York: Institute of Public Administration, 1937), 161–69.

13. Charles E. Lindblom, "Bargaining: The Hidden Hand of
Government (1955)," chap. 7 in *Democracy and Market System*
(Oslo: Norwegian University Press, 1988), 139–70; Charles E.
Lindblom and David Braybrooke, *The Strategy of Decision* (New
York: Free Press, 1963); Charles E. Lindblom, *The Intelligence of
Democracy* (New York: Free Press, 1965). A related criticism was

made by Martin Landau, "Redundancy, Rationality, and the Problem of Duplication and Overlap," *Public Administration Review* (July-August 1969): 346–58.

14. Herbert A. Simon, *Administrative Behavior*, 3d ed. (New York: Free Press, 1976), 61–78; Herbert A. Simon, Donald W. Smithburg, and Victor A. Thompson, *Public Administration* (New York: Knopf, 1950); Robert A. Dahl and Charles E. Lindblom, *Politics, Economics, and Welfare* (New York: Harper Brothers, 1953); Karl, *Executive Reorganization and Reform*, 224–26; and James Q. Wilson, *Bureaucracy: What Government Agencies Do and Why They Do It* (New York: Basic Books, 1989), 315–32.

15. See, for example, Guy Black, *The Application of Systems Analysis to Government Operations* (New York: Praeger, 1968); Robert Haveman, ed., *Public Expenditures and Policy Analysis*, 3d ed. (Boston: Houghton Mifflin, 1983); Ida R. Hoos, *Systems Analysis in Public Policy: A Critique*, rev. ed. (Berkeley: University of California Press, 1983).

16. Wilson, *Bureaucracy*, 113–36.

17. Kelman, *Procurement and Public Management*, 52.

18. The belief that politics and public administration are separate domains of social action was central to the bureaucratic reform vision. This notion has been criticized for decades by academics and educators. According to Wilson, "Political scientists never fail to remind their students on the first day of class [that] in this country there is no clear distinction between policy and administration." *Bureaucracy*, 241. We suppose that these teachings have had sufficient influence to merit focusing attention elsewhere. The bureaucratic paradigm's prescribed separation between substance and institutional administration *within* the administration component of the politics/administration dichotomy has received inadequate notice and scrutiny.

19. Strictly speaking, in the public sector the concepts of *customer* and *service* are typically structural metaphors. Introducing new metaphorically structured concepts into an existing conceptual system makes a difference in how people reason. According to George Lakoff and Mark Johnson, "New metaphors have the power to create a new reality. This can begin to happen when we start to comprehend our experience in terms of a met-

aphor, and it becomes a deeper reality when we begin to act in terms of it. If a new metaphor enters the conceptual system that we base our actions on, it will alter that conceptual system and the perceptions and actions that the system gives rise to. Much of cultural change arises from the introduction of new metaphorical concepts and the loss of old ones. For example, the Westernization of cultures throughout the world is partly a matter of introducing the 'time is money' metaphor into those cultures." *Metaphors We Live By* (Chicago: University of Chicago Press, 1980), 145.

20. The forces making customer service attractive as a conceptual scheme include the emergence of services as the nation's leading sector, a climate that makes privatization in its various forms an ever-present possibility, public discontent with bureaucracy, renewed appreciation for market-oriented forms of social coordination, technological innovation (especially in information systems), directives from the Office of Management and Budget and the Office of the Secretary of Defense, and the availability of training monies. The list could be extended. The social and intellectual history of the movement under way has yet to be written.

21. See the John F. Kennedy School of Government case study "The Army and REQUEST," by Steven Kelman.

22. The point of the example is not that the substitution of a customer orientation for the bureaucratic approach necessarily improves the operation of government; rather, it suggests that applying the customer approach is likely to alter what government agencies do, thereby changing the results of government operations. To evaluate whether the altered outcome constitutes an improvement requires an act of judgment and will. As an empirical matter, the judgment of the Army and its authorizers is that this application is desirable, on the whole.

23. Massachusetts took the first approach—see Massachusetts Department of Revenue, *Annual Reports* (Boston, 1983–84)—while Minnesota took the second (see "A Strategy for the 1990s," n.p., n.d., St. Paul, Minn.).

24. See Ron Zemke, "Putting Service Back into Public Service," *Training* (November 1989): 42–49, on improvements in motor vehicle licensing and registration services. See Mary Faulk,

"Customer Service and Other Unbureaucratic Notions" (Olympia: Department of Licensing, State of Washington, n.d., Mimeographed). The John F. Kennedy School of Government case study "Middlesex County Jury System," C16-86-656, is another illustration.

25. Excellent academic critiques of more general versions of the bureaucratic paradigm can be found in Perrow, *Complex Organizations*, Gareth Morgan, *Images of Organization* (Beverly Hills, Calif.: Sage, 1986), and Wilson, *Bureaucracy*. The service approach is not used by these prominent organizational theorists to critique the theory or practice of bureaucracy. Among the works we draw on in synthesizing the conceptual system of customer service are those written by business school academics and consultants: Theodore Levitt, "The Industrialization of Service," *Harvard Business Review* (September-October 1976): 63–74; Richard B. Chase, "Where Does the Customer Fit in a Service Operation?" *Harvard Business Review* (November-December 1978): 137–42; Thomas J. Peters and Robert H. Waterman, Jr., *In Search of Excellence: Lessons from America's Best-Run Companies* (New York: Warner, 1982); Geoffrey M. Bellman, *The Quest for Staff Leadership* (Glenview, Ill.: Scott, Foresman, 1986); James L. Heskett, *Managing in the Service Economy* (Boston: Harvard Business School Press, 1986); James L. Heskett, "Lessons in the Service Sector," *Harvard Business Review* (March-April 1987): 118–26; Karl Albrecht, *At America's Service* (Homewood, Ill.: Dow Jones-Irwin, 1988); Christian Grönroos, "The Relationship Approach to Marketing in Service Contexts: The Marketing and Organizational Behavior Interface," *Journal of Business Research* 20 (1990): 3–11; William R. George, "Internal Marketing and Organizational Behavior: A Partnership in Developing Customer-Conscious Employees at Every Level," *Journal of Business Research* 20 (1990): 63–70; Christian Grönroos, *Service Management and Marketing: Managing the Moment of Truth in Service Competition* (Lexington, Mass.: Lexington Books, 1990); David E. Bowen, Richard B. Chase, Thomas G. Cummings, and Associates, *Service Management Effectiveness* (San Francisco: Jossey-Bass, 1990); and James L. Heskett, W. Earl Sasser, Jr., and Christopher W. L. Hart, *Service Breakthroughs* (New York: Free Press, 1990). The public sector literature on service man-

agement includes Charles C. Goodsell, ed., *The Public Encounter: Where State and Citizens Meet* (Bloomington: Indiana University Press, 1981).

26. The term *rhetorical* is not meant to be disparaging. On the contrary, rhetoric is a valuable way of mobilizing conceptual resources and evidence. See Giandomenico Majone, *Evidence, Argument, and Persuasion in the Policy Process* (New Haven, Conn.: Yale University Press, 1989). See also Alasdair Roberts, "The Rhetorical Problems of the Manager," paper presented at the Annual Research Conference of the Association for Public Policy Analysis and Management, San Francisco, October 1990.

27. The rhetoric of customer service is becoming ubiquitous in statements of mission and strategy by government organizations. See, for example, U.S. General Services Administration, "1991 Strategic Plan" (Washington, D.C., 1990). It is also becoming commonplace in articles written for public managers. See, for example, Organization for Economic Cooperation and Development, *Administration as Service: The Public as Client* (Paris, 1987); Zemke, "Putting Service Back into Public Service"; Steven Kelman, "The Renewal of the Public Sector," *American Prospect* (Summer 1990): 51–57; David Osborne, "Ten Ways to Turn D.C. Around," *Washington Post Magazine*, December 9, 1990, pp. 19–42; Barbara Bordelon and Elizabeth Clemmer, "Customer Service, Partnership, Leadership: Three Strategies That Work," *GAO Journal* (Winter 1990–91): 36–43; Monte Ollenburger and Jeff Thompson, "A Strategy for Service?" *Public Management* (April 1990): 21–23; George D. Wagenheim and John H. Reurink, "Customer Service in Public Administration," *Public Administration Review* (May-June 1991): 263–70; Tom Glenn, "The Formula for Success in TQM," *Bureaucrat* (Spring 1991): 17–20; and Joseph Sensenbrenner, "Quality Comes to City Hall," *Harvard Business Review* (March-April 1991): 64–75. Professional associations of public administrators are bringing these ideas to the attention of their members. See, for example, the papers presented at the 1990 National Conference of the American Society for Public Administration, published in the Fall 1990 issue of *The Bureaucrat*. Executive education programs, furthermore, are increasingly using the concepts of customers and service.

See Michael Barzelay and Linda Kaboolian, "Structural Meta-phors and Public Management Education," *Journal of Policy Analysis and Management* (Fall 1990): 599–610.

28. In undertaking this task, it is well to bear in mind two observations made many years ago by legal theorist Karl N. Llewellyn. First, "it is hard to take things which are unconventional or otherwise unfamiliar to the addressee and to get them said so that they come through as intended. . . . I say we all know this, and we all try to canvass and prepare, to choose words well and to arrange them better, so that they may become true messengers." Second, "there are no panaceas." *The Common Law Tradition: Deciding Appeals* (Boston: Little, Brown, 1960), 401–3.

29. The concept of the post-bureaucratic paradigm was introduced in Michael Barzelay and Babak J. Armajani, "Managing State Government Operations: Changing Visions of Staff Agencies," *Journal of Policy Analysis and Management* (Summer 1990): 307–38. The term *post-bureaucratic* has also appeared in a review of books on private sector management: Charles Heckscher, "Can Business Beat Bureaucracy?" *American Prospect* (Spring 1991): 114–28. The term is chosen for the same kinds of reasons that the term *post-industrial society* was. Furthermore, *service paradigm* is not an adequate label because we build a new conception of accountability and control into the new paradigm, and we wish to make a clear distinction between the often-conflated concepts of developing a customer orientation and introducing marketlike processes into government.

30. Gordon Chase and Elizabeth C. Reveal, *How to Manage in the Public Sector* (Reading, Mass.: Addison-Wesley, 1983), noted that "overhead agencies use a variety of tactics to frustrate the public manager and maintain control over money and people" (p. 73).

31. The writings that encouraged the executives to use the customer concept included Peter F. Drucker, *Management: Tasks, Responsibilities, Practices* (New York: Harper & Row, 1973); and Peters and Waterman, *In Search of Excellence.*

32. Babak J. Armajani, assistant commissioner, as quoted in "Introducing Marketplace Dynamics in Minnesota State Gov-

ernment," C16-88-826, John F. Kennedy School of Government, 3.

33. In this book, the terms *executives* and *managers* are used in the same sense as they are in Wilson, *Bureaucracy*. The term *employees* is equivalent to Wilson's *operators*. The term *executives* refers to commissioners, deputy commissioners, and assistant commissioners. Examples of managers are the head of purchasing and the head of the materials management division, to whom the head of purchasing reports. In some contexts the term *employees* covers all three groups.

34. Interview with James Kinzie, St. Paul, Minnesota, December 1988, referring to his change of mind in 1986. Kinzie began his career in central purchasing in 1969. The deputy commissioner of administration in 1986 was Babak Armajani. This interview provides evidence for the claim that the kind of cognitive reorganization in which people like Kinzie engage is tantamount to a paradigm shift. On the psychology of paradigm shifts, see, for example, Barker, *Discovering the Future*, 34–39. (We disagree with Barker that thought or behavior leading to such a marked cognitive reorganization as characterizes a paradigm shift is adequately categorized as nonrational.)

35. James P. Kinzie, "From Economy and Efficiency to Creating Value: The Central Purchasing Function," paper presented at the Conference on Managing State Government Operations: Changing Visions of Staff Agencies, John F. Kennedy School of Government, Harvard University, June 19–20, 1989, p. 9; John Haggerty, "From Control—thru Chaos—to Customer Service," paper prepared for the Conference on Managing State Government Operations: Changing Visions of Staff Agencies, John F. Kennedy School of Government, Harvard University, June 19–20, 1989, pp. 7–8; Elaine Johnson, Joe Kurcinka, and Julie Vikmanis, "From Personnel Administration to Human Resource Management: Changing Visions of the Central Staffing Function," paper presented at the Conference on Managing State Government Operations: Changing Visions of Staff Agencies, John F. Kennedy School of Government, Harvard University, June 19–20, 1989, pp. 19–20.

CHAPTER TWO
THE NEED FOR INNOVATIVE STRATEGIES

1. As in many reform states, Minnesota's executive branch was reorganized during the 1920s and 1930s in accordance with the doctrines of honest and efficient government, as propounded by the reorganization and reform movements. Legislation to organize state agencies into departments reporting to the chief executive was passed in the 1920s, along with legislation introducing an executive budget and centralized purchasing. In the late 1930s, the election of Stassen as governor led to the long-awaited passage of civil service reforms and to the creation of a Department of Administration, with responsibility for conducting or overseeing budgeting, accounting, purchasing, printing, and many other administrative practices. See Lloyd M. Short and Carl W. Tiller, *The Minnesota Commission on Administration and Finance, 1925–39: An Administrative History* (Minneapolis: University of Minnesota Press, 1942). For information about reform movements in other contexts, see Richard Hofstadter, *The Age of Reform: From Bryan to F.D.R.* (New York: Vintage Books, 1955), and Edward C. Banfield and James Q. Wilson, *City Politics* (New York: Random House, Vintage Books, 1963), 138–50.

2. The following vignettes from the state of Minnesota bureaucracy were provided by Babak J. Armajani as part of his collaboration on this book. Armajani was deputy commissioner of administration when these events took place, except as otherwise noted.

3. Paraphrased comments of Procurement Director James Weyandt as recalled by then–Deputy Commissioner Babak Armajani.

4. This lease could be executed by the supervisors without the prior approval of central purchasing because the lease of typewriters and other office equipment took place through another division of the Department of Administration.

5. Joan Bartel, "Agency Visit Report" (Minnesota Department of Administration, internal document), October 1984.

6. "Although there are statutory requirements for the Federal Government's accounting systems to adopt accrual accounting, there has been much noncompliance with the regula-

tions. The reason for this is the overemphasis on the budget process within the federal government financial management structure." Ron Points, "Recent Developments in Accounting and Financial Management in the United States," in *Government Financial Management: Issues and Country Studies,* ed. A. Premchand (Washington, D.C.: International Monetary Fund, 1990), 334–36.

7. Paraphrased comments made in the State Departments Subcommittee of the Minnesota Senate Finance Committee during the 1985 legislative session.

8. Assistant Commissioner Armajani, as quoted in Michael Barzelay and Pamela Varley, "Introducing Marketplace Dynamics in Minnesota State Government," C16-88-826.0, John F. Kennedy School of Government, p. 3.

9. Unsatisfactory outcomes are situations, not necessarily problems.

10. On the distinction social scientists and policy analysts make between conditions and problems, see John W. Kingdon, *Agendas, Alternatives, and Public Policies* (Boston: Little, Brown, 1984), 115–21. The literature on problem identification is quite large. For a policy sciences perspective, see Garry D. Brewer and Peter deLeon, *The Foundations of Policy Analysis* (Homewood, Ill.: Dorsey Press, 1983), 35–60. For a symbolic-interactionist perspective, see Murray Edelman, *Constructing the Political Spectacle* (Chicago: University of Chicago Press, 1988).

11. See Giandomenico Majone, *Evidence, Argument, Persuasion, and the Policy Process* (New Haven, Conn.: Yale University Press, 1989), and Charles E. Lindblom, *Inquiry and Change: The Troubled Attempt to Understand and Shape Society* (New Haven, Conn.: Yale University Press, 1990), 17–44.

12. On the family-resemblance theory of human categorization, see the work of Eleanor Rosch, as discussed in Howard Gardner, *The Mind's New Science: A History of the Cognitive Revolution* (New York: Basic Books, 1985), 344–48.

13. See Richard E. Neustadt and Ernest R. May, *Thinking in Time: The Uses of History for Decisionmakers* (New York: Free Press, 1986), 134–56.

14. Lindblom, *Inquiry and Change,* 59–77. See also Joel Arthur Barker, *Discovering the Future: The Business of Paradigms,*

3d ed. (St. Paul, Minn.: ILI Press, 1989), for a discussion of the concept of paradigm paralysis.

15. See, for example, Samuel Bowles and Herbert Gintis, *Democracy and Capitalism: Property, Community, and the Contradictions of Modern Social Thought* (New York: Basic Books, 1986), 27–63, for a general argument.

16. See Albert O. Hirschman, *The Rhetoric of Reaction: Perversity, Futility, Jeopardy* (Cambridge: Belknap Press, Harvard University Press, 1991). See also Majone, *Evidence, Argument, Persuasion, and the Policy Process,* for a related discussion cast in terms of technical and political feasibility.

17. We rely on the readers' lay and professional inquiries to verify that each of these kinds of situations is a recurring phenomenon in American government. So, for example, we believe that writing and reading articles having a script similar to that of "Supply Orders Delayed: School System Failed to Process Pacts," *Boston Globe,* September 24, 1991, p. 33, contributes to verification. The article states, "Three days before the new academic year began, the Boston school system had processed only one of 500 contracts for educational materials, depriving schools of basic supplies, such as textbooks and dictionaries. . . . Mayor Flynn reacted angrily to the reported shortage and blasted the school system's administration for what he characterized as an inability to carry out its responsibilities." On the role of ordinary knowledge in verification of empirical generalizations about the social world, see Lindblom, *Inquiry and Change,* 173–74.

18. Whether a problem is solved is a matter of judgment, requiring the same kind of argument that goes into defining the situation as a problem in the first place. A standard definition of problem solving is the conversion of one state of affairs into another that is considered better.

19. The pervasive consequences of the general fund mentality may be difficult to overcome. But see Allen Schick, "Budgeting for Results: Recent Developments in Five Industrialized Countries," *Public Administration Review* (January-February 1990): 26–34; Premchand, *Government Financial Management;* and David Osborne, "Ten Ways to Turn D.C. Around," *Washington Post Magazine,* December 9, 1990, pp. 19–42.

20. The rest of the chapter focuses on this case. The justifica-

tion for this expositional strategy includes the following elements. First, it is important to ground arguments about conditions and problems in real, factual contexts. Second, the facts about process and outcome in this case are sufficiently simple that our subject of concern—the justificatory structures on which such arguments draw—is highlighted. Third, it is economical to use this case to make the point that reasonable arguments defining recurring situations as conditions can be formulated. If this kind of situation can be categorized as a condition, so can the other situations portrayed above *a fortiori.* Fourth, there is enough experiential similarity between this situation and the others, we think, that arguments about this case will resemble (to varying degrees) arguments about the others.

The general approach of focusing on arguments is also justified. As an empirical matter, social problem solving in a pluralist democracy is influenced to a significant degree by arguments—for example, those about defining troubling situations as conditions or problems. The normative justification is that public deliberation of rival arguments is an essential activity in such political systems. See Martin Shapiro, *Who Guards the Guardians? Judicial Control of Administration* (Athens: University of Georgia Press, 1988); Robert B. Reich, ed., *The Power of Public Ideas* (Cambridge, Mass.: Harvard University Press, 1990); and Hirschman, *Rhetoric of Reaction,* 169.

The effort to identify the justificatory structures underlying rival arguments about particular government activities and policies is increasingly common in the world of scholarship. Two noted examples are Jerry L. Mashaw, *Bureaucratic Justice: Managing Social Security Disability Claims* (New Haven, Conn.: Yale University Press, 1983), and Peter Schuck and Rogers M. Smith, *Citizenship without Consent: Illegal Aliens in the American Polity* (New Haven, Conn.: Yale University Press, 1985).

21. The $50 limit on what is known as local purchasing authority was established in 1939, when the Commission on Administration and Finance was reorganized into the Department of Administration. See Short and Tiller, *Minnesota Commission on Administration and Finance.* The same $50 limit remained in effect until after the change process described in the following chapter began in the mid-1980s.

22. On the economy-mindedness of central purchasing's internal administration before the change process began, see James P. Kinzie, "From Economy and Efficiency to Creating Value: The Central Purchasing Function," paper presented at the Conference on Managing State Government Operations: Changing Visions of Staff Agencies, John F. Kennedy School of Government, Harvard University, June 19–20, 1989.

23. On the unwillingness to give responsibility to lower-echelon professionals, see ibid.

24. Defender's responses to Critic's questions resemble the director of central purchasing's responses to similar questions asked by executives of the Department of Administration during the 1983–85 period. In places, the justificatory argument has been strengthened in ways consistent with the bureaucratic paradigm.

25. This statement abstracts from the role of courts in reviewing whether particular administrative decisions are consistent with law and policy. The bureaucratic reform vision was focused on the executive branch. It took many years after the bureaucratic reform vision was put into place to work out a theory of the role of courts in holding agencies accountable to law and policy. See Shapiro, *Who Guards the Guardians?*

26. The principle at work in this claim is bureaucratic rationality. Bureaucratic rationality has been defined as accurate decision making carried on through processes that appropriately take account of costs. "The legitimating force of this conception flows both from its claim to correct implementation of otherwise legitimate social decisions and from its attempt to realize society's preestablished goals in some particular substantive domain while conserving social resources for the pursuit of other valuable ends. No program, after all, exhausts our conception of good government, much less of a good society or a good life." Mashaw, *Bureaucratic Justice*, 26.

27. Executives of the Department of Administration encountered such arguments for each of the situations described earlier.

28. On the concept of the economic order quantity, see William Baumol, *Economic Theory and Operations Analysis* (Englewood Cliffs, N.J.: Prentice-Hall, 1977), 5–10.

29. For instance, James Q. Wilson's *Bureaucracy: What Government Agencies Do and Why They Do It* (New York: Basic Books, 1989) argues that good ideas about administrative functions tend to founder on the design of the U.S. political order. After pointing out in ch. 17 that the political process can more easily enforce compliance with constraints than attainment of goals (illustrating the point by describing the tension between procurement and the parks department in New York City), Wilson argues in his concluding chapter (pp. 376–78): "Many, if not most, of the difficulties we experience in dealing with government agencies arise from the agencies being part of a fragmented and open political system. . . . The governments of the United States were not designed to be efficient or powerful, but to be tolerable and malleable. . . . In the meantime we live in a country that despite its baffling array of rules and regulations and the insatiable desire of some people to use government to rationalize society still makes it possible to get drinkable water instantly, put through telephone calls in seconds, deliver a letter in a day, and obtain a passport in a week. Our Social Security checks arrive on time. . . . It is astonishing that [all this] can be made to happen at all." Much of the concluding chapter is, however, an argument for attempting to solve what Wilson calls the bureaucracy problem (using deregulation within government as a strategy to focus agencies' efforts on outcomes). Nonetheless, as suggested by the sentences quoted above, a reader can make selective use of Wilson's impressive book to make the argument that routine troubles along the staff/line frontier are conditions, not problems.

30. Most social scientists who study organizations are self-conscious critics of the bureaucratic paradigm. Among the best-known criticisms are those of Herbert A. Simon, *Administrative Behavior: A Study of Decision-Making Processes in Administrative Organization*, 3d ed. (New York: Free Press, 1976); Robert A. Dahl and Charles E. Lindblom, *Politics, Economics, and Welfare* (New York: Harper Bros., 1953); Charles E. Lindblom, *Politics and Markets* (New York: Basic Books, 1977); and Rosabeth Moss Kanter, *The Change Masters* (New York: Touchstone Books, 1983). (As a broad generalization, Kanter argues against the "segmentalist" assumptions of the bureaucratic paradigm's private

sector sibling, whereas the previous generation of critics challenged the rationalism of the bureaucratic paradigm.) Even Mashaw—who rigorously defends bureaucratic rationality as a justificatory structure for official action by government—is a self-conscious critic of the bureaucratic paradigm (see especially "On Living with the Impossibility of Rational Administration," in *Bureaucratic Justice*).

Among the most interesting self-conscious social-scientific attempts to construct alternatives to the bureaucratic paradigm are William A. Niskanen, *Bureaucracy and Representative Government* (Chicago: Aldine, 1971); David A. Lax and James K. Sebenius, *The Manager as Negotiator* (New York: Free Press, 1986); Charles Wolf, Jr., *Markets or Governments: Choosing between Imperfect Alternatives* (Cambridge, Mass.: MIT Press, 1988); Wilson, *Bureaucracy;* and Mark H. Moore, "Creating Value in the Public Sector," book chapter presented at the Annual Research Conference of the Association for Public Policy Analysis and Management, San Francisco, October 1990.

31. For an intellectual history of this form of argument—dubbed the futility thesis—see Hirschman, *Rhetoric of Reaction,* 43–80. He argues, in effect, that the futility thesis is a recurring method (one of three, actually) for arguing that an unsatisfactory situation should be regarded as a condition, not a problem against which human intelligence and effort should be applied: "The demonstration or discovery that [an] action is incapable of 'making a dent' at all leaves the promoters of change humiliated, demoralized, in doubt about the meaning and true motive of their endeavors" (p. 45).

32. "The rational course of action for a legislator is to appeal to taxpayers by ostentatiously constraining the budget for buildings, pay raises, and managerial benefits while appealing to program beneficiaries by loudly calling for more money to be spent on health, retirement, or education. . . . As a result, there are many lavish programs in this country administered by modestly paid bureaucrats working on out-of-date equipment in cramped offices." Wilson, *Bureaucracy,* 119.

33. On this general approach to implementation analysis, see, for example, Graham T. Allison, *Essence of Decision: Explaining the Cuban Missile Crisis* (Boston: Little, Brown, 1971), and Rich-

ard F. Elmore, "Organizational Models of Social Program Implementation," *Public Policy* (Spring 1978): 185–228.

34. On the dilemma of responsiveness, see Wilson, *Bureaucracy*, 326–27. On the concept of bureaucratic personality, see Robert K. Merton, "Bureaucratic Structure and Personality," in *Reader in Bureaucracy*, ed. Robert K. Merton (Glencoe, Ill.: Free Press, 1952), 361–71. In this case, the instrumental value of saving money for taxpayers becomes a terminal value. (See the discussion of bureaucratic personality in Wilson, *Bureaucracy*, 69.) On deriving psychic income from saying "no," see Howell S. Baum: "It is easier to put other people in the category of antagonists than to face the anxiety of trying to develop close working relations with them." *The Invisible Bureaucracy: The Unconscious in Organizational Problem Solving* (New York: Oxford University Press, 1987), 22.

35. "Culture is to an organization what personality is to an individual. Like human culture generally, it is passed on from one generation to the next. It changes slowly, if at all." Wilson, *Bureaucracy*, 91.

36. According to Wilson, *Bureaucracy*, 217: "Executives rarely put [their] energies into administrative matters because they tend to be judged not by whether their agency is well-run but by whether the policies with which they are identified seem to succeed or fail. . . . There are few rewards for being known as a good manager." The same generalization can be made, *a fortiori*, for chief executives and members of legislatures.

37. To reiterate, we are not making predictions about what social scientists would think or say. We are simply asserting that social science research can be used to bolster arguments that aim to categorize as conditions troubling situations we judge to be problems.

38. The delineation of this position was stimulated by reading ch. 6 of Hirschman's *Rhetoric of Reaction*, "From Reactionary to Progressive Rhetoric." He writes: "If the essence of the 'reactionary' futility thesis is the natural-law-like *invariance* of certain socioeconomic phenomena, then its 'progressive' counterpart is the assertion of *similarly law-like* forward movement, motion, or *progress*" (p. 157). Hirschman adds: "Generally, people enjoy and feel empowered by the confidence, however vague,

that they *'have history on their side'* " (p. 158) (emphases in the original).

39. Daniel Bell, *The End of Ideology?* (Glencoe, Ill.: Free Press, 1960); Ronald Ingelhart, *Culture Shift in Advanced Industrial Societies* (Princeton, N.J.: Princeton University Press, 1990). Professor Joan Subirats of the Universitat Autònoma de Barcelona first called to our attention the connection between the end of ideology and the politics of customer service.

40. National Commission on the Public Service, *Leadership for America: Rebuilding the Public Service* (Washington, D.C., 1989).

41. See Michael White, "Major Gambles on Big Idea," *Manchester Guardian*, July 23, 1991, p. 1. See also Robin Oakley, "Broad Sweep to Value-for-Money Citizen's Charter," *Times* (London); July 23, 1991, p. 1: "John Major launched his citizen's charter yesterday and vowed to increase quality and value for money throughout the public services. . . . The remarkable range of proposals, in which Mr. Major has invested considerable personal political capital, was still being dissected at Westminster last night. . . . Conservative MPs hoped that if the government delivers better services, they will produce a significant electoral dividend."

42. We mean to invoke the ordinary sense of the term *bureaucratic politics*, not the specialized sense of Allison's *Essense of Decision*.

43. Robert B. Reich, *The Next American Frontier* (New York: Times Books, 1983), and David A. Garvin, *Managing Quality: The Strategic and Competitive Edge* (New York: Free Press, 1988).

44. Dwight Waldo, *The Administrative State: The Political Theory of Public Administration*, 2d ed. (New York: Holmes and Meier, 1984).

45. Christopher Farrell, "Even Uncle Sam Is Starting to See the Light," *Business Week*, Special 1991 Bonus Issue on the Quality Imperative, October 25, 1991, 134–36.

46. See, for one example, Laurie A. Broedling, "Foreword," *Beyond the TQM Mystique: Real-World Perspectives on Total Quality Management* (Arlington, Va.: The American Defense Preparedness Association, 1990).

47. For the historical processes at work here, see Linda Kaboolian and Michael Barzelay, "Total Quality Management in

the Federal Sector: Discourse, Practices, and Movement," paper presented at the Annual Research Conference of the Association for Public Policy Analysis and Management, San Francisco, October 1990.

48. Lindblom, *Politics and Markets*, 66.

49. Soshana Zuboff, *In the Age of the Smart Machine: The Future of Work and Power* (New York: Basic Books, 1988), 6. In the context of Zuboff's book, these sentences articulate a progressive scenario in Hirschman's sense, not an empirical generalization.

50. See William Strauss and Neil Howe, *Generations: The History of America's Future, 1584–2069* (New York: Morrow, 1991), for a stimulating account of generational identities in the United States. They define a generation as a special cohort group whose length approximately matches that of a basic phase of life, or about twenty-two years. If the head of purchasing in our story had been born in 1940, he would belong to what Strauss and Howe label the Silent generation: the cohort of "men and women who came of age too young for World War II combat and too old to feel the heat of the Vietnam draft." The more junior officials in purchasing would belong to the Baby Boom generation. According to Strauss and Howe, prototypical members of the Silent generation have "a highly refined taste for process and expertise that ties other people in knots. Yet [this generation] has done more than any since Louis Brandeis' to bring a sense of nonjudgmental fairness and open-mindedness to American society" (p. iv). Prototypical Boomers are said to be idealists.

51. See, generally, Kanter, *Change Masters*, especially pp. 37–65.

52. "Just as history produces generations, so too do generations produce history." Strauss and Howe, *Generations*, 8.

53. Albert O. Hirschman, "Introduction: Political Economics and Possibilism," in *A Bias for Hope* (New Haven, Conn.: Yale University Press, 1971), 18.

54. *Possibilism* is a term brought into English usage by Hirschman to characterize his own intellectual posture and vision of social-scientific inquiry. "I have of course not been disinterested in claiming equal rights for an approach to the social world that would stress the unique rather than the general, the

unexpected rather than the expected, and the possible rather than the probable. For the fundamental bent of my writings has been to widen the limits of what is or is perceived to be possible, be it at the cost of lowering our ability, real or imaginary, to discern the probable. . . . In making my proposals, I refuse, on the one hand, to be 'realistic' and to limit myself to strictly incremental changes. At the same time, however, these proposals are not presented as being so revolutionary or so utopian that they have no chance whatever to be adopted in the absence of prior total political change. On the contrary, I feel an obligation to make them in concrete institutional detail thereby deliberately creating the optical illusion that they could possibly be adopted tomorrow by men of good will." Hirschman, *A Bias for Hope*, 28–29.

As will become increasingly evident, one of the key aims of *Breaking Through Bureaucracy* is to add clarity and weight to Possibilist's line of argument (in the context of public management issues) and, hence, to support his conclusion that recurring unfortunate situations along the staff/line frontier are problems, not conditions. We regard Hirschman's statement of possibilism—as well as Lindblom's argument in *Inquiry and Change*—as an endorsement of this approach to professional social inquiry.

55. See discussion of the Army's REQUEST system in chapter 1.

56. See, generally, Jeffrey Pressman and Aaron Wildavsky, *Implementation* (Berkeley: University of California Press, 1973); Walter Williams, *The Implementation Perspective* (Berkeley: University of California Press, 1980); and Steven Kelman, *Making Public Policy: A Hopeful View of American Government* (New York: Basic Books, 1987).

57. On the concept of on-the-spot reflection by professionals, see Donald A. Schön, *The Reflective Practitioner: How Professionals Think in Action* (New York: Basic Books, 1983), 128–67.

58. For a discussion of the importance of employee "ownership" of solutions and the change process, see Herbert A. Simon, Donald W. Smithburg, and Victor A. Thompson, *Public Administration* (New York: Knopf, 1950), 81; and Kanter, *Change Masters*, 180–205.

59. Possibilist could cite many scholarly works—not to mention dozens of examples from personal experience—to justify his concession. See, for example, Willis D. Hawley, "Horses before Carts: Developing Adaptive Schools and the Limits of Innovation," in *Making Change Happen*, ed. Dale Mann (New York: Teachers College Press, 1978), 224–60, and Richard F. Elmore, "Innovation in Education Policy," paper presented at the Conference on the Fundamental Questions of Innovation, Duke University Institute of Policy Studies, Durham, N.C., May 3–5, 1991.

60. On line agency executives who have succeeded in managing change, see, generally, Jameson W. Doig and Erwin C. Hargrove, *Leadership and Innovation: A Biographical Perspective on Entrepreneurs in Government* (Baltimore: Johns Hopkins University Press, 1987). See also Wilson, *Bureaucracy*, 97–98 (case of J. Edgar Hoover at the Federal Bureau of Investigation); Philip B. Heymann, *The Politics of Public Management* (New Haven, Conn.: Yale University Press, 1987), 15–24 (case of Caspar Weinberger at the Federal Trade Commission); Steven Kelman, "The Army and REQUEST," John F. Kennedy School of Government (case of Maxwell Thurman and Army recruiting); Robert Behn, "Management by Groping Along," *Journal of Policy Analysis and Management* (Fall 1988): 643–63 (case of Ira Jackson and the Massachusetts Department of Revenue); Graham T. Allison, Jr., and Mark H. Moore, "Preface," in Gordon Chase and Elizabeth C. Reveal, *How to Manage in the Public Sector* (Reading, Mass.: Addison-Wesley, 1983) (case of Gordon Chase and the New York City Human Resources Administration); "Ellen Schall and the Department of Juvenile Justice," John F. Kennedy School of Government, case C16-87-793.0; Robert D. Behn, *Leadership Counts: Lessons for Public Managers from the Massachusetts Welfare, Training, and Employment Program* (Cambridge, Mass.: Harvard University Press, 1992) (case of Chet Atkins and the Massachusetts Employment and Training System); and Lee Frost-Kumpf, Howard Ishiyama, Robert W. Backoff, and Barton Wechsler, "Transforming Mental Health Services in Ohio: Patterns of Strategic Thought, Language, and Action," paper presented at the National Public Management Research Conference, Maxwell School, Syracuse University, September 20, 1991 (case of Pam Hyde and the Ohio Department of Mental Health).

CHAPTER THREE
INVENTING STRATEGIES

1. The first economy and efficiency commission was appointed by Governor A. O. Eberhart in 1913. See Lloyd M. Short and Carl W. Tiller, *The Minnesota Commission on Administration and Finance, 1925–39: An Administrative History* (Minneapolis: University of Minnesota Press, 1942), 3.

2. On the initial conception of the role of the commissioner of administration in Minnesota, see Leslie M. Gravlin, "Economy and Efficiency Effected through Reorganization of the Minnesota State Government" (n.p., n.d., Mimeographed), 4–6. The document appears to have been written in the early 1940s.

3. The Task Force was also known as the Goff Commission.

4. The Governor's Task Force on Waste and Mismanagement, "Final Report: Governor's Cost Savings Program" (St. Paul, n.p., December 19, 1978, Mimeographed).

5. For examples, see Sandra J. Hale and Mary Williams, eds., *Managing Change: A Guide to Producing Innovation from Within* (Washington, D.C.: Urban Institute Press, 1989), 6. For a specific case, see "Denise Fleury and the Minnesota Office of State Claims," C15-87-744, John F. Kennedy School of Government.

6. Pamela Varley and Michael Barzelay, "Striving towards Excellence in the State of Minnesota," C16-87-737, John F. Kennedy School of Government.

7. Comments by Rudy Perpich at the Conference on Managing State Government Operations: Changing Visions of Staff Agencies, John F. Kennedy School of Government, Harvard University, June 19–20, 1989.

8. See Varley and Barzelay, "Striving towards Excellence," and Sandra J. Hale, "Creating and Sustaining an Environment for the New Vision," paper presented at the Conference on Managing State Government Operations: Changing Visions of Staff Agencies, John F. Kennedy School of Government, Harvard University, June 19–20, 1989.

9. This section draws on Varley and Barzelay, "Striving towards Excellence," and Michael Barzelay and Robert A. Leone, "Creating an Innovative Managerial Culture: The Minnesota

'STEP' Strategy," *Journal of State Government* (July-August 1987): 166–70.

10. Hale's first idea was to name the program Striving Toward Efficiency and Productivity. As she and her team of executives became aware that state employees associated efficiency and productivity with cost-cutting measures rather than with efforts to improve the quality and cost-effectiveness of government, they decided to change the name of the STEP program to Striving Toward Excellence in Performance to reflect the new concept of good management in government.

11. See Varley and Barzelay, "Striving towards Excellence," for a discussion of the roles of others involved in this process.

12. James Hiniker, commissioner of administration under Governor Albert Quie, remained in the new administration as deputy commissioner of administration under Hale for eighteen months. During that period, Hiniker's credibility with the legislature helped ensure that it did not convert revolving funds into appropriations and helped Admin as well as line agencies assume increased responsibilities. For example, Admin was able to increase local purchasing authority to $1,500.

13. See Michael Barzelay and Pamela Varley, "Introducing Marketplace Dynamics in Minnesota State Government," C16-88-826.0, John F. Kennedy School of Government, and chapter 2 of this book.

14. Jeff Zlonis, "Internal Service Activities," paper presented at the Conference on Managing State Government Operations: Changing Visions of Staff Agencies, John F. Kennedy School of Government, Harvard University, June 19–20, 1989.

15. For a discussion of the typewriter repair case, see Barzelay and Varley, "Introducing Marketplace Dynamics."

16. "Executive-Legislative Relations: Opening the Lines of Communication," C16-90-992.0, John F. Kennedy School of Government.

17. One major study of the hiring process was conducted in 1977 by the Legislative Audit Commission.

18. Department of Employee Relations, Staffing Division, "Analysis of System Changes" (St. Paul, n.d., Mimeographed).

19. This section is based on Elaine Johnson, Joe Kurcinka, and Julie Vikmanis, "From Personnel Administration to Human

Resource Management: Changing Visions of the Central Staffing Function," paper presented at the Conference on Managing State Government Operations: Changing Visions of Staff Agencies, John F. Kennedy School of Government, Harvard University, June 19–20, 1989.

20. Julie Vikmanis, manager, Staffing Division, correspondence, December 1, 1989.

21. Johnson, Kurcinka, and Vikmanis, "From Personnel Administration to Human Resource Management," 16–17.

22. Ibid., 6.

23. Ibid., 9.

24. Ibid., 4.

25. Ibid., 22.

26. The extension of the Department of Administration approach to the staffing organization and context suggested that a new vision of staff agencies was beginning to emerge. It was, therefore, possible to convene a conference at the John F. Kennedy School of Government in 1989 on Managing State Government Operations: Changing Visions of Staff Agencies, which was attended by the champions of change in the staff agencies; several other executives (including Finance Commissioner Tom Triplett and Revenue Commissioner John James); a state senator (John Brandl); a state representative (David Bishop); a legislative fiscal analyst (Kevin Kajer); Governor Perpich; a vice-president of the Urban Institute (Stephen Hitchner); staff agency executives from Washington, Texas, and Canada; and professors of public policy, management, political thought, and law from the Kennedy School, Yale University, and Boston University.

27. James Kinzie, "From Economy and Efficiency to Creating Value: The Central Purchasing Function," paper presented at the Conference on Managing State Government Operations: Changing Visions of Staff Agencies, John F. Kennedy School of Government, Harvard University, June 19–20, 1989.

28. Ibid., 9.

29. Ibid.

30. Ibid.

31. John Haggerty, "From Control—thru Chaos—to Customer Service," paper prepared for the Conference on Managing State Government Operations: Changing Visions of Staff Agen-

cies, John F. Kennedy School of Government, Harvard University, July 19–20, 1989, 2–3.

32. Judith A. Pinke, "Managing Internal Services: The Inter-Technologies Group," paper presented at the Conference on Managing State Government Operations: Changing Visions of Staff Agencies, John F. Kennedy School of Government, Harvard University, June 19–20, 1989. The name given to the bureau in 1968 was the Computer Services Division.

33. This section draws on Barzelay and Varley, "Introducing Marketplace Dynamics," 5.

34. Phyllis L. Kahn, "Information Resources Management in Minnesota," in *Government Infostructures*, ed. Karen B. Levitan (New York: Greenwood Press, 1987), 123–46.

35. *Minnesota Statutes, 1987 Supplement*, §16B.41, subd. 2.

36. Pinke, "Managing Internal Services," 1.

37. In what follows, we use the term *enterprise management*, even though this term came into use a few years after the presentation to overseers discussed in this section.

38. They were similarly concerned about their ability to oversee line agencies that derived revenue from sources other than appropriations, such as user fees.

39. "A Strategy for Funding and Managing Department of Administration Activities," 30.

40. For example, the financing of Information System Architecture, Standards, Contracts, and Enterprise Analysis was to change from revolving funds to general funds, in accord with the yet-to-be-implemented agreement to create the IPO. Similarly, the legislature agreed in 1986 to fund Capitol Complex Buildings and Grounds (plant management) with revolving funds rather than appropriations. (Ceremonial space remained generally funded.) In many cases, changes in funding bases had been agreed to by the legislature even before the strategy was discussed. For a listing of activities within each category, see appendix 1.

41. If legislators were dissatisfied with the performance of utilities, their remedies included expressing displeasure, exercising leadership, criticizing the department in statements to the media, and issuing specific commands in legislative acts (for

example, specifying the rates to be charged in the appropriations bill).

42. Privatization was a program neither of the governor nor of the legislature.

43. On exceptions to the principle of financing service activities with revolving funds, see the strategy document reproduced as appendix 1.

44. In financial management terminology, such an action is sometimes called "appropriating revolving funds."

CHAPTER FOUR
REWORKING THE CULTURE AND PRODUCING RESULTS

1. "Manager Feedback—Core Program" (Minnesota Department of Employee Relations, internal document), October 28, 1987.

2. Elaine Johnson, Joe Kurcinka, and Julie Vikmanis, "From Personnel Administration to Human Resource Management: Changing Visions of the Central Staffing Function," paper presented at the Conference on Managing State Government Operations: Changing Visions of Staff Agencies, John F. Kennedy School of Government, Harvard University, June 19–20, 1989, 24.

3. Three separate teams served administrative agencies, technical and scientific agencies, and social service agencies. The underlying idea was that many occupations were highly represented in only one of these subsets of agencies. Agency services teams could seek to achieve some reasonable level of consistency in the management of people engaged in similar work in different agencies. Not all staffing employees were assigned to the agency services section. A technical services section was created to provide assistance to other staffing units and to state agencies' personnel officers by developing policies, procedures, and guidelines explaining how to perform technical personnel work within the system. An applicants' services section advertised jobs and handled contacts with job applicants.

4. "Long time staff . . . felt it naïve to suggest that the department could be a service agency to managers when a goodly share

of the reasons for the department's being was to control agencies from trammeling the rights of applicants and employees." Johnson, Kurcinka, and Vikmanis, "From Personnel Administration to Human Resource Management," 18.

5. Julie Vikmanis, "Service and the System: Some Philosophical Thoughts" (n.p., n.d., Mimeographed), 4.

6. Ibid., 5.

7. Johnson, Kurcinka, and Vikmanis, "From Personnel Administration to Human Resource Management," 38.

8. Elaine Johnson, presentation to a research symposium on service management sponsored by the U.S. Office of Personnel Management, Washington, D.C., November 12, 1990.

9. "The newsletter format was selected in preference to an earlier idea of a one time guidebook explaining the total system to managers. A newsletter was thought to be more suitable to the amount of time managers have available to pay attention to personnel issues. It also renews interest in a positive way at periodic intervals and reminds managers of the connection between them and the personnel system." Johnson, Kurcinka, and Vikmanis, "From Personnel Administration to Human Resource Management," 36.

10. Exemplified by the issue reproduced as appendix 2.

11. Johnson, Kurcinka, and Vikmanis, "From Personnel Administration to Human Resource Management," 48.

12. Department of Employee Relations, " 'Personnel Office Extra' to *Smart Staffing* Issue: Beyond the Eligible List, October 1988," 1.

13. The 1987 conference, for example, dealt with such topics as how to resolve conflicts, how to collaborate with customers, and the new service delivery system. Johnson, Kurcinka, and Vikmanis, "From Personnel Administration to Human Resource Management," 31–34.

14. Ibid., 35.

15. James Kinzie, "From Economy and Efficiency to Creating Value: The Central Purchasing Function," paper presented at the Conference on Managing State Government Operations: Changing Visions of Staff Agencies, John F. Kennedy School of Government, Harvard University, June 19–20, 1989, 18.

16. Jeff Zlonis, lecture given to a research symposium on ser-

vice management sponsored by the U.S. Office of Personnel Management, Washington, D.C., November 12, 1990.

17. Kinzie, "From Economy and Efficiency to Creating Value," 12.

18. Ibid., 6.

19. Interview with James Kinzie, September 24, 1991.

20. Kinzie, "From Economy and Efficiency to Creating Value," 19.

21. Ibid., 27.

22. Purchasing's method for improving turnaround times was inspired by the quality-management movement. See John Haggerty, "From Control—thru Chaos—to Customer Service," paper presented at the Conference on Managing State Government Operations: Changing Visions of Staff Agencies, John F. Kennedy School of Government, Harvard University, June 19–20, 1989.

23. Information Policy Office, *Charting Your Course: Strategic Information Planning for the '90s* (St. Paul, 1989), 41.

24. The people principle was that "information systems extend human capacities when people define the purposes of their organization and structure the design and use of information to implement those purposes." The management principle was that "information systems, like other important resources such as personnel and budget, are fundamental management responsibilities which should not be merely delegated to operations staff." Ibid., 43.

25. Ibid., 42.

26. Not only were compliance costs reduced, but the contract offered agencies a 40 percent discount on microprocessing equipment.

27. Information Policy Office, *Recommendations for Funding State Information Systems: FY 1990–91 Change Level Requests* (St. Paul, January 1989), 76.

28. Ibid., 15.

29. Information Policy Office, *Inside Information: Strategies for Information Management* (St. Paul, September 1989), 2.

30. Lecture by Larry Grant, assistant commissioner of administration, at the John F. Kennedy School of Government, Harvard University, November 9, 1990.

31. Summary minutes of Information Policy Office's annual stakeholders meeting, St. Paul, February 1, 1990.

32. Data are from "InterTech and Department of Human Services: Cost Management Issues and Proposals" (Department of Administration, internal document), June 26, 1990.

33. Thirty-eight respondents answered this question. The standard deviation was 1.46. The survey was conducted as part of the research for this book and administered by the author.

34. Elaine Johnson, personal communication.

35. Judith A. Pinke, "Managing Internal Services: The InterTechnologies Group," paper presented at the Conference on Managing State Government Operations: Changing Visions of Staff Agencies, John F. Kennedy School of Government, Harvard University, June 19–20, 1989, p. 12.

36. The printing activity was protected from competition from vendors on certain product lines.

37. "Proposal to Change State Records Center to a Revolving Fund" (Minnesota Department of Administration, internal memorandum), May 11, 1990, p. 1.

CHAPTER FIVE
CHALLENGING FINANCIAL PARADIGMS

1. The concept of champions is prevalent in literature on innovation, product development, and organizational change. See, for example, Rosabeth Moss Kanter, *The Change Masters: Innovation and Entrepreneurship in the American Corporation* (New York: Simon & Schuster, 1983), 296–98, and literature cited therein.

2. Finance commissioners in the mid-1980s did support the enterprise-management strategy discussed in previous chapters and summarized in appendix 1. For the most part, these executives' agendas were too crowded to resolve conflicts surrounding its implementation.

3. The term *new vision* was proposed in Michael Barzelay and Babak Armajani, "Managing State Government Operations: Changing Visions of Overhead Agencies" (Cambridge, Mass., n.p., 1989), which was discussed formally at a June 1989 conference on accumulated experience in Minnesota's staff agencies held at

the John F. Kennedy School of Government. The paper argued that the emerging pattern of staff/line/overseer relations departed from the bureaucratic reform vision and, hence, should be understood as reflecting a new vision. From that point forward, the term was used by the champions to denote the overall approach to staff/line/overseer relations that was still unfolding.

4. Armajani, as mentioned in the preface, had moved from Admin to Revenue in 1987, where he remained a principal champion of the "new vision." He had been in close contact with Hutchinson, both professionally and personally, for nearly twenty years.

5. In this section I draw on information provided in a background paper written in 1991 by Hutchinson.

6. Hutchinson conjectured that "in the bureaucratic vision, central decision making was seen as a check on agency excess. There was no need to charge for capital since the central process was assumed to be successful." "Background Paper" (St. Paul, n.p., 1991), 3.

7. The 1990 bonding bill also provided for the establishment of an executive/legislative task force to determine how to make the capital budgeting process work better.

8. On the Revenue Department's budget practices, see "The Executive Branch and the Legislature: Opening the Lines of Communication in Minnesota," C16-90-991, John F. Kennedy School of Government.

9. Hutchinson, "Background Paper," 7.

CHAPTER SIX
MORE PROBLEMS, FEWER CONDITIONS

1. The intended outcome of supplementing possibilist arguments with information drawn from the Minnesota case is not the acceptance of such claims. Rather, the intended outcome is well-probed volitions in Charles E. Lindblom's sense of informed and reflective judgments. See *Inquiry and Change: The Troubled Attempt to Understand and Shape Society* (New Haven, Conn.: Yale University Press, 1990), 17–44. The presumption is that volitions will not be well probed unless deliberators are exposed to high-quality possibilist arguments. If deliberators

reach a reflective judgment, after hearing possibilist arguments supplemented by information presented here, that any or all of the troubling situations in their context should be defined as conditions, the objective of this chapter will have been accomplished.

2. This strategy taps into traditions of thought about social problem solving and the planning of change. See, for example, Charles E. Lindblom, "The Science of Muddling Through," *Public Administration Review* (Spring 1959): 79–99; Charles E. Lindblom, "Still Muddling, Not Yet Through," *Public Administration Review* (November-December 1979): 517–26; Warren G. Bennis, Kenneth D. Benne, Robert Chin, and Kenneth E. Corey, eds., *The Planning of Change,* 3d ed. (New York: Holt, Rinehart & Winston, 1976); John Friedmann, *Planning in the Public Domain* (Princeton, N.J.: Princeton University Press, 1987); Garry D. Brewer and Peter deLeon, *The Foundations of Policy Analysis* (Homewood, Ill.: Dorsey Press, 1983); and Donald A. Schön, *The Reflective Practitioner: How Professionals Think in Action* (New York: Basic Books, 1983).

3. We have the impression that even ordinarily optimistic policy analysts and program managers, when they think about most staff functions, are pessimistic about change. An example is Gordon Chase and Elizabeth Reveal, *How to Manage in the Public Sector* (Reading, Mass.: Addison-Wesley, 1983). We also have the impression that this temper is common within schools of public policy. We conjecture that the historic gulf between schools of public administration and schools of public policy is both a cause and consequence of this temper.

4. When Minnesota belongs to the audience's reference group, this assumption is reasonable. Empirical research on the diffusion of innovation provides ex ante criteria for discerning whether Minnesota is within the reference group of a possibilist's locale. For a noted example of this kind of research, see Jack L. Walker, "The Diffusion of Innovations among the American States," *American Political Science Review* (September 1969): 880–99.

5. For purposes of this discussion, the facts that German immigration was larger than Nordic immigration and that the population is increasingly heterogeneous are irrelevant.

6. On the distinction between cosmopolitan and local orien-

tations, see Charles H. Cooley, *Human Nature and the Social Order* (New York: Scribner's, 1902).

7. The problem of inducing change in locales where few if any people are cosmopolitans in the sociological sense is an interesting one. I have explored this challenge in Michael Barzelay, "Managing Local Development: Lessons from Spain," *Policy Sciences* (November 1991): 271–90. One of my conclusions is that people can understand unfamiliar information and arguments as long as these are related to—and illuminate—their direct experience.

8. The pattern was sufficiently clear by 1986 that Admin executives decided to write and present "A Strategy for Funding and Managing Department of Administration Activities" (appendix 1).

9. This category scheme makes use of a concept, accountability, that is meaningful to overseers, executives, managers, and operators. Focusing on accountability enables deliberators to consider the effects of the interaction of such factors as organizational culture, constraints, incentives, and routines; it does not steer deliberators toward a diagnosis focused exclusively on incentives. For discussions of the precise but limited effects of incentives on human behavior in organizations, see Herbert A. Simon, Donald W. Smithburg, and Victor A. Thompson, *Public Administration* (New York: Knopf, 1950); Charles Perrow, *Complex Organizations: A Critical Essay*, 2d ed. (New York: Random House, 1986); and James Q. Wilson, *Bureaucracy: What Government Agencies Do and Why They Do It* (New York: Basic Books, 1989).

10. The private sector literature on strategy and structure is extensive.

11. On the hidden rationality of sequential problem solving, see Albert O. Hirschman, *The Strategy of Economic Development* (New Haven, Conn.: Yale University Press, 1958). On the related concept of sequential attention to goals, see Richard M. Cyert and James G. March, *A Behavioral Theory of the Firm* (Englewood Cliffs, N.J.: Prentice-Hall, 1963).

12. James Kinzie, "From Economy and Efficiency to Creating Value: The Central Purchasing Function," paper presented at the Conference on Managing State Government Operations:

Changing Visions of Staff Agencies, John F. Kennedy School of Government, Harvard University, June 19–20, 1989.

13. Another way to describe the cultural shift is in terms of the development of new missions, mandates, and principles of management for staff agencies. These are discussed in chapter 7. If one prefers historical continuity over novelty, an attractive way to describe the shift is that it brought into currency two strands of eighteenth- and nineteenth-century thought concerning the relationship between individual and social rationality that had been left out of the bureaucratic reform vision: the strands are the thesis of the natural identity of interests and the principle of the fusion of interests. The principle of the artificial identity of interests was downgraded but not wholly removed from staff agency cultures. For background, see Elie Halévy, *The Growth of Philosophical Radicalism* (London: Faber and Faber, 1928).

CHAPTER SEVEN
MANAGING CUSTOMER-FOCUSED STAFF AGENCIES

1. The concept of a principle is usefully developed in Eugene Bardach, "From Practitioner Wisdom to Scholarly Knowledge and Back Again," *Journal of Policy Analysis and Management* (Spring 1987): 188–99. According to Bardach, "A good principle should help a manager make sense of the complex and often dangerous world that he or she inhabits. . . . A 'bad' principle is not 'false' but unilluminating or misleading. It displaces attention from important features onto unimportant ones. This does not, however, imply that a good principle brooks no exceptions—only that the exceptions are simply not worth making explicit."

2. Leslie M. Gravlin, "Economy and Efficiency Effected through Reorganization of the Minnesota State Government" (n.p., n.d., Mimeographed), ca. 1942, 4–6.

3. The arguments made for a state business manager—based on the premise that centralization is necessary for economical and efficient production—can be discerned not only in the document just cited but also in a 1941 speech made to the Women's Division of the Minnesota Republican State Central Committee,

published as Leslie M. Gravlin, "The Department of Administration: Its Place in Minnesota's State Governmental Organization," *Information Please Series: Know Your Minnesota Government* (St. Paul, March 1941).

4. On the relative competences and incompetences of command and market systems, see Charles E. Lindblom, *Politics and Markets: The World's Political-Economic Systems* (New York: Basic Books, 1977), 65–89. For a classic analysis of the concept of economizing, see Robert A. Dahl and Charles E. Lindblom, *Politics, Economics, and Welfare*, 2d ed. (Chicago: University of Chicago Press, 1976).

5. The belief that needs to be rejected is that the centralization of responsibility for and authority over the provision of inputs used by line agencies results in more economical and efficient government. This belief tended to justify the expansion of the commissioner's activities into new domains. During the Depression, for example, internal services were called on to reduce line agencies' expenditures on inputs. A central motor pool was created, purchases of state-owned cars were scrutinized, reports on the use of such cars were instituted, and provision of telephone, telegraph, and lighting services was centralized. In the 1960s, data processing was centralized.

6. For a classic statement of this argument in the context of resource consumption decisions, see F. A. Hayek, "The Use of Knowledge in Society," *American Economic Review* (September 1945): 519–30.

7. Herbert A. Simon, Donald W. Smithburg, and Victor Thompson, *Public Administration* (New York: Knopf, 1950), 534.

8. The statement that follows bears a family resemblance to the general aspects of a prototypical mandate as well as a resemblance to an organizational mission. An accepted general definition of the term *mandate*—whether of an organization, functional area, or position—is a description of the substantive purposes to be accomplished, the authority and resources to be employed, and the conditions and expectations for their use. See David A. Lax and James K. Sebenius, *The Manager as Negotiator* (New York: Free Press, 1986), 263. A mission has been defined as a clear statement of organizational purpose universally understood and as the organization's true internal and external com-

mitments. See Philip Selznick, *Leadership in Administration: A Sociological Interpretation*, rev. ed. (Berkeley: University of California Press, 1984), 65–74.

9. Throughout his career, Charles E. Lindblom has criticized this habit of thought. See, for example, a 1955 article entitled "Bargaining: The Hidden Hand in Government," published in his *Democracy and Market System* (Oslo: Norwegian University Press, 1988), 139–70. See also Albert O. Hirschman and Charles E. Lindblom, "Economic Development, Research and Development, and Policy Making: Some Converging Views," *Behavioral Science* (April 1962): 211–22; Charles E. Lindblom and David Braybrooke, *A Strategy of Decision* (New York: Free Press, 1963); Charles E. Lindblom, *The Intelligence of Democracy* (New York: Free Press, 1965); and Charles E. Lindblom and David K. Cohen, *Usable Knowledge: Social Science and Social Problem Solving* (New Haven, Conn.: Yale University Press, 1979). As far as I know, Lindblom never traced this habit of thought directly to the bureaucratic reform vision or the more general progressive outlook. However, he has sometimes appeared to trace it to the scientific problem-solving paradigm of policy analysis.

10. In what follows, I presume that concepts structure understanding and that understanding influences action.

11. We regard this as a reliable rule in Bardach's sense. This rule does not necessarily apply to work units *within* staff agencies, some of which might usefully identify citizens or private firms—such as job applicants or vendors—as customers.

12. The division is Minnesota's contemporary version of the centralized organization inspired by the scientific management movement.

13. Interview with Terry Bock, director of the management analysis division, cited in Pamela Varley and Michael Barzelay, "Striving towards Excellence in the State of Minnesota," C16-87-737, John F. Kennedy School of Government.

14. Principle 3 applies to staff functions as a whole, not to all of their parts. Within purchasing and staffing it might be a good idea to create control-oriented work units, such as one responsible for auditing line agencies' use of local purchasing authority.

15. Our procedure for defining the term *customer relationship*

is to highlight those aspects of the term's meaning in the source domain—the world of commercial relations—that are helpful to understanding and acting purposefully within the target domain of staff/line/overseer relations. The following definition therefore consists of the most important implications of saying that a user is a customer of a provider A, rather than a list of features of a prototypical customer service relationship (which include, for example, the voluntary exchange of services for money). The justification for this approach is derived from cognitive science, as expounded by George Lakoff, *Women, Fire, and Dangerous Things: What Categories Reveal about the Mind* (Chicago: University of Chicago Press, 1987).

16. Peter F. Drucker claims that the purpose of the organization lies outside the organization. *Management: Tasks, Responsibilities, Practices* (New York: Harper & Row, 1973), 61. On the purposive nature of serving customers, see Thomas J. Peters and Robert H. Waterman, Jr., *In Search of Excellence: Lessons from America's Best-Run Companies* (New York: Warner, 1982).

17. For a most careful analysis of the pros and cons of this prudential outlook, see Frank H. Knight, "The Ethics of Competition," in his *The Ethics of Competition* (New York: Harper & Row, 1935). For a careful analysis of the concept of informed and reflective judgments, or volitions, and their relationship to social problem solving, see Charles E. Lindblom, *Inquiry and Change: The Troubled Attempt to Understand and Shape Society* (New Haven, Conn.: Yale University Press, 1990), 17–44.

18. This presumption is not necessarily germane to a client relationship. In client relationships, unlike customer relationships, the judgments made by a provider's peers are often regarded as more relevant information about whether the provider's service meets user needs than a client's own judgments. One reason to use the customer concept instead of the client concept is to remind providers and users of the implication noted in the text.

19. This definition of accountability adds a psychological dimension to classical notions such as responsibility and answerability. The recognition of this dimension is even apparent in Bernard Rosen's otherwise traditional account of the concept: "Achieving accountability as a normal part of supervision is nei-

ther easy nor certain because accountability is, among other things, a *state of mind.* Do the individual employees—technicians, professionals, managers—find their work meaningful? Do they take pride in their own work? If so, they are more likely to *feel* accountable and have a strong desire to understand what is expected and then fulfill those expectations" (emphasis added). See *Holding Government Bureaucracies Accountable,* 2d ed. (New York: Praeger, 1989), 34. Significantly, Rosen does not discuss accountability to customers but only supervisory direction and review, the budget process, internal audit, and various forms of external evaluation.

20. Presumably, the views of the chairpersons of the subcommittees that appropriate funds to control activities contain more evidence of customer needs and satisfaction than those of a rookie legislator belonging to the minority party whose committee assignments are unrelated to the oversight of staff agencies. Between these two extremes, judgment is required. A related category of political-management work is to integrate and balance the interests of the chief executive with those of members of the legislature. See, generally, Philip B. Heymann, *The Politics of Public Management* (New Haven, Conn.: Yale University Press, 1987).

21. The reason for making this point is that recipients of organizational messages often believe, incorrectly, that a positive message is pregnant with a further statement in negative form. For example, "When the Social Security Administration communicates via its medical listings that certain specified medical conditions are per se disabling, it also seems to communicate a negative pregnant: conditions that do not satisfy the medical listings are presumptively nondisabling. Despite SSA's many attempts to stamp out this notion, it persists." Jerry L. Mashaw, *Bureaucratic Justice: Managing Social Security Disability Claims* (New Haven, Conn.: Yale University Press, 1983), 66.

22. What this particular stakeholder relationship entails is a matter for deliberation and political management, as described in the section on the enterprise-management strategy in chapter 3.

23. See appendix 1, part 2.

24. Since the legislature permitted line agencies to purchase

training services from private vendors, it is hard to argue that employee relations' mandate included rationing training services so as to produce some kind of egalitarian outcome in this area. Moreover, the governor did not generally support administrative policies rationing access to particular inputs after the 1983 freeze.

25. The U.S. Office of Personnel Management has made increasing use of revolving funds to finance training services provided to federal agencies, with apparently desirable results. Interview with Assistant Director Robert Agresta, U.S. Office of Personnel Management, November 1990.

CHAPTER EIGHT
THE POST-BUREAUCRATIC PARADIGM
IN HISTORICAL PERSPECTIVE

1. The concepts of program budgeting, program evaluation, and policy analysis broadened and improved the bureaucratic paradigm and provided some of the seeds for the post-bureaucratic paradigm, but they did not challenge the bureaucratic paradigm's conception of administration, production, organization, and accountability.

2. James Q. Wilson, *Bureaucracy: What Government Agencies Do and Why They Do It* (New York: Basic Books, 1989), 369–76.

3. David Osborne and Ted Gaebler, *Reinventing Government: How the Entrepreneurial Spirit Is Transforming the Public Sector* (Reading, Mass.: Addison-Wesley, 1992). The term was used in the 1991 inaugural address of Massachusetts Governor William Weld. See "What 'Entrepreneurial Government' Means to Governor Weld," *Boston Globe*, January 8, 1991, 17–18.

4. On the quality movement in government, see Christopher Farrell, "Even Uncle Sam Is Starting to See the Light," *Business Week*, Special 1991 Bonus Issue: "The Quality Imperative," October 25, 1991, 132–37. On the origins of quality management concepts and practices, see David A. Garvin, *Managing Quality: The Strategic and Competitive Edge* (New York: Free Press, 1988). TQM's influence in the defense department can be seen in, e.g., Tom Varian, "Beyond the TQM Mystique: Real-World Perspectives on Total Quality Management" (Arlington, Va.: American

Defense Preparedness Association, 1990); Defense Communications Agency, "Vision 21/TQM: Venturing Forth into the 21st Century," 2d ed. (Washington, D.C., March 1989); Navy Personnel Research and Development Center, "A Total Quality Management Process Improvement Model" (San Diego, Calif., December 1988). Any scholarly literature on total quality management in government has yet to appear.

5. Donald B. Shykoff, "Unit Cost Resourcing Guidance" (Washington, D.C.: Department of Defense, n.p., October 1990), cited in Fred Thompson and L. R. Jones, "Management Control and the Pentagon," book manuscript, October 1991, 16.

6. Project 1988, "Round II: Incentives for Action: Designing Market-Based Environmental Strategies" (Washington, D.C., 1991); and Robert N. Stavins, "Clean Profits: Using Economic Incentives to Protect the Environment," *Policy Review* (Spring 1989): 58–63.

7. Malcolm K. Sparrow, Mark H. Moore, and David M. Kennedy, *Beyond 911: A New Era for Policing* (New York: Basic Books, 1990).

8. Beth A. Stroul and Robert M. Friedman, "A System of Care for Severely Emotionally Disturbed Children and Youth" (Washington, D.C.: Georgetown University Child Development Center, July 1986).

9. "Middlesex County Jury System," John F. Kennedy School of Government case C16-86-656.0.

10. Theodore R. Sizer, *Horace's Compromise: The Dilemma of the American High School* (Boston: Houghton Mifflin, 1984); and Paul T. Hill and Josephine Bonan, "Decentralization and Accountability in Public Education" (Santa Monica, Calif.: RAND, 1991).

11. John E. Chubb and Eric A. Hanushek, "Reforming Educational Reform," in *Setting National Priorities*, ed. Henry Aaron (Washington, D.C.: Brookings Institution, 1990), 213–47; and John E. Chubb and Terry M. Moe, *Politics, Markets, and America's Schools* (Washington, D.C.: Brookings Institution, 1990), 185–229. For a critical book review of Chubb and Moe by Richard F. Elmore, see *Journal of Policy Analysis and Management* (Fall 1991): 687–94.

12. A paradigm is an experientially grounded conceptual sys-

tem. More specifically, a paradigm might be thought of as a system of awarenesses, mental schemes, commonsense theories, and general reasons for action. To see how such a system is structured, consider an important concept in the paradigm of modern society: production. The concept of production heightens awareness of certain kinds of work processes (such as factory work) and downplays others (such as domestic work). The concept entails a complex mental scheme, which includes such other concepts as workers, tasks, machines, specialization, skills, organization, supervision, throughput, work-in-process inventory, bottlenecks, defects, inspection, rework, costs, and efficiency. This complex mental scheme structures commonsense theories about production. A historically important commonsense theory held that modern prosperity and convenience required efficiency; efficiency required reducing production costs; and costs could be reduced through task specialization, close supervision of workers, and rational organization. Out of this commonsense theory came a general reason for action in industrial society: efficiency.

13. On mappings from source to target domains, see George Lakoff and Mark Turner, *More Than Cool Reason* (Chicago: University of Chicago Press, 1989), 57–65.

14. These reforms included introduction of civil service protections, the short ballot, reorganization, the executive budget process, and competitive purchasing.

15. The concept of the public interest has been ably scrutinized by political scientists over the years. See, for example, Charles E. Lindblom, "Bargaining: The Hidden Hand in Government (1955)," chap. 7 in *Democracy and Market System* (Oslo: Norwegian University Press, 1988), 139–70. Historian Richard Hofstadter points out that in general the public interest was what reformers—principally middle-class professionals and elites who had lost power to political machines—thought would make America a better society. See *The Age of Reform: From Bryan to F.D.R.* (New York: Vintage, 1955), 174–214.

16. Some may criticize the use of any concept such as the public interest. Arguments can be found in the literature on public deliberation and public management to support our premise that if the public interest rhetorical category is suppressed, it should be replaced by a functionally similar idea. See Steven Kelman,

Making Public Policy: A Hopeful View of American Government (New York: Basic Books, 1987), 215. See also Robert B. Reich, ed., *The Power of Public Ideas* (Cambridge, Mass.: Harvard University Press, 1990); Dennis F. Thompson, "Representatives in the Welfare State," in *Democracy and the Welfare State*, ed. Amy Gutmann (Princeton, N.J.: Princeton University Press, 1988), 136–43; and Mark H. Moore, "Creating Value in the Public Sector," book manuscript in progress. Support for the premise that rhetoric contributes to deliberation can be found in such diverse works as Donald N. McCloskey, *The Rhetoric of Economics* (Madison: University of Wisconsin Press, 1985); Warren Bennis and Richard Nanus, *Leaders: Strategies for Taking Charge* (New York: Harper & Row, 1985); David Johnston, *The Rhetoric of* Leviathan (Princeton, N.J.: Princeton University Press, 1986); and Giandomenico Majone, *Evidence, Argument, and Persuasion in the Policy Process* (New Haven, Conn.: Yale University Press, 1989).

17. We simplify here by omitting discussion of the concept of economy. Economy was the watchword of those who wanted to reduce government expenditures and taxes; efficiency was highlighted by those who wanted to improve government performance. We also simplify the discussion of efficiency here by focusing on the scientific management movement and factory administration. For a more complete discussion of the concept of efficiency in early public administration, see Dwight Waldo, *The Administrative State*, 2d ed. (New York: Holmes and Meier, 1984).

18. By knowledge in this context we mean ordinary knowledge as discussed in Charles E. Lindblom and David K. Cohen, *Usable Knowledge: Social Science and Social Problem Solving* (New Haven, Conn.: Yale University Press, 1979), 12–14. On mappings from source to target domains, see Lakoff and Turner, *More Than Cool Reason*, 57–65.

19. Robert B. Reich, *The Next American Frontier* (New York: Times Books, 1983), 22–82.

20. Alfred D. Chandler, Jr., "Mass Production and the Beginnings of Scientific Management," in *The Coming of Managerial Capitalism: A Case Book in the History of American Economic Institutions*, ed. Alfred D. Chandler, Jr., and Richard S. Tedlow (Homewood, Ill.: Richard D. Irwin, 1985), 465.

21. "Systematic bookkeeping was revolutionizing control over industrial production, pointing out the direction not only of efficiency and greater profit but honesty as well." Barry Dean Karl, *Executive Reorganization and Reform in the New Deal* (Cambridge, Mass.: Harvard University Press, 1963), 35. In stressing the role of industry as a source domain of knowledge about efficient government, we do not claim that other sources of knowledge were irrelevant. Indeed, Karl points out that early reformers were influenced by city management in Germany and the British parliamentary system, although the influence of these models was mediated by knowledge of business and industry in the United States. See *Executive Reorganization and Reform*, 95–96. Karl also argues that the power of arguments about industrial practice was enhanced by moral outrage against corruption and waste. See *Executive Reorganization and Reform*, 141–43.

22. What explains this puzzle? One argument might be that the outputs of government are different from the outputs of factories. But that argument fails because the concept of product could have served as a structural metaphor—as it does today—in efforts to conceptualize the relation between organizational goals and organizational work. One might argue, against this view, that reformers did not know how to think metaphorically. But the concept of an efficient government entails the use of the structural metaphor "Government is industry." Whether reformers knew they were speaking metaphorically is largely irrelevant. We conjecture that the concept of product was left out because reformers were committed to rationalism and professionalism and shunned market processes and commercial values in the context of government. The influence of legal conceptions of organization was also felt.

23. See Herbert A. Simon, *Administrative Behavior*, 3d ed. (New York: Free Press, 1976), 134–45. Simon restates arguments for respecting lines of authority irrespective of the merits of the particular decision.

24. On the importance of integrating functions and adapting organizations to the environment, see Kenneth R. Andrews, *The Concept of Corporate Strategy*, rev. ed. (Homewood, Ill.: R. D. Irwin, 1980).

25. The word *efficiency* does not appear in the index of either Michael E. Porter, *Competitive Advantage: Creating and Sustaining Superior Performance* (New York: Free Press, 1985), or of James L. Heskett, W. Earl Sasser, Jr., and Christopher W. L. Hart, *Service Breakthroughs* (New York: Free Press, 1990).

26. The information provided in chapters 3–5 of this book is evidence for this claim.

27. On rival definitions of the concept of product, see Derek Abell, *Defining the Business: The Starting Point of Strategic Planning* (Englewood Cliffs, N.J.: Prentice-Hall, 1980). For discussions of the concept of value creation, see Porter, *Competitive Advantage*, 33–61; and David A. Lax and James K. Sebenius, *The Manager as Negotiator* (New York: Free Press, 1986), 63–116. The concept of value creation in both works fits in the broad tradition of welfare consequentialism. See Amartya Sen and Bernard Williams, eds., *Utilitarianism and Beyond* (Cambridge, England: Cambridge University Press, 1982).

28. On the role of ad hoc arguments in practical reason and social science, see, respectively, Joseph Raz, *Practical Reason and Norms* (Princeton, N.J.: Princeton University Press, 1990), 28–35; and Charles E. Lindblom, *Inquiry and Change: The Troubled Attempt to Understand and Shape Society* (New Haven, Conn.: Yale University Press, 1990), 169–70.

29. On classical organization theory, see Gareth Morgan, *Images of Organization* (Newbury Park, Calif.: Sage, 1986), 19–38.

30. For a classic argument that administration is an identifiable domain of governmental activity, see Woodrow Wilson, "The Study of Administration," *Political Science Quarterly* (June 1887): 197–222.

31. National Commission on the Public Service, *Leadership for America: Rebuilding the Public Service* (Washington, D.C., 1989), 173–75.

32. Rosabeth Moss Kanter, *The Change Masters: Innovation and Entrepreneurship in the American Corporation* (New York: Simon & Schuster, 1983), 56–58.

33. National Commission on the Public Service, *Leadership for America: Rebuilding the Public Service*, 21–41.

34. For a discussion of process control, see Robert H. Hayes, Steven C. Wheelwright, and Kim B. Clark, *Dynamic Manufac-*

turing: Creating the Learning Organization (New York: Free Press, 1988), 185–341; and Heskett, Sasser, and Hart, *Service Breakthroughs*, 112–58.

35. This empirical claim cannot be substantiated on the basis of social scientific research. It rests on anecdotal evidence derived from extensive contact with public sector managers and from conducting field work for "Denise Fleury and the Minnesota Office of State Claims," John F. Kennedy School of Government case C15-87-744.0.

36. Marshall Bailey of the Defense Logistics Agency argues that process analysis is a way to combat the PHOG (Prophecy, Hearsay, Opinion, and Guesswork) that impairs employee commitment and organizational performance.

37. One interviewee for the Denise Fleury case reported that before engaging in process flow analysis, coworkers viewed one another as job categories; afterward, they viewed one another as people.

38. Some activities in government, such as minting currency and making weapons, are more like manufacturing than like service delivery. Most compliance activities are more similar to services than to manufacturing. *Winning compliance to norms* is an appropriate term for production in a compliance context.

39. The typical accounts of total quality management fail to make the vital distinction between industrial production and service delivery. For a discussion of this distinction, see James L. Heskett, *Managing in the Service Economy* (Boston: Harvard Business School Press, 1986). Indeed, the source domains for total quality management practices are industries and utilities. Viewed at close range, the failure to make the service/industry distinction is a significant handicap of TQM.

40. A background reason was the influence of machine metaphors on organizational thought. See Morgan, *Images of Organization*, 19–38.

41. See JoAnne Yates, *Control through Communication: The Rise of System in American Management* (Baltimore, Md.: Johns Hopkins University Press, 1989), 1–20. According to Yates, the notions of control and systems were developed into a management philosophy during the 1890s.

42. For a discussion of frequent mismatches between rules

and operational realities, see James Q. Wilson, *Bureaucracy*, 333–345; and Steven Kelman, *Procurement and Public Management: The Fear of Discretion and the Quality of Government Performance* (Washington, D.C.: American Enterprise Institute, 1990), 88–90.

43. As mentioned above, the total quality management movement has not focused on compliance processes. If such a focus were to be developed, it might begin by pointing out the similarities between enforcement approaches to compliance and inspection approaches to quality assurance. In diagnosing problems with the enforcement approach, experience with inspection could serve as a useful source domain. Similarly, as a heuristic device to structure a better approach to compliance, TQM's preferred alternatives to inspection should be used as a source domain. From a post-bureaucratic perspective, TQM should not be the only such source domain. Other source domains include the liberal and civic republican strands of American political theory and recent experience with service management.

44. For a discussion of this consequence of an enforcement orientation in the context of social regulation, see Eugene Bardach and Robert A. Kagan, *Going by the Book: The Problem of Regulatory Unreasonableness* (Philadelphia: Temple University Press, 1982), 93–119.

45. See J. Richard Hackman and Greg R. Oldham, *Work Redesign* (Reading, Mass.: Addison-Wesley, 1980).

46. See generally, Joseph Raz, "Introduction," *Authority*, ed. Joseph Raz (New York: New York University Press, 1990), 1–19.

47. See the discussion of good and bad apples in Bardach and Kagan, *Going by the Book*, 124.

48. See Jeffrey A. Roth and John T. Scholz, eds., *Taxpayer Compliance: Social Science Perspectives*, vol. 2 (Philadelphia: University of Pennsylvania Press, 1989); Malcolm K. Sparrow, "Informing Enforcement" (Cambridge, Mass.: n.p., December 1991); Mark H. Moore, "On the Office of Taxpayer and the Social Process of Taxpaying," *Income Tax Compliance*, ed. Philip Sawicki (Reston, Va.: American Bar Association, 1983), 275–92; Manuel Ballbé i Mallol, Catherine Moukheibir, Michael Barzelay, and Thomas D. Herman, "The Criminal Investigation and Prosecution of Tax Fraud in Advanced Societies" (Madrid: Ministry of Economy and Finance, Instituto de Estudios Fiscales,

September 1991); and State of Minnesota, Department of Revenue, "Strategies for the '90s" (St. Paul, 1990).

49. For the classic statement of the difference between organizations as technical instruments and as committed polities, see Philip Selznick, *Leadership in Administration: A Sociological Interpretation* (New York: Harper & Row, 1957). For a recent argument along similar lines, see Albert O. Hirschman, *Getting Ahead Collectively: Grassroots Experiences in Latin America* (New York: Pergamon, 1984).

50. Robert A. Dahl and Charles E. Lindblom, *Politics, Economics, and Welfare* (New York: Harper Bros., 1953), and Charles E. Lindblom, *Politics and Markets* (New York: Basic Books, 1977).

51. Alfred D. Chandler, Jr., *Strategy and Structure* (Cambridge, Mass.: MIT Press, 1962).

52. Another valuable concept is strategy, especially as defined in Lax and Sebenius, *Manager as Negotiator*, 261–68.

53. This definition is influenced by Mark H. Moore, "What Sort of Ideas Become Public Ideas?" *The Power of Public Ideas*, ed. Robert B. Reich (Cambridge, Mass.: Harvard University Press, 1990), 55–83; and Ronald Jepperson and John W. Meyer, "The Public Order and the Construction of Formal Organizations," in *The New Institutionalism in Organizational Theory*, ed. Walter W. Powell and Paul J. DiMaggio (Chicago: University of Chicago Press, 1991), 183–203.

54. As mentioned above, services and products in the public sector are often defined metaphorically. The role of structural metaphors in public sector management thought and practice deserves substantial attention. For a beginning, see Michael Barzelay and Linda Kaboolian, "Structural Metaphors and Public Management Education," *Journal of Policy Analysis and Management* (Fall 1990): 599–610.

55. See the principles discussed in chapter 7.

56. The bureaucratic paradigm focused attention on functions and nonoperational goals rather than producing desired states of affairs. The term *outcome* has a different meaning in this context than in the academic public policy literature, where the concept of outcome generally refers to the ultimate intended consequences of a public policy intervention. As used here, an outcome can be proximate results of an organization's work. For

example, desired outcomes of a plant management operation include clean buildings and satisfied customers.

57. Herbert A. Simon, Donald W. Smithburg, and Victor A. Thompson, *Public Administration* (New York: Knopf, 1950), 513.

58. The argument that accountability is a psychological state of affairs that can be influenced by the individual's environment is developed in Hackman and Oldham, *Work Redesign*, 71–98. In a similar vein, other social psychologists conclude on the basis of experiments that accountability raises "concerns about social evaluation, so that an individual's interest in appearing thoughtful, logical, and industrious overcomes motivation to loaf." See Elizabeth Weldon and Gina Gargano, "Cognitive Loafing: The Effects of Accountability and Shared Responsibility on Cognitive Effort," *Personality and Social Psychology Bulletin* (1988): 160, cited in Robert E. Lane, *The Market Experience* (Cambridge, England: Cambridge University Press, 1991), 49.

59. Robert Nozick, *The Examined Life: Philosophical Meditations* (New York: Simon & Schuster, 1989), 174. Nozick also argues, in effect, that being accountable in this sense is necessary for a full, moral life. Drawing on Lockean political theory, Rogers M. Smith makes a similar argument. See *Liberalism and American Constitutional Law* (Cambridge, Mass.: Harvard University Press, 1985), 205–6.

60. Hackman and Oldham, *Work Redesign*, 77–81. For a recent summary of the literature on intrinsic and extrinsic motivations at work, see Lane, *Market Experience*, 339–71.

61. Simon, Smithburg, and Thompson, *Public Administration*, 508–9.

62. Allen Schick presents a nuanced statement of this aspect of the bureaucratic paradigm: "Spending agencies usually behave as claimants, but most have procedures to conserve the resources available to them. . . . Similarly, the central budget office has a lead role in conserving resources, but it occasionally serves as a claimant for uses that it favors. It is not uncommon for the budget office to argue that some programs should be given more funds than have been requested." See "An Inquiry into the Possibility of a Budgetary Theory," *New Directions in Budget Theory*, ed. Irene S. Rubin (Albany: State University of New York Press, 1988), 65.

63. See Peter Hutchinson, Babak Armajani, and John James, "Enterprise Management: Designing Public Services as if the Customer Really Mattered (Especially now that Government Is Broke)" (Minneapolis: Center of the American Experiment, 1991); as well as the fiscal 1992–93 budget instructions for Minnesota state government, reproduced as appendix 3.

64. Many readers will recognize these responsibilities as a subset of the classic POSDCORB role frame. The definitions of planning, organizing, directing, and coordinating are informed by Luther Gulick, "Notes toward a Theory of Organization," in *Papers on the Science of Administration*, ed. L. Gulick and L. Urwick (New York: Institute of Public Administration, 1937), 3–45; Joseph L. Massie, "Management Theory," *Handbook of Organizations*, ed. James G. March (Chicago: Rand McNally, 1965), 387–401; and Simon, *Administrative Behavior*, 123–53.

65. Among the many authors who have formulated, elaborated, restated, and/or popularized such concepts are Mary Parker Follett, Peter Drucker, Herbert Simon, Philip Selznick, Warren Bennis, Donald Schön, J. Richard Hackman, Harold Leavitt, James Q. Wilson, Rosabeth Moss Kanter, James Sebenius, James Heskett, Robert Behn, Philip Crosby, Thomas Peters, and Robert H. Waterman, Jr. These conceptual themes continue to be extended in the public management literature by such writers as Jameson Doig, Steven Kelman, Mark Moore, Ronald Heifetz, Philip Heymann, and Robert Reich.

66. The change process in Minnesota, described in chapters 3–5, accelerated after such arguments—informed by the results of the research leading to this book—were made.

Name Index

225

Subject Index

Printed in the United States
1385300001B/132